The Leading-Edge Manager's Guide to Success

Strategies and Better Practices

DAVID PARMENTER

WILEY

John Wiley & Sons, Inc.

Published by John Wiley & Sons, Inc., Hoboken, New Jersey.

Published simultaneously in Canada.

For general information on our other products and services or for technical support, please contact our Customer Care Department within the United States at (800) 762-2974, outside the United States at (317) 572-3993 or fax (317) 572-4002.

Wiley also publishes its books in a variety of electronic formats. Some content that appears in print may not be available in electronic books. For more information about Wiley products, visit our web site at www.wiley.com.

Library of Congress Cataloging-in-Publication Data

Parmenter, David.
   The leading-edge manager's guide to success: strategies and better practices/David Parmenter.
       p. cm.
   Includes index.
   ISBN 978-0-470-92043-5 (hardback); ISBN 978-1-118-02310-5 (ebk);
ISBN 978-1-118-02311-2 (ebk); ISBN 978-1-118-02312-9 (ebk)
   1. Executive ability.   2. Management.   3. Leadership.   4. Success in business.
I. Title.
   HD38.2.P375 2011
   658.4'09–dc22

                                                                    2010045217

10   9   8   7   6   5   4   3   2   1

To my friend Michele who, one evening asked "What are all the facets of leadership?" This question, which I could not answer, inspired me to complete this work.

Contents

Preface

Many of us have drifted into management without adequate preparation, very much in the way we drifted into adulthood. In many cultures, the transition into adulthood is managed very carefully—the Australian Aborigines by the "walkabout," the New Guinea highlanders by formal ceremonies, and the Zulus by hunting game. If we are to be successful in management, we need guidance from our extended family, our managers, our colleagues, our heroes, and our mentors.

This book is designed to share the peer wisdom that you might get if you are lucky enough to be in uenced by a gifted leader—one who, like a passing comet, gathers others and drags them upward until they themselves have the momentum to make it to the top.

The better practices listed here are like the buckshot from a shotgun. Many of the buckshot will miss their target—either they are not appropriate or you are already doing something similar. However, some better practices will hit the target and these will hopefully make a difference in your current and future management positions.

Please note that I do not view my management experiences as being anything like those of the great managers and leaders I feature here. That is not my purpose. I fervently seek to ensure that the reader does not perform in the naive and fault-ridden way that characterized my own management years. This book is about better practices that will help you become a leader who will make a difference—a *serving leader*.

While this book incorporates many of the latest management techniques it cannot replace regular management training or the attendance of a residential management course.

How to Use This Book

This book is for all those talented managers who are making a difference but acknowledge that some of the building blocks were never put in place properly. It targets the staff person about to become a supervisor, who needs to process the first section, as well as CEOs who, behind closed doors, may find some tips to help them score more goals.

Using Part One: Selecting the Mountain and Your Guides   It helps to have an idea of what you want to achieve—otherwise, as Lewis Carroll said, "Any road will take you there." If you want to climb Mount Everest, you will obviously need a high degree of skill and preparation on all types of challenging terrain. If you want to be a CEO of a major corporation, you will likewise need to have that vision early on and carefully map your career moves to ensure you are gaining the requisite skills.

All successful mountaineers need to select their guides carefully. These guides in the business world are your mentors. Your mentors will help prepare you for the challenges ahead and save you from falling into the crevasses. Mountaineers carefully pack their rucksack. They cannot afford to carry excess baggage as this would limit their chances of success. This section of the book will help you; minimize your own personal baggage, find you mentor(s), spur you on to find your vision, and assist you to find the right organization to work for.

Using Part Two: Getting Prepared for Management   Many of us embark on management with limited knowledge and skills, having at best read a collection of management books and attended a management training course some five or six years ago. For various reasons, the building blocks are not complete. This section of the book is aimed at providing the missing building blocks to give you a sound basis for summiting the management mountain. It covers creating winning personal habits and developing winning work habits.

Using Part Three: Being a Better Manager   This part covers those skills and experiences you need to have in order to move onward and upward. It covers creating improved team performance, better recruiting, becoming more financially aware, developing your selling skills, and working smart with the outside world.

Using Part Four: Being a Leader Who Makes a Difference   This part covers those skills and experiences you need to have gained in order to successfully reach the top of the mountain (become the CEO) and return safely, ready for the next mountain. It covers understanding how Key Performance Indicators (KPIs) can transform your organization, reporting performance measures in a balanced way, finding your organization's *critical success factors*, stories about some special organizations and people, obtaining feedback on performance, adopting twenty-first-century performance management techniques, ways you can destroy value quickly if you are not careful and becoming a *serving leader*.

Why Feature Leadership Stories throughout This Book?

During the journey of writing this book I have been captivated by the stories of some great leaders. When researching them I have found that their messages are very powerful. In this book I feature lessons from Sir Ernest Shackleton, Sir Edmund Hillary, Sir Winston Churchill, and other leaders less well known. I have deliberately woven them throughout the book to give the reader a sense of continuity and perspective and some relief from the technical topic areas that are covered here.

Electronic Media Available

To support you in implementing the strategies and better practices in this book, the following electronic media are available (some for a small fee):

- Numerous webcasts (see www.davidparmenter.com/webcasts/). These are free to everyone.
- On my website (www.davidparmenter.com) I have placed some complementary electronic media that will be helpful to readers. The website will refer to a word from a specific page in this book which you can use as a password.
- Most of the checklists, agendas, and report formats can be purchased from www.davidparmenter.com using a PayPal link on the site.

The following icons relate to what types of media are available throughout this book:

 All exhibits with this icon are available electronically (some for free, some for a small fee).

 I have performed a webcast on this topic for you (see www.davidparmenter.com/webcasts).

 An article on this subject is available for free on my website (www.davidparmenter.com).

As an alternative to reaching the author's Web site, you can access the material by going through the publisher's link: www.wiley.com/go/leadingedge

Acknowledgments

I would like to acknowledge the commitment and dedication of Waymark Solutions staff members over the years it took to complete this project (Dean, Roydon, Matt, Louis and Jennifer). I thank my partner, Jennifer Gilchrist and children, Alexandra and Claudine, who are so understanding during my absences which are so much a part of being a writer and speaker.

I am also grateful to all those managers who have shared their ideas on management and leadership with me over the years.

I want to thank Harry Mills, Matt Clayton, and Jeremy Hope for their ongoing sage advice and Sheck Cho for getting this book published in the first place.

Special appreciation goes to my parents, who, encouraged all their four children to be independent and confident in their own endeavours. To all of the above mentioned people and all the other people who have been an influence in my life, I say "*thank you*" for providing me the launching pad for the journey I am now on.

PART I

Selecting the Mountain and Your Guides

CHAPTER 1

Creating a Vision of What You Want to Achieve

If you have only a few minutes to skim over this chapter, this is what you should focus on:

- Neuro-Linguistic Programming

It helps to have an idea of what you want to achieve, otherwise, "Any road will take you there."[1] If you want to climb Mount Everest, you will obviously need a high degree of skill and preparation on all types of challenging terrain. If you want to be a CEO of a major corporation, you will likewise need to have that vision early on and carefully map your career moves to ensure you are gaining the requisite skills. It is worth noting that becoming a CEO of a major corporation seldom happens by chance.

It is worth understanding the power of the subconscious. As I understand it, the subconscious does not know the difference between right and wrong; it does not know the difference between what is real and what is imagined in the future or the present; it does not know its limitations.

In the book, *The Winning Zone*,[2] Al Smith states that "the more vivid the imagination, the more real the subconscious thinks the picture is; eventually, the subconscious will believe it is reality and allow the body to perform the task."

Neuro-Linguistic Programming

Many readers will be aware of this term, even attended a course on it, and yet this concept has been left in the deep recesses of the brain, unused. At its basic level it is the most effective form of behavior alignment one can do. By using your five senses you create visions of achievement you have yet to attain. You smell, you see, you feel, you hear, you touch, all in your mind, the event you want to achieve. Your *subconscious* is now in a dilemma. It needs to close the gap between now and this future reality. Because it knows no bounds, it will lift your performance, the only limiting factor being your *consciousness*, which as always will interfere and will sabotage progress, if allowed to.

Al Smith, a sport psychologist, sat his son down to watch hours of videotape of the top-ten bowler, Marshall Holman. After a week and a half of focusing on Holman's delivery and visualizing the same approach and motion when he bowled, his son's average moved from the 120s to the 185s! There are many more sporting analogies highlighting the power of vision.

Sir Edmund Hillary and Tensing Norgay are reputed to have visualized being the first person to climb Mount Everest. It is no surprise that they should meet each other in the best-organized attempt on Mount Everest. Upon meeting, they soon realized their compatibility and joined together as a two-man climbing team, performing feats of endurance designed to catch the eye of Lord Hunt, the Expedition leader. They naturally were then selected to be the second summiting team. The first team met a problem they could not surmount, whereas when Sir Edmund Hillary approached the final barrier, now known as the Hillary step, he developed a new climbing technique, at 27,000 feet, to get around the problem. One wonders how much Sir Edmund's and Norgay's shared vision was the differentiating factor between the two separate summiting attempts.

Influencing the Environment

There are people who believe that one's thoughts can influence the environment around you. For those readers who think I have lost the plot, I ask you to do an exercise. Pick a busy shopping day where parking will be a nightmare. Now think precisely where you want to park—the most convenient busy road where parking is available. On the journey, think of an empty parking spot. Now that you are thinking the positive thoughts you will be amazed at the results you get. It is as if the universe has linked into another driver and stimulated him to move his car just as you are arriving; or looking at this another way you are more open to the opportunities that are always there. Many cars will be leaving their spots during peak times!

By creating visions of where you want to be, you are, according to this school of thought, *creating* the opportunities and being *receptive* to them as they arise. It is worth attending courses on neuro-linguistic programming, meditation, and visualization, which lock in practices better than any book on the subject.

Notes

1. Lewis Carroll, *Alice's Adventures in Wonderland*, (Tribeca Books).
2. Al Smith, *The Winning Zone*, 1st Books Library, 2002.

CHAPTER 2

Find Out about Yourself

If you have only a few minutes to skim over this chapter, this is what you should focus on:

- The Enneagram
- The personal baggage checklist

Personal Baggage

We will always be running with a few cylinders misfiring unless we fully understand our behavior patterns and those of the people around us. Skip the section on personal baggage and I promise you that you will never reach your potential. You will never be able to successfully implement large change as this requires advanced interpersonal skills.

We inherit *baggage* from our ancestry, along with many great things. This baggage is added to by our parents, with either too much smothering, too little attention, too much criticism, too little quality time (need I go on?). One course I attended, called "Turning Point," stated that we all have baggage; our role in life is to lighten the load so that it is not crippling when we decide to start "management summiting."

My point is, you owe it to your colleagues, staff, suppliers, contractors, family, partner, and offspring to do something about your personal baggage.

We have a choice: to grow and to challenge those behavior traits that will create havoc in the workplace, or to ignore them and seek new jobs like we do new partners, hooked on the romance period and leaving when the going gets tough. To make a major contribution, you will need to achieve through the contribution of others. This means acquiring a suite of behavioral skills.

Let us be clear: To be a leader today you do not have to have handled all your personal baggage. There are plenty of leaders "crippled" with the weight of their personal baggage who are causing havoc within every organization that they work for. Yet there are those *Iconic leaders* who are a pleasure to work with that demonstrate the benefit of minimizing one's own personal baggage.

Courses to Attend

As I said before, you owe it to your colleagues, staff, suppliers, contractors, family, partner, offspring, and golfing partners to do something about it. Here are six courses that everybody needs to do as a basic minimum.

Course 1: The Enneagram

"The enneagram is a profound, elegant, and compassionate approach to people and their relationships. It describes nine basic world-views and nine different ways of doing business in the world. Each of the nine personality types is something of a pathway through life, with likely obstacles and pitfalls along the way."[1]

Your principle motivation should be a better understanding of how you work and what will benefit your family, friends, and colleagues. A by-product will be that you will have an understanding of the likely worldview/personality type of your boss, and thus be in a better position to make the relationship work. (See www.enneagraminstitute.com/ennagram.asp.)

Course 2: Hermann's Thinking Preferences

This entertaining workshop looks at the way people think. It is broken into four types. It is important to understand the thinking preference of your boss, colleagues, and staff reporting to you so you can communicate effectively with them. Attend a local course as soon as you can or visit www.hbdi.com/

Course 3: Myers-Briggs Profiling

This helps you understand how you perceive the world and make decisions. It is particularly useful to use it as a team exercise so members can better understand each other. Even though there are only 16 different profiles you will be surprised how accurate the profiling is for you.

Visit www.myersbriggs.org and read *Quick Guide to the 16 Personality Types in Organizations: Understanding Personality Differences in the Workplace.*[2]

Course 4: Neuro-Linguistic Programming

The importance of Neuro-Linguistic Programming has been discussed in Chapter 1. Go on the Web and search "NLP+course +New York"(your location) to find a local course.

Course 5: Transactional Analysis

Transactional analysis says that each of us is made up of three alter egos parent, adult, child. When we communicate, as a manager to our staff, we need to understand that it will be more productive if we communicate as an "adult" rather than reverting to our parent or child egos. In addition we need to be aware when having a discussion with a staff member what ego they are using. If a staff member is emotional they are using their child ego thus it is not productive to use one's adult ego (structured reasoning) as the staff member needs your nurturing side (parent ego) for the communication to work effectively.

I hope I have said enough to encourage you to explore more in this area. A practical explanation can be found on www.businessballs.com/transact.htm.

Attending a Transactional Analysis course will helps you understand communication styles and why sometimes our communication does not work. It is particularly useful in improving relationship communication with our direct reports, our partner, and our family members.

Course 6: Intensive Life Skills Course

Life skills courses have various titles. I have attended courses called "Turning Point," "Point of Choice," and "Essentially Men;" there are many others, such as "Money and You." Some of your friends and relatives will have attended a course. Go to one that is highly recommended and that has made a difference to that person. The personal development courses of longer duration have the most chance of changing your behaviors. The experts in behavioral change say that it takes up to 12 to 16 weeks of weekly exercises to change behavior. These courses help you to develop a decent toolkit to handle disappointment, anger, and loss. If you do not learn to handle these events, there will be plenty of opportunities for them to screw up your life.

I went to one course, as a skeptical accountant would, expecting to be mildly challenged. It turned out to be a vastly more challenging and rewarding experience. I soon realized the extent of my baggage. Part
(Continued)

of the major load was that I had never grieved properly for the loss of my dear sister-in-law, who died of cancer before she reached 30. With the flowing of my tears I have found life more rewarding, as I now am able to express sadness and loss as any normal person would do.

Locking in a New Behavior Trait

If you ask management at a weight-loss company or at a fitness gym how long it takes for clients to lock into a new behavior, one they will continue with, they may well say "at least 16 weeks." It is no wonder that very often training does nothing to influence behavior change. Yet behavior change is the fundamental thing that is necessary if an organization is to lift itself to another level.

To make any breakthrough you have got to realize the impact of your current behavior on the organization. The behavior change process takes so long because you need to travel along a path of enlightenment as set out in Exhibit 2.1.

Exhibit 2.2 provides some of the basic behaviors that will make a difference. How do you score?

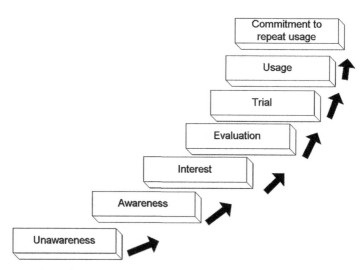

EXHIBIT 2.1 Behavior Change Process

EXHIBIT 2.2 Personal Baggage Checklist[a]

Focus

Do you allocate large parts of your time to the major goals in your life? (as per your treasure map)	☐ Yes	☐ No
Have you determined what your goals are for the next two to three years?	☐ Yes	☐ No
Do you treat email as you would mail and read it at an appropriate time? (you can set up filters to help manage your emails and better channel your time)	☐ Yes	☐ No
Do you avoid being sucked into "nonurgent, not important" issues?	☐ Yes	☐ No
Do you inoculate yourself from the diversion disease?	☐ Yes	☐ No
Do you have a clear understanding of all the loose ends that are outstanding?	☐ Yes	☐ No
Do you carefully check the purpose and intent of a meeting before you agree to attend?	☐ Yes	☐ No

Ability to Finish

Do you have specific times for finishing (e.g., a finishing week or two weeks each month)?	☐ Yes	☐ No
Do you minimize your involvement in new projects until your previous ones are finished?	☐ Yes	☐ No
Do you occasionally work away from your office (from home or a quiet location) so that you can focus on projects uninterrupted?	☐ Yes	☐ No

Interpersonal Skills

Are you able to make sufficient eye contact, at least 50% of the time, when a conversation is taking place?	☐ Yes	☐ No
Are you able to demonstrate "humility" when you consider yourself an expert in the subject matter? (showing that you are open to others' suggestions and opinions)	☐ Yes	☐ No
Can you remain open to ideas, which initially you would like to reject out of hand?	☐ Yes	☐ No
Do you listen to tone and context of the spoken words so as to ascertain what the person really means? (the poor choice of words commonly leads to misunderstandings)	☐ Yes	☐ No
Do you allow others to complete their conversations?	☐ Yes	☐ No
Are you using your mind to create more linkages from the conversation?	☐ Yes	☐ No
Do you show interest and give back verbal and nonverbal signals that you are listening?	☐ Yes	☐ No
Are you aware of all the nonverbal cues you are giving from your body language?	☐ Yes	☐ No

(Continued)

EXHIBIT 2.2 (Continued)

Can you be courteous with people and ruthless with time?	☐ Yes	☐ No
Can you be as patient with other people as you would wish them to be with you?	☐ Yes	☐ No

Calm in Adversity

Can you avoid taking adversity personally?	☐ Yes	☐ No
Can you look at the funny side when adversity strikes?	☐ Yes	☐ No
Can you realize that adversity is part of life and deal with it?	☐ Yes	☐ No
Can you still be courteous to people when you are on a tight deadline?	☐ Yes	☐ No

Addiction Management

Do you limit stimulants that adversely affect your behavior? (e.g., caffeine can make a substantial impact on how argumentative you might become especially if you have more than two strong coffees during the working day)	☐ Yes	☐ No
Have you limited any addiction to the adrenaline rush of completion in the 11th hour?	☐ Yes	☐ No
Have you controlled the need to work harder (or longer) than anyone else on your team?	☐ Yes	☐ No

Anger Management

Do you see anger as a negative trait rather than a good release valve?	☐ Yes	☐ No
Do you handle your angry feelings in a safe way?	☐ Yes	☐ No
Are you aware that you have a choice and alternatives? (there are many good behavioral change programs)	☐ Yes	☐ No
Are you aware that frustration with oneself is one of the great initiators of anger?	☐ Yes	☐ No
Do you use the "time-out" technique to avoid expressing anger to your colleagues, staff, and family?	☐ Yes	☐ No
Do you view events as challenges to be overcome rather than roadblocks to your progress?	☐ Yes	☐ No

Personal Learning and Growth

Have you attended any personal development courses to overcome the defense mechanisms that you have put in place from childhood onward which may be limiting your effectiveness?	☐ Yes	☐ No
Have you attended any personal development courses to challenge your negative behavior traits? (we all have them)	☐ Yes	☐ No
Do you know where you lie on the Enneagram? (a worldwide program to help individuals understand their behavioral weaknesses)	☐ Yes	☐ No
Do you know your Myers-Briggs personality type? (a worldwide program to help individuals understand their personality type)	☐ Yes	☐ No
Have you attended a "Transactional Analysis" course?	☐ Yes	☐ No
Have you run a Myers-Briggs team wheel course for your team?	☐ Yes	☐ No

EXHIBIT 2.2 (Continued)

Creating Win-Win Situations		
Do you analyze the situation from the other side?	□ Yes	□ No
Can you honestly say you are focused on a mutual win-win?	□ Yes	□ No
If your trade suppliers, customers, and others were contacted, do you think they would say you are fair and reasonable?	□ Yes	□ No
Functioning Team Member		
Are you able to curb your own desires in order to function fully as a team member?	□ Yes	□ No
Are you able to put other team members' needs alongside yours?	□ Yes	□ No
Do the administration staff willingly help you? (because you have linked well with them)	□ Yes	□ No
Do you share praise from others with the team rather than "bag it" for yourself?	□ Yes	□ No
Your score of "yes" ticks.		
Your mentor scoring you, number of "yes" ticks.		

Number of Ticks	My Advice to You
less than 20	Treat it as an urgent priority
20–25	Time to get serious with personal development
25–30	Still more could be done
over 30	Congratulations, you have made good progress minimizing your personal baggage (suggest you get a number of your staff to score you—there may be a difference)

Inner Disarmament

The Dalai Lama talks about inner disarmament. It is a beautiful concept, one that says we must invest time and energy to find our inner peace. It is an endless search, I know, but as you get closer to your hidden treasure, it has significant impact on all your relationships. Your colleagues, boss, partner, children, and extended family will all notice and appreciate the difference. You owe it to yourself and them.

Lack of anger management is the real relationship destroyer. The aggressor often believes that saying "I'm sorry" sets all things right, whereas the recipient can remember each incident as if it were yesterday. A number of us, myself included, suffer or have suffered from an abusive behavior pattern; we have a tendency to be sarcastic, antagonistic, and take it out on those around us—our colleagues and family. This problem needs to be dealt with before it creates havoc in the workplace and at home.

One of Sir Edmund Hillary's selection criteria was to find people who could see the funny side in a crisis. He pointed out that when he was selecting staff for his expeditions he was looking for people who were self-effacing, and could handle adversity with a smile. It is a special gift. So many of us can very easily add to the problem with more personal drama—"Why me? Why has this happened to me?" We need to accept crisis as a part of life. Graham Dingle, a mountaineer and explorer, says that life is about "95% hard work and 5% joy."[3]

An interesting point made by Professor Marshall Cook is that "by venting your anger, you're actually feeding it, becoming more angry for a longer time. You're also compounding the harm to your body and psyche by prolonging the physiological responses (adrenaline surge, rapid heartbeat, elevated blood pressure)."

Thus, sorting out an anger management problem is beneficial to your health, your colleagues, staff, and, of course, your family and friends.

It took a failed marriage for me to realize that I had an anger management problem. The classic trait was that when I was frustrated about my own performance, I would take it out on those close to me—my colleagues and partner. I went to an anger management course that provided a learning venue for those who expressed their anger violently and those, like myself, who expressed it verbally. After eight weeks, I figured it out. I realized that the anger was in most cases transference. In addition I realized that I had a *choice* whether to get angry or not. Now I never lose my temper. Soon after the course a flooring company laid my entire house with the wrong patterned carpet! I worked my way around the problem without ever losing my temper, to the amazement of the flooring company CEO. I created a win-win and at the same time felt very proud of my newfound skill.

Notes

1. Michael J. Goldberg, *Getting Your Boss's Number: And Many Other Ways to Use the Enneagram at Work*, HarperCollins, 1996.
2. Linda V. Berens, Sue A. Cooper, Linda K. Ernst, and Charles R. Martin, *Quick Guide to the 16 Personality Types in Organizations: Understanding Personality Differences in the Workplace*, Telos Publications, 2002.
3. *Management*, New Zealand Institute of Management, December 2002.

CHAPTER 3

Locating a Mentor

If you have only a few minutes to skim over this chapter, this is what you should focus on:

- Why you need a mentor
- A mentor checklist

Why You Need a Mentor

All successful mountaineers need to select their guides carefully. These guides in the business world are your mentors. It always amazes me, when I address an audience, how few people have a mentor. Your mentors will help prepare you for the challenges ahead and save you from falling into crevasses. The different visions that people in management have are as varied as the mountains around the world. You may wish to be a senior manager in an international bank, a CEO of a fast-growing technology company, or a CEO of a major multinational. But the pathway to each of these positions is quite different:

- The CEO of a bank would require at least ten years of banking experience, including multinational banking in the major financial centers.
- A CEO of a fast-growing technology company would need to have demonstrated entrepreneurial skills and the ability to relate to technology staff; they might possibly (but not necessarily) need over five years of sector experience.
- A CEO of a major multinational would need blue-chip experience with other similar-sized multinationals.

Most of us recognize that we need to seek advice. The problem is that we are often not selective enough when we start to pour out our problems to untrained ears. Your best friend, parents, or work colleagues may not be skilled enough to give you the balanced feedback you need for your career.

The answer is very easy: Find an "Obi-Wan Kenobi," someone who will coach you to find the "force within you." Typically, these mentors reek wisdom; they are wise owls who have seen it all before and are gracious enough to merely raise an eyebrow when you talk about some madcap action you are about to take. They talk you through it and let the enlightenment strike by itself.

One corporate accountant I know was offered some confidential information about intended legislation. The legislation that was going to be passed affected his organization. Instead of thinking about the ramifications of receiving the information and talking with his mentor, he let curiosity win the day and looked at the document. The information was so hot that as soon as he read it he realized that he would now have to disclose the information to his company colleagues, who were duty-bound to disclose it to the stock market. The massive fallout in the press had the corporate accountant as the guilty party for the drop in share price. The corporate accountant was roasted in front of a governmental subcommittee and featured for over a week on the front pages.

Richard Branson, a modern-day hero, consulted with Freddie Laker before he went into the airline industry. The advice he was given helped him avoid the pitfalls that proved too much for Laker Airways, the pioneers of the cheap travel we have today.

In this day and age, only the foolish venture forward without having a mentor supporting them from behind the scenes. A mentor is normally someone older than you, wiser, and with more gray hairs, who knows something about what you are doing. It could be a retired CEO of the business, a retired board member who has known you for a while, a professional mentor, or someone in the sector where there is no conflict of interest.

A good mentor will save your career a number of times. With the advent of email, a career-limiting event is only a "click on the send button" away! The mentor is someone whom you ask, "Please look at this. I am thinking of forwarding it on to the CEO," to which the mentor replies,

"Let's have a coffee first before it is sent," after which, when asked about the email, you reply, "What email?"

Mentors are also well connected and will often further your career during discussions on the 19th hole. Some receive as payment a good meal once a quarter, while others will do it for a living.

How to Find a Mentor

When looking for a mentor, start at the top and work down. Most successful people are happy to mentor up-and-coming "young guns." Asking someone to become your mentor is one of the greatest compliments you can give. Exhibit 3.1 will help you find a mentor.

How to Ask Someone to Be Your Mentor

You can ask someone to mentor you in a number of ways:

"Pat, I would really appreciate the opportunity to meet you over lunch sometime soon to discuss a few work issues. I have the utmost respect for your judgment and experience and I would find such a meeting most valuable." *There is no need to mention the word mentor because Pat has never been a mentor before.*

"Pat, I have recognized that if I am to grow as a manager I need to seek advice from time to time from wise people. I was wondering

EXHIBIT 3.1 Mentor Checklist

1. Understands the sector you are in	☐ Yes	☐ No
2. Has reached a senior position, not necessarily a CEO	☐ Yes	☐ No
3. Has had a broad career experience	☐ Yes	☐ No
4. Has a quick and incisive mind	☐ Yes	☐ No
5. Is a person you look up to and respect	☐ Yes	☐ No
6. Is normally significantly older than you	☐ Yes	☐ No
7. Has good contacts	☐ Yes	☐ No
8. Is well respected by others	☐ Yes	☐ No
9. Is well read	☐ Yes	☐ No
10. Is patient and tolerant	☐ Yes	☐ No
11. Sees his or her role as mentor as important and thus commits to making meeting dates	☐ Yes	☐ No

(You need to find someone who scores over 6)

if you could spare a lunch or dinner once every quarter so I can cover issues with you. Occasionally, I might need your thoughts on an urgent matter that I might be having some problems with. My boss is very supportive of this and is happy to pay for the meals and any incidental expenses that you may incur." *In this situation it is made clear to Pat that this relationship is supported by the company.*

"Pat, I am aware that you are mentoring a few people. I would benefit greatly if this service could be extended to me. My manager has set aside an amount of money for my mentoring. Could I come to see you to discuss how we might make this happen?" *In this scenario Pat is a paid professional mentor, so a more direct approach is possible.*

Types of Mentors

In a very readable book Mick Ukleja and Robert Lorber[1] have talked about four different types of mentors. I give you the four types in their words.

Upward Mentors: These are the people to whom you look up. They have helped and are still helping you become who you are. They can be a parent, grandparent, coach, author, pastor, rabbi, or boss. They may be someone you haven't met.

Friendship Mentors: These are the people with whom you experience life. You have gone through various stages with them—college, career, or family, and work life. They are your peers, and you've learned from them in a mutually giving way.

Sandpaper Mentors: You don't have to look for them; they always find you! These are people who rub you the wrong way. Don't reject all that they say simply because they are critical or cranky. In reality they can help you—if you are observant, open, and non-defensive.

Downward Mentors: These are the people in whom you are invested. They may be younger than you, but not necessarily. When you invest in others in a giving relationship, you actually learn a lot about yourself. You experience what's important to you and what should be emphasized and reinforced in your own professional and personal life.

I subscribe to their views and believe that having mentors covering these characteristics will aid you on your journey.

Some Mentoring Better Practices

To give you an idea of mentoring, here are some better practices:

One health-sector organization has established a mentorship program for all managers reporting to the general managers. The program is to support these managers for their first six months until they have developed their own support network. In the past they had found that managers had become isolated, which had led to some questionable decisions and actions.

Government groups have developed a mentoring system where the mentors have received training and meet together to discuss issues that affect their "students." At first, management did not understand the distinction between a mentor and a manager, but now they accept that a mentor must *not* be in direct line of control of his or her student.

One government group's graduate program has a mentoring facility for all new recruits. Typically, the graduate will first work for the mentor (who has had a two-day course in mentoring skills); this ensures a good start to the process. The graduate has the same mentor for the ensuing two years, although he or she will have several managers during the period.

We all need heroes. They help create vision and sometimes a piece of their magic rubs off on you. Remember those days when you were young, the dreams of hitting that tennis ball in the Wimbledon final, sinking that last putt on the 18th hole to win the open, or scoring the final goal? You still need those dreams now, but in a different context.

Dreams create visions; visions create spotlights on pathways; pathways get you where you want to be. It is that simple.

Many great heroes, from Alexander the Great to Sir Edmund Hillary, also hero-worshipped. The difference between them and us is that they made their dreams become reality.

Notes

1. Mick Ukleja and Robert Lorber, *Who Are You and What Do You Want?*, PERIGEE, 2009.

CHAPTER 4

Finding the Right Organization for You

If you have only a few minutes to skim over this chapter, this is what you should focus on:

- Finding the right manager to work for
- Move-or-stay-put checklist

It is often said that the best jobs never hit the papers. These are either filled through "head hunters," via the extended network of the senior management team, or from approaches made by proactive managers. Organizations, not surprisingly, cannot fail to be impressed by good candidates who have done their homework and made an innovative approach to them.

Working under a Great CEO

The more senior you are, the more important it is to know what the current CEO is like. From my exposure to CEOs through consulting and auditing, the truly great ones who change all those whom they contact are less than one in every hundred. So if you hear about a great CEO, move heaven and earth to get a job at their organization.

Here are some of the approaches you could adopt:

- Ask all of your contacts: "Who is the best CEO you have worked for?" and "What made the CEO so good?" For every good CEO there are about nine average ones.
- Read better-practices books as stories will emerge about the work styles of these truly great CEOs.
- Monitor all the major social media and take note of the CEOs who are talking about making change, challenging the mindset—these are the ones you want to work for.

Working for a Great Manager

I was giving a course in Australia and after the session I was having a drink with some of the attendees. One attendee, who had attended with his boss, asked me about a dilemma he faced. He had been approached by a head hunter to join another company. I asked about his boss. This is what he said: "She is incredibly supportive and innovative—for example, she attended this course with me today. She is so good that she was brought in by the CEO who had worked with her previously. She is most certainly a high flyer."

I had already met her in the course so I was not surprised by the comments. When I pointed out that having one manager like that in a career is considered lucky, he immediately could see that moving was not the right decision to make.

While being sought after by another company is very flattering, remember the following:

- The worst managers are generally the biggest con artists. They promise everything and deliver on few of their promises. Talk is cheap for these people—they have to be good at lying because no one would work for them if they told the truth!
- Good and great managers have staff members who have stayed on a long time. So if a manager's direct reports are turning over quickly, you know that it is a dysfunctional team/organization.
- Each move is a risk and you need to be compensated for it. Why move for less than a 20% increase unless you know that the other organization/ CEO/manager is truly great? In that circumstance moving for a pay cut could be a worthwhile investment.

Before changing jobs, check your score on the checklist in Exhibit 4.1.

A Great Leader

I recently met George Hickton, one of New Zealand's most successful CEOs, a week or so before he left Tourism New Zealand (TNZ). Arriving at the head office you are immediately struck by how different it is from many other government institutions/departments in Wellington. There is a large reception area that is used for team gatherings. It is an *open-plan office* with workstations and not an office desk in sight. A quiet buzz of activity permeates the office space. This is very different from the Tourism Board that Hickton inherited.

Having arrived early I decided to go down and get myself a latte. In the elevator I spoke to a young staff member. "What is it like to work at TNZ? What is it like to work with George?" Besides saying she loved the job and how great George was, she said, "George addressed me by my first name when we met in the elevator and it was my second week and I was only working on a part-time basis." Track back and see his history, interview his staff, and the same will be said: "The last of the true gentleman CEOs," "The nicest CEO I have ever worked for," "A legend in this own lifetime."

I believe great leadership is like a fingerprint, unique to the individuals who exude it. We can, however, glean much by understanding the great masters of leadership—the leaders who have made a real difference. George Hickton is one such leader. I am analyzing Hickton against a model I developed when looking at "The Boss": Antarctic explorer Sir Ernest Henry Shackleton (1874–1922), one of the greatest leaders of the 20th century.

Exhibit 4.1 Move-or-Stay-Put Checklist

Current Manager		
Do you enjoy working with your manager?	☐ Yes	☐ No
Are you still learning from your manager?	☐ Yes	☐ No
Is your manager well-respected and liked in the organization?	☐ Yes	☐ No
Has your manager had a good career to date?	☐ Yes	☐ No
Is your manager in the inner circle with the CEO?	☐ Yes	☐ No

Current Organization		
Is there further potential for you in the organization?	☐ Yes	☐ No
Are there other managers in the organization you would enjoy working with?	☐ Yes	☐ No
Are you proud about working for your organization?	☐ Yes	☐ No
Is your current rate of pay in the top third for your position and experience?	☐ Yes	☐ No
Are you given good training and development opportunities?	☐ Yes	☐ No

Number of Ticks	Advice to You
7–10	Really stupid to leave, the grass is not greener on the other side of the fence.
6–7	Only move on if the organization or manager is changing for the worse.
3–5	Start looking for a new position elsewhere, but only leave when you have another job lined up.
<3	You should have left ages ago.

Crisis Management

If you think you have a crisis, think of what Hickton has faced. In the space of one week, the terrorist attacks of September 11 and the collapse of the Australian Airline, Ansett, had occurred. Like Shackleton, Hickton is at his best in a crisis. He has noted that in some cases life is simpler when most of the extraneous activities are shed and you have fewer "balls in the air" to juggle.

Staff report that they have never seen Hickton in a panic. In this crisis he focused on and dealt with the issues that mattered: "communicating with the operators in the tourism industry."

If you have worked for a boss who gets stressed in a crisis, please note this is a habit to avoid. Great leaders rise every time to meet the challenge and inspire their staff to do likewise.

Recruiting

Hickton always looks to recruit senior management positions from within. This approach is common in great companies like Toyota. It is so important to ensure that there is an in-depth understanding of the culture and operations among the senior management team (SMT).

Hickton has a knack of building a great team around him. He does not have to bring in a team from his previous company. He works with the existing senior management in developing their often-unseen potential.

Optimism

Some say great leaders can be made. I personally do not think so. While one's leadership can improve greatly, certain traits needs to be hardwired genetically. One of these is optimism. Hickton always remains optimistic, no matter what is thrown his way. This optimism is not just for morale; it lies much deeper. Optimistic people always see the glass half full rather than half empty.

Optimism is contagious; it helps organizations overcome horrendous difficulties; it enables the human spirit to achieve the seemingly impossible.

Managing Results and People

The Monday-morning staff meeting is quick and focused on the achievements of the previous week. Hickton has developed some techniques that have been with him wherever he goes:

- At a government agency he developed the "Nine O'clock News," a snapshot metrics report that showed how well all the branches were operating.
- He had a simple vision that everybody could understand: "Greater tourist numbers visiting New Zealand and getting them to spend more while they are here."
- The Monday meeting, with all the Wellington staff, covers progress, people, policy, and points of interest. While addressing the needs of over 20 people, the duration of the meeting never exceeds 30 minutes.
- On the importance of an annual conference, Hickton says, "You need a grand finale, something to work toward." The annual conference is a two-day event that everybody attends. It is heralded as an opportunity to communicate, to celebrate.

When Hickton first introduced this concept to the employment service there was a certain amount of skepticism. Hickton said to the executive team, "I wish to acknowledge a member of staff who has gone beyond the call of duty to deliver a stunning service." The executive team replied, "You cannot do that—by singling out an individual you will ostracize the rest." Hickton nodded and said, "I accept your point of view but we will go ahead."

On the day when Hickton started to give the acknowledgment, there was a silence in the room. Upon announcement of the named individual, there was a spontaneous ovation. Everybody was not only recognizing the individual but also celebrating that the organization was happy to make the acknowledgment as well.

As Hickton recounts it, tears flowed and the recipient had to rush out of the hall to call his wife to share the first recognition in 20 years of service.

In TNZ they give out rocks as awards, New Zealand rocks fashioned by nature over millions of years, and as the advertisement goes, "given away in a moment—priceless." The recipients are called "rock stars." I was lucky enough to sit next to a recipient of this award on a plane trip. She recalled to me the shock, gratitude, and buzz over the acknowledgment, and she, too, had to rush out to share the news with the folks at home.

Why do we place a tax on recognition? Why is it that we are scared to celebrate the individual? I certainly do not subscribe to "Employee-of-the-Month" awards as it indicates that only one can receive it. Why not have "Employees-of-the-month?" We should celebrate with recognition *all* those who have achieved.

A Born Psychologist

All great leaders are naturally good motivators. They have a built-in radar that warns them who needs to be monitored, helped, and recognized.

When Hickton was promoted to a leading hand on the Ford assembly line at 18, he was given an almost impossible task.

Over the weeks he had one-to-one consultations with his staff, many of them old enough to be his parents. He calmly said, "We need to work well as a team, for if we don't, you will need to work with that miserable sod over there," as he pointed to a worker who was second in line for the job and considered by many to be a pain-in-the-neck. It was not long before the team was working like a well-oiled machine.

Conveying the Vision

Hickton is a born communicator. In order to create a vision you need to communicate a simple message. Hickton used this technique to great effect. His message to overseas travelers was, "Come now, do more, and send others." Like all great messages, it passes the *14-year-old test*. If a 14-year-old understands what you are talking about, it is likely that almost everyone will.

His message to government agency staff was, "Provide a fast and accurate income support service to customers." As Hickton points out, by making business simple, staff get engaged. He also likes to make strategic plans flexible so they can change with the circumstances.

Engage and Develop Staff

Hickton and his team are among the few organizations in New Zealand that have a leadership development program run by the SMT. This exercise is great for the bonding of all those involved and at the same time ensures the executive team members get a refresher themselves. When he was at a government agency, they trained 150 managers and supervisors in three courses run each year. That is what I call commitment to development.

Induction is something that Hickton takes very seriously. A new member is formally welcomed by all staff. The "Maori welcome" that is performed for the benefit of the new recruit is one of the most powerful experiences in their lives and the full turnout of staff makes a lasting impression. The ceremony is conducted in Maori, the native language of New Zealand, and involves oratory, song, and the acceptance of a gift by the new recruit.

Hickton recalls when he first raised his wish for a one-week orientation course run by the executive team. They looked at him and said, "George, can we afford the time?" As with all SMTs he has worked with, they knew to trust George and of course they were converts after the first induction program.

Constantly Reinventing Yourself

Unlike many CEOs, Hickton likes to read the latest management literature. He mentioned the impact that Gary Hemel's *Harvard Business Review* article, "Moon Shots for Management," had on him.

He likes to challenge the "status quo of operations." One week a year the executive team ran part of the business with the existing staff by their side, showing them the ropes. His executive teams have run the Happy Road Employment Centre, a betting agency, an unemployment benefit center, and a tourist information center.

During the one-week training session, the executive team, duty-bound to undertake mundane tasks, asked the staff, "Why am I having to copy this out three times?", "Why do I need a hard copy when I have an electronic copy?", "Why do I have to enter so much detail in the database?" The staff replied, "These are the procedures that you approved!" On returning from these one-week sessions, the executive team is refreshed and is a tighter knit group whose priorities have changed completely. Now they focus on initiatives that will help the staff at the workplace service their clients better.

Managing Results and People

Hickton has always combined the importance of performance with a focus on the happiness of the staff. I was lucky to witness the setting up of an income-support service, an agency to support the unemployed and sickness beneficiaries, in the early 1990s. He had all the internal walls removed from the head office areas and his newly recruited executive team looked, at first, bewildered at the vast empty space where there was no protection from staff coming up to ask a question or seek guidance. The "Nine O'clock News" was developed, a daily report that gave the statistics of performance of each income-support office. The high performers celebrated and the branches lower down the table knew the extent of the gap that they needed to close.

"It is so important for the executive team to work on the environment, not in it," Hickton says. By keeping in the helicopter overlooking the whole operation and not on the ground getting stuck into detail, the executive team allows the supervisors and staff to do their job, to make their decisions, and to run the day-to-day operations while the executive team can look out further afield.

Embody the Values

Hickton arrives at work to sit at a new workstation every day. His dedicated executive assistant has already arrived in order to position it in a new place. All staff at TNZ head office work at a different workstation each day. For many readers, this would sound impossible, disruptive, and inefficient, and yet, on reflection, it is profoundly logical.

Toyota has the five S's: *Sort, Straighten, Shine, Standardize,* and *Sustain.* Jeffrey Liker has explained this and the other 14 management principles of Toyota in his masterpiece, *The Toyota Way¹.* To be efficient, we all would agree, everything should be able to be filed in the right place so it can be found. The staff at the TNZ have:

- All their work saved electronically on shared drives on the server
- A small filing area for personal possessions, which is repositioned every day
- The filing of all papers into a suite of filing cabinets, organized so all can access them
- The same computer equipment
- A corporate uniform that supports the values of this great entity

Nothing more typifies the values that Hickton embeds in the organizations he works for than TNZ's "NZ rugby ball" display structure, which shows off New Zealand scenery to all visitors. This rugby ball pavilion, over 40 feet high and 70 feet long, travels around the world, popping up at exotic locations like one of those "stolen garden gnomes" (e.g., under the Eiffel Tower!). From the vision of the concept came the confirmation that technically it was possible; then came the approval from the Minister, with the caveat, "This better bloody well work" and then the speedy approval from the French government. No barrier was deemed too hard to climb by the staff involved.

Early Leadership Experiences

Hickton points out the importance of taking on leadership positions early on (e.g., in school, university, social clubs, sports teams, etc.). It is through these experiences that you can become a student of "practical" psychology.

Mentorship

Like all great leaders, Hickton has had many mentors on his journey. From the Ford manager who took him under his wing to Andy Kirkland and Jas

McKenzie, two of New Zealand's leading managers. To all you managers out there: Get yourself a mentor who is wiser than you and has more gray hair than you and whose advice you respect.

For more on leadership, see Chapter 32.

Notes

1. Jeffery Liker, *The Toyota Way*, McGraw-Hill, 2003.

PART II

Getting Prepared for Management

CHAPTER 5

Creating Winning Personal Habits

I f you have only a few minutes to skim over this chapter, this is what you should focus on:

- Treasure mapping
- The treasure map in Exhibit 5.1
- Recognition
- How to "Post-It" Reengineer

Treasure Mapping

What is a *treasure map?* In using the *mind-mapping* technique, it is the combined pictures of the outcomes you are seeking (Exhibit 5.1). On a large piece of paper (fanfold 17 × 12 inches/A3 size), you set out all the areas in your life where you want to score goals, state the goals, and stick on pictures to help you visualize the outcomes you seek. The more pictures the better—magazines and journals are an excellent source. (For example, if you want to be more physically fit, then choose a picture of a person similar to you with the body shape you aspire to; if you want to practice yoga daily, then get a picture of a person like yourself doing yoga, etc.)

My first treasure map had a picture of a particular bike—a BMW R100RS—a reasonably rare bike. Two years later, I owned the exact replica of the bike in the photo, with even the same paint combination. Read any self-help book and ask any achiever, and they will tell you that *visualization* is the key.

The more you *picture* the precise goals you want to achieve, the more you will achieve. In his book, *To the Top*, Sir Edmund Hillary comments that he had visualized summiting Mount Everest in this own mind many times. The great golfer, Jack Nicklaus, commented that he always visualized the precise flight of the ball before he commenced his swing. His vision is of the ball traveling over the out-of-bounds fence and drifting back onto

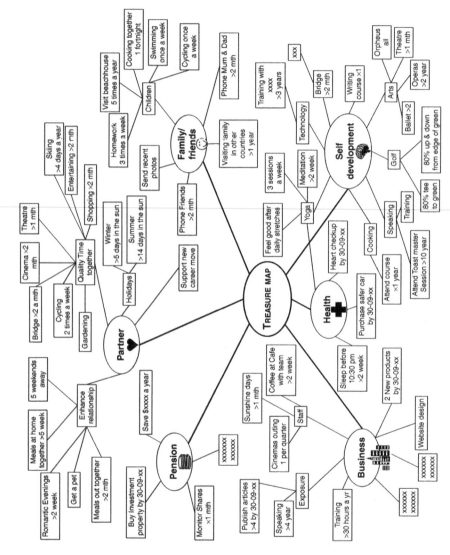

EXHIBIT 5.1 Treasure Map

EXHIBIT 5.2 Treasure Mapping Checklist

Have you included a section on your partner?	□ Yes	□ No
Have you included a section on family and friends?	□ Yes	□ No
Have you included a section on living environment? (your house, the area where you want to live, etc.)	□ Yes	□ No
Have you included a section on hobbies and interests?	□ Yes	□ No
Have you included a section on personal development? (in its wider context, including spiritual)	□ Yes	□ No
Have you included a section on health and well-being?	□ Yes	□ No
Have you included a section on career?	□ Yes	□ No
Have you included a section on pension planning?	□ Yes	□ No
Does each section have clearly stated goals that are quantified (e.g., go away for six romantic weekends a year or play tennis twice a month)?	□ Yes	□ No
Does it fit on one page?	□ Yes	□ No
Have you stuck the map where you can see it each day?	□ Yes	□ No

the fairway, having taken the shortest route to the hole. Light years from our vision—the out-of-bounds fence!

A useful technique is to pick a special day each year to update and revise your treasure map (e.g., a public holiday, birthday, etc.). Initially, you may want to change and amend your treasure map two or three times in the first year; in subsequent years you may find that an annual update is sufficient.

The treasure map needs to be stuck on a door or a wall where you can see it each day. It is important to note that this treasure map is yours and thus it is put in a private place for your eyes only. I used to have mine on the inside of my closet door. While you will want to have things on it that your partner agrees with, it is not meant to be a treasure map for two, as this typically will delay the implementation.

Treasure mapping is so important that I am giving you tips on how to complete each section of your own treasure map. Exhibit 5.2 provides a treasure-mapping checklist. You can access a help-list to build a treasure map on the website www.davidparmenter.com.

Self-Recognition

One of the most important traits to have is an inner recognition of what you have, what you are, and what you are capable of achieving. You see it in people you meet who say, "Look at this great job I have done," "I had a great round of golf today," "The report I wrote was received very well," and so forth. These individuals might sound overconfident and full of themselves, and we think that we would *never* say such things about ourselves.

Yet these confident individuals have developed a valuable trait, that of inner recognition. Every day we need to combat the negative thoughts we have and the negative environment we live in by developing our self-recognition.

Every day you can celebrate the following:

- If you have made an effort to look nice, then celebrate that you look like a million dollars.
- If you have a beautiful and therapeutic home, then celebrate the achievement before you leave for work.
- Celebrate your achievements at work.
- Talk to your colleagues and ask them about the things you do well and the things you can improve on.
- Every time you tackle a difficult issue and succeed, celebrate the achievement.
- At least three times a day recognize the things you are doing well.
- As an exercise, practice telling a close friend what you are doing well. At first it will feel uncomfortable; yet you will feel the power of *hearing* as well as thinking these recognition statements. (Your friend will also enjoy the experience.)
- When you start having those negative thoughts about your performance, those "*should-have* thoughts," listen, and stop yourself. Say to yourself, "I am not a *should-have* person." Simply treat these events as learning experiences. Look to change the behaviors that have created the problem.

> One of the most influential people in my life was my grandmother, a very positive woman. She encouraged me to say, "Every day, in every way, I am getting better and better." Try this saying yourself. You will soon feel a sense of belief in yourself that you are moving forward.

Recognition of Others

I have for a long time been aware of the significance of recognition, but only recently have I been aware that it is fundamental to all our relationships, both personal and business. The ability to appreciate and recognize all those we come in contact with defines us as a person and defines how successful, in the broadest terms, we can be.

EXHIBIT 5.3 Weekly Recognition Checklist

	Suggested frequency	4 weeks ago	3 weeks ago	2 weeks ago	Last Week	Date if not in last 4 weeks
Our partner	Daily/weekly					
Our children	Daily/weekly					
Our staff	weekly					
Our work colleagues	weekly					
Our boss	weekly					
Our friends & relatives	monthly					
Our key suppliers	quarterly					
Our mentor	quarterly					
Our key customers	quarterly					

Many of us will need to *count* the recognitions until it becomes a natural part of our makeup. I suggest you count them for the next 12 weeks as a starting point (see Exhibit 5.3).

For some of us the simple task of recognizing all the types of support we receive will be unnatural. If you are having difficulty trying to recognize contributions, think of:

- The **home**-building activities of your partner that give you a safe and secure place to return to
- The **actions** done by others that make your life easier at work and at home
- The **love** from family and friends that nourishes you
- The **support and commitment** from those at work and at home

We all appreciate recognition especially when we do not have to wait for it. Some managers have found some clever ways, such as handing out film tickets, vouchers for two at a good restaurant, and so forth, to reward staff who have gone the extra mile.

Making Decisions

The inability to make decisions is a very damaging trait that needs to be tackled head-on. Why is it that one person does her Christmas shopping all in one afternoon while another takes weeks if not months agonizing as to what to buy? Let us analyze decision making:

- No matter how much you pour over the decision, you will never know whether it is the right or wrong one until later.
- By not making a decision you have made a decision.
- There is a huge cost to not making a decision (in the Christmas shopping example, some of the costs could include multiple parking charges and cost of transportation there and back).
- Many successful people say that a quick wrong decision is better than a slowly drawn-out one that may be right.
- Very few of our decisions are life-or-death decisions when it comes to ourselves, our loved ones, or the public at large—just get on with it!
- Celebrate every quick decision you make.

For all major decisions and all those decisions you are having difficulties with, it is a good idea to **FRAME** them:

F   **Financial**: Ensure that you can afford any potential downside.

R   **Research**: Look back on your own experiences or those of people you know who have made the same decision in the past, and learn from them (history has a habit of repeating itself!).

A   **Avoid**: looking back after the decision is made; just move on and modify your course as needed, just as an ocean liner modifies its course during its journey. It is important to avoid being a should-have person.

M   **Mentor**: Always discuss major decisions with your mentor.

E   **Evaluate**: Study the pros and cons of the decision (see Exhibit 5.4).

Sleep on It Rather Than Sending It Out

When you have finished a major report, are about to make a major decision, or are about to send that terse email, sleep on it. This is especially important when you do not have a mentor or are unable to bounce the problem off someone. While you are asleep your subconscious will be thinking about the issues and you will find that you have a clearer view the next day.

Pros-and-Cons Schedule

A useful technique is to list the pros and cons of the decision. Exhibit 5.4 separates the major issues from the minor ones. I would advise against

𝓔 EXHIBIT 5.4 Pros-and-Cons Schedule

Major	Pros	Cons
	1.	1.
	2.	2.
	3.	3.
	4.	4.
	5.	5.
	6.	6.
	7.	7.
	8.	8.
	9.	9.

Minor	Pros	Cons
	1.	1.
	2.	2.
	3.	3.
	4.	4.
	5.	5.
	6.	6.
	7.	7.
	8.	8.
	9.	9.

scoring them as this is trying to create precision in a *subjective* area. This list, if completed properly, should help you make the right decision most of the time. Remember: You will never make the right decision all of the time.

Do Not Run Out of Fuel

Stop your wheels from falling off by maintaining your fluids and nutrition. I can hear you thinking, "the author has lost the plot." But if you skip this section you may as well skip the rest of the book, because you will never have the mental horsepower or the energy to do half the things I am going to introduce to you.

How many times have you worked all day on an empty stomach, not having time to eat, and in fact never noticing it? The task was so important that there was not enough time for breakfast or a sandwich for lunch!

With our many deadlines, and long, 14-hour days during the critical times, many of us fall into this trap all the time. Have you examined the times when you tend to lose your marbles? I'll wager they tend to occur after three hours without food and or fluids. Let me explain.

First look at one of the most productive managers in your organization, the one who has bountiful energy and makes great decisions, and I will show you someone who is on top of one of the secrets of successful management. She is managing her nutrition, hydration intake, and regular exercise during the working day! Yes, you have to look at the working day as if you were an athlete in the Olympics doing a marathon. You have to be as focused on these issues as these top athletes are.

If you lose 2% of body weight through dehydration, your brain cannot function. This has been proved in studies. Thus for an 85 kilo (13.5 stones) person this is 1.7 kilos or 1.7 liters (3.5 pints) of water. By working in an air-conditioned office you will lose this amount quicker than you think. Without adequate water intake your brain and muscles will cease to operate effectively and thus your energy and concentration will falter.

Understanding nutrition and its impact on your productivity is very important and I would recommend that you attend a short course on it. Start studying about the importance of balancing protein, carbohydrates, and natural oils together. It will make a profound impact on your physical condition, sense of well-being, and lifestyle. For more information see www.prozone.co.nz.

I once had a job as a corporate accountant for a radio network. They should never have appointed me, because my direct report, while not yet qualified, was very capable of doing the job. I had no experience in running the complex general ledger. I started working 14-hour days, drinking so much coffee that my hands began to shake. Every month something went wrong and the month-end was a disaster. I was asked to leave after three months of torture. Through joining the union I was able to negotiate a staggered departure, as the company had been ultimately at fault because there was no disclosure of the job skill requirements.

I am now sure that if I had managed my nutrition and hydration I would have been able to think more clearly and operate past the obstacles instead of chasing my tail.

Continuous Innovation

This is the lifeblood of an organization and one where new recruits have an advantage because they are full of new ideas and are not yet paralyzed by the company's red tape.

For one high-performance team, innovation is discussed at the end of every day in a *debriefing*. But in many organizations that I have worked in and visited, this is not the case. Innovation needs to be on every agenda; it needs to be pushed so that staff members know what is expected—otherwise, we are simply standing still. I get the impression that in many organizations staff members have the perception that innovation is not required. The same person who is "building his yacht in his backyard" after work is also performing the same unproductive tasks day after day like a laboratory rat hunting for its cheese. How is it that organizations can take an individual who is innovative at home and turn him into an automaton at work? There are many aspects of the culture that need to change. There should be more delegation, more risk taking, less witch-hunting, and more celebration of success. Then, you truly can have continuous innovation.

> In his book, *Screw It, Let's Do It*[1] Sir Richard Branson points out that his style is to *not* second-guess all ideas that come up to him. If the downside is less than the upside, and there is no obvious reason not to do it, he will go ahead. Staff thus are exposed more frequently to the possibility of making mistakes, but at the same time they are responsible for initiatives that really make a difference.

Some suggestions where you can score goals are given in Exhibit 5.5.

EXHIBIT 5.5 Innovation Checklist

Investigate the three main processes that your team spends the most time on	□ Yes	□ No
Attend courses/continuous improvement on total quality management	□ Yes	□ No
Reduce the number spreadsheets used by replacing them by more robust applications	□ Yes	□ No
Clarifying the myriad spreadsheets	□ Yes	□ No
Eliminate inefficient customer or supplier interfaces	□ Yes	□ No
Establish a national supplier arrangement that includes some transfer of the processing activities	□ Yes	□ No
Month-end processes (management and board reports)	□ Yes	□ No
Annual budget process	□ Yes	□ No

Worldwide Toyota is credited with implementing over 90,000 employee initiatives a year. That is nearly 300 for every day of the year. How many staff-generated initiatives have you implemented in the finance team in the past 12 months?

Learn How to "Post-It" Reengineer

"Post-It" reengineering will revolutionize the finance team's effectiveness and efficiency. Replace detailed process mapping with a "Post-It" solution (see Exhibit 5.6). A demonstration can be seen on www .davidparmenter.com.

Obtain different-colored Post-It pads, one for each team involved in the process, and ask the staff to write down on separate Post-Its each action they undertake. Hold a workshop of all teams and stick all the Post-Its on one wall in time bands. Then ask the team members to brainstorm to look at removing various activities. The questions that need to be asked are:

- Do we need to do this action?
- Can it be done earlier?
- Can it be done differently?

EXHIBIT 5.6 "Post-It" Reengineering in Action

All procedures that are deemed surplus to requirements are removed and stuck on another wall, and each such action should be celebrated as it represents a substantial saving.

Mind Mapping

Far too frequently we go around in circles trying to solve problems, in both our personal and working lives. We visit the same place time and time again, have the same thoughts, and end up doing nothing useful.

The technique of *mind mapping* was developed by Tony Buzan[2] to help tackle these problems in a number of ways:

- Mind mapping encourages you to see the structure of the problem or issue as you ask yourself: What are the main issues here?
- It encourages more original thought as new ideas can be entered on the map immediately and require less editing.
- As the mind map develops, headings can be easily moved across to more appropriate groups.
- It puts everything down on one page—sometimes a fan fold size of paper (11 × 17 inches) is necessary.
- It creates a diagram that is easily remembered and thus is an ideal tool for good exam technique.
- It gets you started on the report without having to worry about writer's block.
- It ensures that you always see the big picture.

After 30 years' experience with mind maps (see Exhibit 5.7), I offer this advice:

Step one: Place the issue in the forefront and think carefully about the title (e.g., "Best Location for Factory," is better than simply "Factory").

Step two: Think of the main issues and write them in as headings around the central point and connect them via arrows (e.g., for a factory it could be the history (or background), resource availability, labor issues, transportation issues, closeness to market, cost to build, cost to operate, proximity to key suppliers, etc.).

Step three: Brainstorm each issue in turn. If a point is suggested that is better in another section, write it in that section. Occasionally you get an entirely new issue raised; with these you simply add another arrow from the center.

Step four: Make sure you have enough facts, examples, references, and so forth; these will be in the third or fourth tiers of arrows.

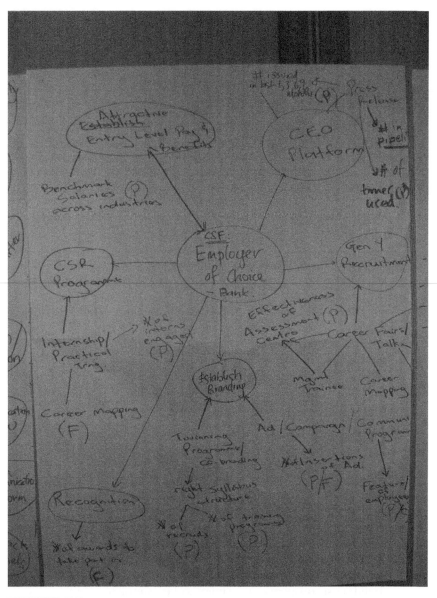

EXHIBIT 5.7 Mind Map from a Key Performance Indicator Workshop

Business Etiquette

This is an area that often holds back the accountant. In the desire to be a more efficient processing machine, we forget that most of what we are doing is not the really important stuff. In fact, *managing relationships* should be right at the top of the list.

Managing Relationships

One's career can be reviewed from a series of standpoints. How open was I in taking up opportunities as they presented themselves to me? How equipped was I to succeed? How well did I nurture the relationships around me? I believe the "nurturing of relationships" is often undervalued by the corporate accountant. We are working so hard that we have little or no time to grow a network of supporters. In fact we do the opposite—we often alienate ourselves from the senior management team through undertaking tasks they hate, such as the annual planning process!

I had been working in London on a consultancy assignment for three months as a contract worker for an investment bank that had grandiose plans with little idea how to achieve them. I was conscientious, as were all the employees, struggling to see the forest for the trees. One Friday I had decided to leave early to avoid the traffic en route to Liverpool. I had asked my manager if it was okay a few days earlier. The manager, as you can imagine, was under a lot of stress because nobody in the team was getting very far with their project work. She stormed in at 4:00 P.M. trying to locate me, only to find that I had already left work. She chose to forget the earlier conversation we had had and complained to my firm.

On the following Monday I was taken off the job. Six months later she was laid off and applied to join the firm I was working for. I was consulted. While I tried to remain positive I explained that there was always a risk with her interpersonal skills. She lost out. It goes to show how small the world really is and how making unwise moves has a tendency to come back and haunt you.

Cell Phone Etiquette

How many times have you been in a meeting when someone has taken a call or answered a text that was not very important? How many times have you heard every word of someone's conversation on public transportation? In one case I nearly went up to the person and said "Count me in on the deal!"

In some countries it is common practice to cover your mouth when speaking on a cell phone, thus not allowing the sound waves to travel. Otherwise, you will, like the rest of us, simply raise your voice on the misguided belief that the mobile microphone needs a bit of help.

Have you ever taken someone out on what you thought was going to be a hot date, having gone to a lot of trouble in organizing what you thought was going to be a memorable night, and found the person spending the whole time answering one call after another? The trouble is, you could be like this at work!

I believe running one's life via mobile phone indicates a flaw in one's personality. I have seen it in many people. By responding to a call or text coming in while in another's presence, you are telling the person that you are with that she is less important than the message you are about to respond to. While we all can justify having our cell phones on all the time (e.g., I could get a call from my sick parents), in reality it is an addiction. Few of us are brain surgeons; few of us have people depending on us for their lives to justify being in contact 24/7. Try turning it off. You might get to like it. To warn your callers you could leave something like the following message:

I am on a behavioral change program, freeing my life for success, and my cell phone will be off more than it is on. Please do not take offense— leave a message or send a text or an email. I will get back to you within 24 hours.

Greeting the Guest

I have met many managers over the years and none have greeted me in the way I was treated by a CEO.

I will never forget the day I visited the CEO of Pilkington Automotive Glass in New Zealand. On arrival, the security man at the gate was expecting me. Once I was at the ground-floor reception area, instead of going up to the executive floor the CEO came down and greeted me. This was the first and only time this has happened. During the discussion I asked about the total quality management (TQM) practices that they were famous for, such as the way any worker on the factory floor has the right and obligation to stop a production batch if he thinks there is something wrong.

I ended up asking the CEO why he came downstairs to meet me, to which he replied, "I take great care vetting meetings. Once I have agreed to a meeting, I will personally greet my guests at reception and return them there after the meeting. It is a sign of respect." Yes, it is, and one that I have never forgotten.

Remember You/Remember Me

They say that the most important word to us all is our own name. Great CEOs have the ability to remember names and even any small incidents relating to the last meeting to show that they remember you. This skill makes a lasting impression and is one of the reasons why President Clinton is still so popular.

There are a number of tricks to remembering names. One is to look at the person and consider whether they remind you of another person with the same name; another is to ensure that you use the person's name as much as you can while in conversation with the individual. Finally never *say* you are bad at remembering names, as you are effectively telling your subconscious to wipe this information out of your memory banks!

Disengaging Swiftly and Politely

Many of us can be seen as a little too abrupt. As thinking people, we want to move on as soon as we have discussed the issues we wanted covered. We have other things to do. The skill to learn is how to disengage swiftly and politely.

I was in discussion with a health club manager, and a new client arrived. She had a marvelous way of touching me on the arm and saying "excuse me." I, however, am appalled at some of the ways I disengage. It is an art to disengage swiftly yet politely. Develop some catch phrases, such as:

- "I am scheduled to make a call to Pat; I've so enjoyed . . ."
- "Thank you for your card. I will call you next week to discuss this issue further. I look forward to continuing our discussion then."
- "My apologies [touching the person on the arm]. I need to catch up with a few acquaintances here today; could we meet up in the near future? I will send you an email."

Full Attention at Meetings

Many times, pressing issues will mean that your attention will be elsewhere. It might be a family issue, a work issue, or a worrying quirk in your golf swing (just kidding). Attending a meeting with your mind wandering is in fact worse than *not* attending. The attendee's perception of you will be negative and that impression unfortunately will remain weeks after the meeting. Do the wise thing. If you cannot give full attention at a meeting, do not go.

I once met a person who had a shocking habit at meetings—he would fall asleep! The pinnacle was reached when he fell asleep in a one-on-one with his manager. I was brought in to be his mentor. I soon discovered that this individual had a rocket scientist's brain capacity and thus the thinking speed of those around him seemed so slow to him that he could listen to the conversation while day dreaming with his eyes closed.

His behavior was turned around by ensuring that he attended only essential meetings; his contribution was handled first on the agenda, after which he was excused, and while at the meetings he was encouraged to take notes. The interesting point was that the notes were not for his benefit; he did not need them for he had total recall. The notes were to keep him busy and at the same time say to all those who were there, "What you are saying is important."

After the meeting he would dispose of the notes (out of sight of the attendees).

It never ceases to amaze me when people answer their phone while they are having a meeting in their office. How long does it take to shut off the phone or put it on vibrate? What is the good of saying "I am in a meeting, please call me back?" Let them leave a message and call them back later, thus avoiding one conversation that cannot go anywhere.

Returning Phone Calls

Probably the easiest way to lose credibility at home and at work is not to return calls. How does one return calls and yet be efficient at work? My suggestion is to set aside specific times in the day to do this, such as right after lunch and in the last hour of the day, and book these times in your schedule. Naturally, there will be those return calls to the CEO or your partner that are done immediately. The rest, however, can wait.

Golden Rules with Email

If you are receiving over 50 emails a day here are some golden rules to save you time.

Rule #1: Never open emails before 10.30am.

In the good old days, we would handle mail at 10:30 A.M. when the mail finally arrived from the mailroom. We thus started the day with scoring a goal—undertaking a service delivery activity. Now the first thing we do is open up the email and suddenly one hour has evaporated. Some of us even get interrupted every time a new email arrives.

As a therapy I suggest not opening your email until after your morning coffee and then only looking at emails at one or two more intervals during the day. If something is very important you will get a phone call. This technique will help you get more 1.5-hour blocks of concentrated time in your day. See Exhibit 5.8.

Rule #2: You are not Barrack Obama so do not live and sleep with your Blackberry!

Most of us (fortunately or unfortunately) are not heart or brain surgeons. Our work is not critical to life. Many emails we handle have little or no relevance to where we or our organizations want to go. The silliest thing is surely to handle an email twice, once on the Blackberry "Will get back to you when in the office" and once in our computer.

Rule #3: The five sentence rule.

Treat all email responses like SMS text messages and limit them to something you can count easily—five sentences. A campaign has been started see www.five.sentenc.es. Ensure all terms, conditions, papers are attached to the email. This has the added benefit of ensuring that your email will not be a critical company document. This way you have a full record filed in your document management system.

Rule #4: Have an attention grabbing header.

Make the header the main message of the email. If you cannot think of a good email header maybe you should not send the email

Rule #5: Actively terminate email exchanges.

Manage your email exchanges. If you needed feedback in order to get to a closure, often a phone call is better. Ping pong emails on the same topic are screaming out "Lets speak tomorrow!" Think about your desired outcome and promote a course of action to avoid the table tennis. If necessary use the "No more emails on this one thank you."

Rule #6: Promote yourself by your endeavors not by your use of broadcast emails, reply all, or copy correspondence (cc).

Avoid sending broadcast emails unless you are prepared to call up each person to advise them that there is a key document that they need to read. Ensure that you do not add to the "spam" in your organization. Forwarding business material may be well meaning but it is creating havoc in many organizations, where frequently managers are receiving up to 240 emails a day. Ask yourself is it necessary to copy the CEO—just for visibility?

Rule #7: If you would not put your words in a letter do not put them in an email.

Far to often the content of emails, while amusing, is not appropriate. Be careful about being the bearer of silly jokes. Today many people seem to want to be remembered by their joke telling. Now, don't get me wrong, I love a joke, but when you are sent a couple a week by the same person you do wonder what they do all day. Remember, perception rules everything. You do not want to be perceived as a person whose prime focus is to entertain. You want to be thought of in more positive terms.

Rule #8: Master your email application's tools.

The boffins have been busy improving the ways we can handle emails. The applications you use for emails will have many features you have never opened! Many readers have mastered word and spreadsheet applications yet the one application you use the most is in reality least known about. Master the new features, it will take a 30 minute session with a techo. You need to know and master:

- How to turn off auto-notifiers
- How to use filters to sort and prioritize
- Getting newsletters to automatically go straight to a folder which you access twice weekly
- Setting up auto responders to acknowledge and advise response time
- filters, flags, colors, sorting tools

Rule #9: Your Inbox is not a storage area.

The inbox should be for collection only, just like your in-tray! Messages should be deleted, auctioned, or filed. Do you keep all your texts and phone messages. NO! be ruthless with deletions. You have only gone far enough when you start having to ask people to resend their message.

Rule #10: Have a night's sleep before you send a complaint/rebuff email.

For complex responses, complaints, rebuffs, etcetera draft the email and file in the draft section, of your email application, overnight, as you may well have second thoughts. It is a good idea to discuss these emails with your mentor. Many a career has been dented by a poorly thought through email written in anger.

EXHIBIT 5.8 Checklist for Making Your Email Usage More Efficient

Making your Email usage more efficient checklist		
Are you applying the golden rules of email		
Rule #1 Never open emails before 10.30am	☐ Yes	☐ No
Rule #2 You are not Barrack Obama so do not live and sleep with your Blackberry!	☐ Yes	☐ No
Rule #3 The five sentence rule	☐ Yes	☐ No
Rule #4 Have an attention grabbing header	☐ Yes	☐ No
Rule #5 Actively terminate email exchanges	☐ Yes	☐ No
Rule #6 Promote yourself by your endeavors not by your use of reply—all or cc	☐ Yes	☐ No
Rule #7 If you would not put your words in a letter do not put them in an email	☐ Yes	☐ No
Rule #8 Master email application's tool section	☐ Yes	☐ No
Rule #9 Your Inbox is not a storage area	☐ Yes	☐ No
Rule #10 Have a night's sleep before you send a complaint/rebuff email	☐ Yes	☐ No
Other useful email habits		
Always use the spell check (ensure that the appropriate dictionary is set up)	☐ Yes	☐ No
Just because emails are an instant communication it does not mean the issue is urgent, prioritize your time responding in relation to the importance of all your priorities	☐ Yes	☐ No
Set up a folder in your inbox called "I do not need this information" for all those emails you do not need to receive and send a standard reply to them when you have time (see suggestion below)	☐ Yes	☐ No
Ask yourself if it is better to respond in person or over the phone, e.g. Delicate issues are obviously better handled "eyeball to eyeball"	☐ Yes	☐ No
Monitor how many emails are not furthering your goals, your team goals, or your organization's goals	☐ Yes	☐ No

Notes

1. Sir Richard Branson, *Screw it, Let's Do it: Lessons in Life*, Virgin Books, 2006.
2. Tony Buzan, *The Mind Map Book: Unlock Your Creativity, Boost Your Memory, Change Your Life* , BBC Active, 2009.

CHAPTER 6

Developing Winning Work Habits

If you have only a few minutes to skim over this chapter, this is what you should focus on:

- Attend a weeklong management course
- Ban morning meetings
- The 4:00 P.M. Friday weekly planner
- Quality assurance checks
- Better-practice graphics
- Deliver bulletproof PowerPoint presentations

Attend a One Week Management Course

Many of us have little or no preparation for management. It is totally different from working as a direct-report team member. Your success now depends on how you can obtain output from your staff. It is hard to make the transition and far too easy to value your contribution on what output you create rather than looking at the collective whole.

A weeklong management course will help you to:

- Learn how to handle different situations through creative role playing.
- Create a useful network with your peers from different organizations (I have remained in contact with three members that I met over 18 years ago at a management course).
- Help prepare a shift in thinking.
- Understand the dynamics of a good team.

The things you need to look for in good management courses are in the checklist in Exhibit 6.1 and an example is provided in Exhibit 6.2.

EXHIBIT 6.1 Good Management Course Attributes Checklist

General

1. Residential course of at least five days	☐ Yes	☐ No
2. Based around some team exercises and role playing	☐ Yes	☐ No
3. Some prereading requirement	☐ Yes	☐ No
4. Your manager being required to complete a needs analysis and assessment of your current skill base	☐ Yes	☐ No
5. Course providers happy to give you contacts of previous participants	☐ Yes	☐ No
6. Follow-up courses offered post the management course	☐ Yes	☐ No
7. Course presenters have had in-depth management experience	☐ Yes	☐ No
8. Good range of age and experience of other participants	☐ Yes	☐ No

Course Content

9. Current management thinking and practice	☐ Yes	☐ No
10. How to manage teams effectively	☐ Yes	☐ No
11. Enhancement of communication skills	☐ Yes	☐ No
12. Leadership practices	☐ Yes	☐ No
13. Completing personal development plan	☐ Yes	☐ No
14. How to set strategy	☐ Yes	☐ No
15. Business disciplines at a strategic level	☐ Yes	☐ No
16. Impact of culture	☐ Yes	☐ No
17. Preparing plans that are adaptable in today's changing environment	☐ Yes	☐ No
18. Managing a budget (being fiscally responsible)	☐ Yes	☐ No
19. Analyzing and solving complex problems	☐ Yes	☐ No
20. Negotiating	☐ Yes	☐ No
21. Resolving conflict	☐ Yes	☐ No
22. Delegating responsibility	☐ Yes	☐ No
23. Recruiting successfully	☐ Yes	☐ No
24. Finding a mentor	☐ Yes	☐ No
25. Handling difficult staff and peer relationships	☐ Yes	☐ No
26. Understanding one's own personality traits, strengths, and weaknesses	☐ Yes	☐ No

How to Help Your Boss Be Successful

I have been lucky enough to hear the Dalai Lama. He talked about many things; one was "inner disarmament." It put quite clearly the issue that we cannot have peace at home, at the workplace, or between countries if we do not have inner peace. The converse of inner peace must be inner conflict, and this permeates through to how we work with our colleagues and how we relate to our boss.

EXHIBIT 6.2 Management Course Outline Example

Part I: Overview of Management
- What is management and what role does it play?
- What do effective managers actually do?
- Selecting the appropriate management strategy
- Managerial competencies
- Mentorship and its importance to you

Part II: Self-management
- Making the transition from staff member to person in charge
- Determining individual competencies
- Managing time and setting priorities

Part III: Managing Others
- Planning the work—goal setting
- Organizing the work
- Choosing strategies for training, coaching, and delegation
- Communication skills and techniques
- Recruiting well—why it is the most important thing you do
- Principles and practices making up transactional analysis
- Motivating others through the feedback process
- Giving performance appraisals
- Monitoring the work
- Handling managerial challenges—counseling
- Servant Leadership—lessons from great leaders

Part IV: Action Plans for the Future

Methodology
This highly interactive program will provide individual exercises that allow you to work through the various management processes by interfacing with other soon-to-be managers. Case studies, role play, and group exercises are also utilized as a means of reinforcing what you have learned so that you are able to apply this in a practical, day-to-day manner.

The talk got me thinking about how many firms I have seen where there is disharmony between the manager and the staff. It is easy to blame the manager in this situation, yet when you look deeper you see a different picture. Many staff, when interviewed, had trouble with their last three managers, yet they fail to see the correlation.

A good relationship between the manager and staff is expressed by rock climbing, as illustrated in Exhibit 6.3.

EXHIBIT 6.3 A Rock-Climbing Relationship between the Manager and Staff

This exhibit tells many stories. Let's take the time to understand them:

- The person in front is your boss. He has the experience and technical knowledge (in most cases) to lead the team up known and uncharted routes.
- The leader needs to ensure his team is educated so that they can follow at a reasonable pace. The leader cannot climb successfully alone; he can only summit small mountains on his own.
- The staff should ensure that the boss is kept up to date on important conditions so correct decisions can be made.
- There is a degree of trust and respect as mountaineers' lives depend on their gear and fellow climbers.
- The first company I worked for had a recruiting diagram that showed each person up the rope wanting you to take their place so that they could move on themselves. The firm truly believed in the concept and it was an experience I have not had again.

So, if I were asked what advice I would give a keenly motivated individual, I would say, "Help your boss summit those high peaks." How? Simply look at the picture in Exhibit 6.3 again and it all becomes clear.

Focus on Your Boss's Goals

Concentrate on your boss's goals and make them your goals. Your goals should be a subset of what your boss is trying to achieve. If there is total discord, you will need to appraise why you are in your current job, or work to change the focus of your boss.

Stop Commenting on Your Boss's Weaknesses to Others

We all have weaknesses; why not focus on the strengths, and start talking about them to other people? You may just find that the more positive you are the more your boss's performance improves. Nobody, including you and your boss, can survive for long in a negative environment.

Understand What Makes Your Boss Tick

A good starting point is to take courses covering the Enneagram, Hermann's thinking preferences, and Myers-Briggs personality profiles; these will help you work better with your manager and colleagues.

Encourage Your Boss to Celebrate Success

Try an outing to a matinee film show—yes, you invest your lunch break, the boss invests the rest; make sure every birthday is celebrated, and remember staff with young children do not have extendible evenings!

Help Your Boss to Become a Finisher

One suggestion that worked for me is to work on a week-on/week-off basis—one week on a "finishing" focus and the other working on those nice new projects we so love to start. On the finishing week, nothing—I mean *nothing*—new can be started. Even the very thought is banned. Start finishing off those projects that your boss wanted but now has forgotten about or has put into the "too-hard basket."

See the checklist in Exhibit 6.4 for ways of helping your boss.

How to Handle a "Bully of a Boss"

The most important point is that you can never change someone else's behavior. Only they can. The best help to you is your mentor, who will have handled this situation before. Start off by learning to help your manager summit. This will improve the relationship and may lead to his departure to greener pastures.

If you have tried everything and life at work is miserable, you owe it to yourself to find an alternative position within the organization or as a last measure in another organization. No matter how bad it is, never resign, as you will find that the euphoria of being at home while others

⚙ EXHIBIT 6.4 Helping Your Boss to Succeed Checklist

1. Are you helping your boss become more computer literate?	☐ Yes	☐ No
2. Do you provide your boss with decision-based reports?	☐ Yes	☐ No
3. Do you focus on your boss's goals?	☐ Yes	☐ No
4. Have you stopped commenting on your boss's weaknesses?	☐ Yes	☐ No
5. Do you understand what makes your boss tick?	☐ Yes	☐ No
6. Do you help make work fun by organizing team functions?	☐ Yes	☐ No
7. Do you help your boss to become a finisher?	☐ Yes	☐ No
8. Are you looking for other mountains for your boss to climb?	☐ Yes	☐ No
9. Do you enjoy your boss's successes as you have helped create them?	☐ Yes	☐ No
10. Can you take criticism in a positive light?	☐ Yes	☐ No
11. Do you accept differences and just get on with it?	☐ Yes	☐ No
12. If you want to be emotional about your relationship with your boss or other employees, do you keep it to "one minute?"	☐ Yes	☐ No
13. Have you invested time and energy to find your inner peace?	☐ Yes	☐ No

are suffering at work is short-lived and career damaging. Always look for a new job from a position of power (i.e., while employed).

Time Management: The Basics

There is a vast array of books and courses on time management. My suggestion is that you attend such a course every five years, to reenergize yourself. Writers on this topic talk about spending time on the key building blocks first. A good example I have seen delivered by Stephen Covey[1] is to ask a member of the audience to put rocks, pebbles, and sand in a container. The only way it can be done is to put the rocks (key tasks) in first, the pebbles (other service delivery tasks) in second, and the sand in last (the day-to-day dramas, meetings, etc. that sabotage our work). See Exhibit 6.5.

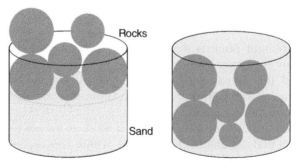

EXHIBIT 6.5 Putting the Rocks in First

𝓔 EXHIBIT 6.6 Work/Home Balance Planner

<table>
<tr><td rowspan="8">Urgent</td><td>Work</td><td>Home</td></tr>
<tr><td>1.</td><td>1.</td></tr>
<tr><td>2.</td><td>2.</td></tr>
<tr><td>3.</td><td>3.</td></tr>
<tr><td>4.</td><td>4.</td></tr>
<tr><td>5.</td><td>5.</td></tr>
<tr><td>6.</td><td>6.</td></tr>
<tr><td>7.</td><td>7.</td></tr>
</table>

<table>
<tr><td rowspan="8">Nonurgent</td><td>Work</td><td>Home</td></tr>
<tr><td>1.</td><td>1.</td></tr>
<tr><td>2.</td><td>2.</td></tr>
<tr><td>3.</td><td>3.</td></tr>
<tr><td>4.</td><td>4.</td></tr>
<tr><td>5.</td><td>5.</td></tr>
<tr><td>6.</td><td>6.</td></tr>
<tr><td>7.</td><td>7.</td></tr>
</table>

Check to see that you have activities within these sections of your treasure map (tick if some action is happening).

Partner	Family	Living Environment	Health	Hobbies	Personal development	Work	Pension

Another technique I use is to list all work and life activities into urgent and non-urgent categories, as shown in Exhibit 6.6. The schedule will help ensure you have balance in your life and that you tackle the urgent things first. The key of course is to tackle as many as possible while they are non-urgent! See Exhibit 6.7 for a time management checklist.

A philosophy professor is lecturing to his students. He brings out an empty jar and golf balls. Filling the jar with the golf balls, he asks if it is full. "Yes," they reply. Then he lifts a container of dried peas and pours them in. "Is it full?" "Yes," they reply. Then he lifts a container of sand and pours it in around the golf balls and peas. "Is it full?" "Yes,

(Continued)

definitely," they reply. Then he pours in a cup of coffee. He explained, "Golf balls are the important things in your life—you must put them into your life first, otherwise you can't fit them in. Dried peas—are the next most important things. Sand—thoughts, hobbies, holidays, daily chores."

"So why the coffee?" a student asks. "To remind you to always have the time for a coffee with your friends," the professor replied.

EXHIBIT 6.7   Time Management Checklist

Basics

1. Have you attended a time management course?	☐ Yes	☐ No
2. Are you spending at least half your time in the important-not-urgent quadrant?	☐ Yes	☐ No
3. Have you read any of the Covey books (*first things first*)?	☐ Yes	☐ No
4. Do you run an electronic calendar that reminds you of meetings, etc.?	☐ Yes	☐ No
5. If Microsoft scheduler is used in your company, do you block two-hour chunks of time so meetings are not allowed to decimate your day?	☐ Yes	☐ No

Better-Practice Time Management Habits

6. Do you avoid crisis by planning in advance?	☐ Yes	☐ No
7. Do you avoid commitments that do not fit into key result areas?	☐ Yes	☐ No
8. Are you courteous with people and ruthless with time?	☐ Yes	☐ No
9. Do you have set meetings with yourself planning the next few days, weeks, months and assessing progress in your key result areas?	☐ Yes	☐ No
10. Do you allow enough time between meetings in case one runs overtime?	☐ Yes	☐ No
11. Do you think that arriving just in time is actually being late, in other words, for a 9 A.M. meeting you arrive at 8:45 to 8:50 A.M.?	☐ Yes	☐ No
12. Do you work back from the time you need to be there and schedule in some contingencies?	☐ Yes	☐ No
13. Do you avoid taking that last call as you are running out the door?	☐ Yes	☐ No
14. Do you treat your electronic calendar alarm as a signal to get up and go (not as a flag to complete some new small exercise that will surely make you late)?	☐ Yes	☐ No
15. Do you plan for the next day, next week, next month on a rolling basis?	☐ Yes	☐ No
16. Do you focus back on your goals daily?	☐ Yes	☐ No

It is important to run your week in the most efficient way to service your customers and your workload. Thus, the number-one rule is not to allow others to disorganize you.

It is important to avoid having meetings during your key productive time. Yet that is the very thing we all tend to do.

Ask anybody about his or her productivity and you will find frustration about how time has been taken away in nonproductive activities. It never ceases to amaze me how many people schedule meetings in their prime thinking time, the first part of the morning. Would it not be better to schedule meetings toward the tail end of the day and leave the first two hours of the morning for working on your projects? Exhibit 6.8 depicts the impact on the working day. In other words, limit or ban morning meetings.

The main change in Exhibit 6.8 is that there are larger chunks of service-delivery time (the time spent catching up on projects, answering emails and phone calls, and so forth) and meeting times are rescheduled to the afternoons, allowing us to be more relaxed, having scored some early goals. In order to make this possible there need to be fewer meetings, and here are some suggested rules that might be useful:

- Avoid opening emails until 10:30 A.M.—this is covered later in this chapter.
- Have meetings only when all actions have been undertaken from the previous meeting.
- Block your service-delivery time three months ahead, so that your working day cannot be ambushed by others accessing your electronic calendar.

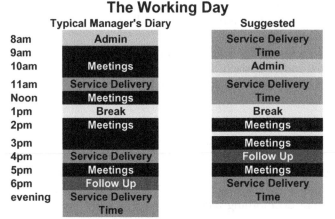

The Working Day

	Typical Manager's Diary	Suggested
8am	Admin	Service Delivery
9am		Time
10am	Meetings	Admin
11am	Service Delivery	Service Delivery
Noon	Meetings	Time
1pm	Break	Break
2pm	Meetings	Meetings
3pm		Meetings
4pm	Service Delivery	Follow Up
5pm	Meetings	Meetings
6pm	Follow Up	Service Delivery
evening	Service Delivery Time	Time

EXHIBIT 6.8 Working-Day Schedule

EXHIBIT 6.9 Costing Managers' Time

A manager's year may look like this:	Weeks	
Vacations (including public holidays)	6	
Sick leave	2	
Training and updating	2	
Time spent travelling to other offices, to training courses, to suppliers, stakeholders etc.	2	
Time spent handling "non-service delivery" communications, emails, phone calls (e.g Supplier marketing, company newsletter, handling spam etc.) say half a day a week	4	
Time spent on annual budget process (including time spent reporting against it)	6	
Time left for manager to spend on service delivery activities	30	weeks
Total	52	weeks
Service delivery hours per year (30 weeks × 45 hours a week)	1350	hours
Cost per hour base on the salary of $75,000	$56	per hour
Cost per hour base on the salary of $100,000	$74	per hour
Cost per hour base on the salary of $125,000	$93	per hour

- Cost all meetings (as a guide, each manager will be effectively costing the organization somewhere between $60 to $100 an hour; see Exhibit 6.9).
- Insist on outcomes from every meeting.
- Team leaders should monitor all meeting requests endeavoring to deliver the service rather than attending the meeting to discuss the service request.
- Attendees provide satisfaction ratings on meetings utilizing simple but effective intranet-based survey technology or the old-fashioned form (poor chairpersons would soon get the message).

> By blocking off the mornings from meetings I now have the luxury of performing strategic, project-related tasks every morning. While for many readers this will not be totally achievable, you can start by blocking off the morning with project work and letting your peers know that "you do not do morning meetings."

EXHIBIT 6.10 4:00 P.M. Friday Planner Checklist

1. Arrange a get-together with colleagues to ask for their opinion on something	☐ Yes	☐ No
2. Arrange to meet those new colleagues who have arrived recently for a coffee	☐ Yes	☐ No
3. Write down some open-ended questions for meetings scheduled for next week	☐ Yes	☐ No
4. Think of the colleagues you are having the most problems with, reflect on the differences in a positive way and plan to say something positive to them next week	☐ Yes	☐ No
5. List all the deferred decisions you have, pick one, undertake the pros-and-cons exercise, and make a call, NOW (You will enjoy the weekend immensely)	☐ Yes	☐ No
6. Follow-up on a training session you have had and see how you can apply the lessons next week	☐ Yes	☐ No
7. Think about whom you can give positive recognition to, and make three phone calls now and make their weekend, and yours!	☐ Yes	☐ No
8. Do at least two actions from the meetings you have attended and send the material on to the appropriate person	☐ Yes	☐ No
9. Organize your network meetings for the next two weeks	☐ Yes	☐ No
10. Think about what innovation you will bring to the operation in the following week	☐ Yes	☐ No

The 4:00 P.M. Friday Weekly Planner

A sound practice I have seen is the planning of the next week on a Friday afternoon (see checklist in Exhibit 6.10). It has a number of benefits:

- It means that you can start Monday on the front rather than on the back foot.
- It can be followed by a team debriefing, which means everybody knows what they are doing the next week and thus there is no need to have the dreaded Monday-morning team meeting.
- It has the benefit of holding something in your mind and letting the subconscious do a bit of processing over the weekend.

Power Dressing

Some readers will have heard the saying, "Look a million dollars, feel a million dollars." Power dressing is very important as perception is the key factor here. Observe those who you admire and look at how they are dressed, and over time, as funds permit, replicate the look. You will find it does wonders for your confidence, especially in challenging situations when you know you are one of the best-dressed people in the room.

A good starting point if you are not known for your color sense is to get yourself color-charted. The experts in color have broken colors down to the four seasons. You are either a person who looks better in spring, summer, autumn, or winter colors. They will show you techniques to bring a traditional dark suit back into the color that suits you best through a suitably colored shirt, tie, silk handkerchief (positioned in the top pocket of the jacket), or broach in the lapel.

Preparing for Your Performance Review

Here are suggestions for preparing for a performance review:

- Prepare a mind map on your performance.
- Spend time thinking about positive outcomes even from those less than emeritus activities you performed within the progress review period.
- Think about the emotional drivers your manager will have and sell yourself around these (e.g., if your manager is concerned about the profile of the unit, think of ways you can help promote the unit by simplifying a procedure, by reducing requirements that are not needed, or by suggesting a more informative team intranet page that you personally manage).

Preparing a Monthly Progress Report

As mentioned earlier a monthly progress report should be brief and prepared quickly, via the use of a mind map. The one-page snapshot report should take no more than 30 minutes to write and five minutes to read. Remember that this report is important, so never issue it on the same day you wrote it. You need to sleep on it and review it for completeness the next day. See Exhibit 6.11 for suggested headings and layout.

Quality Assurance Checks

Far too often, in the pursuit of expediency, managers issue reports without spending enough time doing the quality assurance. See Exhibit 6.12 for a quality assurance checklist. The quality assurance of a report should include:

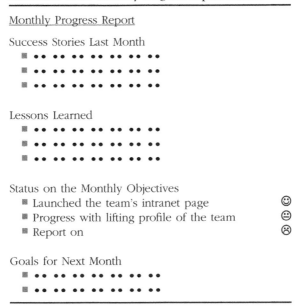

EXHIBIT 6.11 Monthly Progress Report Format

Monthly Progress Report

Success Stories Last Month

Lessons Learned

Status on the Monthly Objectives
- Launched the team's intranet page ☺
- Progress with lifting profile of the team ☺
- Report on ☹

Goals for Next Month

- **An allowance for a final quality assurance check.** Here are some basic quality assurance tips to help ensure that your work is of a high standard. It reminds me of a story about a good friend of mine who had to work all through the night to meet a tight deadline. Due to tiredness, his last version of the report was not checked thoroughly, and the result was a substandard piece of work. When he offered the excuse of being up all night, his manager had little sympathy. No matter how hard you have worked, always allow enough time for a read-through and other quality assurance checks.
- **The two-person read-through.** The only surefire way of picking up all errors is to have a call-through. What I do is have a staff member sit at my desk while I have the hard copy. The staff member reads out loud and I follow the words on my copy. We are in tandem. By hearing it read aloud, I can check the "dance of the words"—their rhythm—and thus amend to make it an easier read.
- **Computer read-back facility especially for people suffering from dyslexia.** Dyslexia is a crippling syndrome and many of us suffer from it. It means that we can easily transpose words or completely leave words out. Reviewing one's own work with this disability is totally worthless. A must for any person suffering from dyslexia is to acquire a voice-recognition package that will also include the more valuable

EXHIBIT 6.12 Quality Assurance Checklist

1. Ensure all spreadsheets used have built-in cross checks	☐ Yes	☐ No
2. Look for unnecessary detail that can be removed (e.g., never show numbers that are less than 10% of the total)	☐ Yes	☐ No
3. Check to ensure there are enough suggestions on the next steps, thus ensuring implementation issues have been thought about adequately	☐ Yes	☐ No
4. Have you looked for what is missing?	☐ Yes	☐ No
5. Have you allowed at least one night between finishing the writing and the final review?	☐ Yes	☐ No
6. Perform a call-through (one person reads aloud to another who reads an identical version silently)	☐ Yes	☐ No
7. Cross check all references (appendices, headings, numbers)	☐ Yes	☐ No
8. Page through all printed copies (to avoid missing pages, poor printing, pages wrong way up)	☐ Yes	☐ No
9. Avoid last-minute changes to tables as it is likely that cross references may become out of sync	☐ Yes	☐ No
10. Check all graphs back to source to ensure that they are the final version	☐ Yes	☐ No
11. Change the print cartridge if you have a major print run to avoid print cartridge failure (you can always reuse the partly used one)	☐ Yes	☐ No
12. Use high-quality paper for those special reports where color graph reproduction is important	☐ Yes	☐ No
13. Seek a third-party review of logic and content (specifically ask them to ignore grammar, syntax, and so forth as this will limit their high-level review; you want them to keep on "seeing the forest as opposed to looking at the trees")	☐ Yes	☐ No
14. In every piece of work look, for the last two errors (Often you will not make the changes—they will never spot them!)	☐ Yes	☐ No

tool, the *read back*. This tool can be acquired as freeware (such a package is called "Via Voice"). The computer-aided read back should not replace the two-person read-through on those important reports because you will miss out on some collective editing that occurs when two minds are working on the one document.

- **A final look for those last two errors.** This is what I call the two-gremlin rule, which states that in every piece of work there are always at least two gremlins that sneak through. If I find them and they are minor, I leave them and release the report. If you do not find them, look again or someone else will spot them.

Remember that you need a sense of perspective here; if the error is minor, do not alter the report as the cost both in time delays and reprinting may not merit the change. If someone else spots an error, you simply congratulate the person, saying "Well spotted." Never mention these errors. Let your manger find them if she can.

I would always correct typos on the first couple of pages or in the recommendations section, as these can undermine the report.

If time is really pressured, spend five minutes searching for the two gremlins, especially on the first few pages.

Contributing to Your Organization's Intranet

It is important to start good practices now. So learn how to maximize your use of the company's intranet as it will become a bigger feature in the future of all rising stars. (See Exhibit 6.13 for a checklist of the things you can do immediately.)

Making the Most out of Your Computer Applications

While some of the current senior management team may be technological dinosaurs, very soon being technically competent will be a prerequisite for all senior managers. Exhibit 6.14 provides some guidelines to ensure you make the most out of technology.

EXHIBIT 6.13 Checklist for Contributing to the Company's Intranet

1. If there is a knowledge database in your organization, ensure your CV is loaded up	☐ Yes	☐ No
2. Access the knowledge database for experts to help you	☐ Yes	☐ No
3. Be proactive and help update your section's Web pages every week	☐ Yes	☐ No
4. Look for new applications that can be added to the intranet and be a vocal supporter	☐ Yes	☐ No
5. Understand all sections of the intranet	☐ Yes	☐ No
6. Get onto some project teams that will bring additional features to the intranet	☐ Yes	☐ No
7. Report to the webmaster any omissions or errors on the intranet	☐ Yes	☐ No
8. Ask people from other departments what they like and dislike about your team's intranet Web page and suggest changes based on their feedback	☐ Yes	☐ No

⌘ EXHIBIT 6.14 Computer Applications Checklist

1. Attend "update" training courses at least every two years	□ Yes	□ No
2. It is better to use your existing applications more efficiently than to spend all your training time understanding the next upgrade, as many of the changes may have little benefit to you	□ Yes	□ No
3. Build a contacts database for your team if you do not already have one; it will be very useful and a good training exercise	□ Yes	□ No
4. Learn good file structure techniques if your organization does not already have a documentation management system	□ Yes	□ No
5. Be proficient with word processing, spreadsheet, database, email, and presentation software	□ Yes	□ No
6. For databases, the table structure should enable a minimization of repeated common data (e.g., company details should be in a separate linked table rather than repeating them for every contact person within that company)	□ Yes	□ No
7. Regularly search the internet for the latest free offering on using the technology you are having the most problems with	□ Yes	□ No
8. Visit application gurus you have in the office whenever you are about to embark on a major development. They will have useful tips not covered in any manuals and they will be more than happy to help if asked nicely	□ Yes	□ No
9. Learn a new application at least once a year; this will help remove possible barriers you may have to new technology	□ Yes	□ No

In Pursuit of Slow

Early on in your career it is important to understand the importance of slow times. These are times when you have a chance to unwind and stand back. Many great managers have this ability. Instead of rushing off to the gym or going for a punishing 10 km run, think about an activity that is profoundly "slow." For example, slow activities include: a lunch time walk, gardening, fishing, making something with your hands, or restoring a vintage bike, boat, or car. Carl Honour's[2] book, *In Praise of Slowness,* points out the benefits of many slow activities.

Better-Practice Graphics

Data visualization is an area that is growing in importance. No longer is it appropriate for well-meaning accountants and managers to dream up report formats based on what looks good to them. There is a science behind what makes data displays work. The expert in this field is Stephen Few. Stephen Few has written the top-three best-selling books on Amazon on data visualization.

A must-visit for all corporate accountants, analysts, and managers is Stephen Few's company's website where he has lodged many high-quality whitepapers on the topic of graphical displays (www.perceptualedge.com/library.php).

Dashboards, where data is summarized for senior management or the board on one page in a combination of tables and graphs, is very common. In fact, in some companies the one page looks like the dashboard of a car, where the term originated from. Few has come up with a very useful list of common pitfalls in dashboard design, which are explained in detail in his whitepaper on the topic, "Common pitfalls in dashboard design," on www.perceptualedge.com/articles/Whitepapers/Common_Pitfalls.pdf.

While graphs are an art form and not a science, there are definitely good and bad graphs. The key is that they convey the message to the user, support the argument being made, and do not try and cover too many issues. Spreadsheet applications are the normal source for graphs and this means that most staff in the organization will be able to update and amend. If you are using a specialized graphics application, you may be drawn into the more scientific graphs, which are more are suitable to a thesis than a business communication. Examples of good graphs are shown in the material that is available to readers of this book (see www.davidparmenter.com), and see Exhibit 6.15 for a better-practice graphics checklist.

EXHIBIT 6.15 Better-Practice Graphics Checklist

1. Insert graphs into tables in the Word document; this enables you to put formatted text underneath it or to the side, without complex tab arrangements. This also means that the graphs will auto-size to the width of the table when you paste them in, saving on formatting time.	☐ Yes	☐ No
2. Show 15 to 18 month trend analysis. That way you can compare last month against the same month last year and observing the trends leading up to these two months.	☐ Yes	☐ No
3. Avoid more than three trend lines as they will cross over numerous times and make the whole picture confusing.	☐ Yes	☐ No
4. With line graphs thicken the standard line so the color comes through clearer.	☐ Yes	☐ No
5. Use a pale-yellow background as all other colors sit well against this background.	☐ Yes	☐ No
6. Avoid more than five divisions in a stacked bar.	☐ Yes	☐ No

(Continued)

EXHIBIT 6.15 (Continued)

7. Wherever possible print in color.	□ Yes	□ No
8. Use a high-quality paper for the final copy.	□ Yes	□ No
9. Put the title of the graph in the table rather than on the graph; it enables you to make an 11th-hour change without having to go back to the source graph.	□ Yes	□ No
10. Organize your workbook so that the worksheet names clearly show what graphs are in each sheet.	□ Yes	□ No
11. Limit four graphs to a worksheet so that they can be seen on the one screen, this avoids hunting among spreadsheets for graphs six months later when you have forgotten which worksheet they are in.	□ Yes	□ No
12. Keep it simple; there are many graphical options that may be fully understandable by yourself but do not convey the message quickly to the user. (Radar, bubble, and 3D surface graphs are so hard to read that two individuals can read the same graph and come to widely varying conclusions.)	□ Yes	□ No
13. When paste linking graphs into the document, select "manual link" option as opposed to "automatic." Word attempts to update all automatic links when opening the document and this can corrupt graphs or lock up the machine if the source worksheet is not opened beforehand.	□ Yes	□ No
14. Integrate your graphs with the text and avoid at all costs placing the graphs in an appendix.	□ Yes	□ No
15. Mock up several different graph types when you are displaying data you have not shown in a graph form before. This way you can quickly see which type will suit the data best.	□ Yes	□ No
16. If you have more than six lines of data split into multiple graphs showing an average (for a graph with absolute numbers) or total (for a graph with relative ratios).	□ Yes	□ No
17. On common spreadsheets change the font on the graph. Disable auto-sizing as the text will dominate the graph when you enlarge it.	□ Yes	□ No

Delivering Bulletproof PowerPoint Presentations

This is a skill you need to adopt before you can be an effective manager. So it is best to start now. I will assume that you have attended a presentation skills course, a prerequisite to bulletproof PowerPoint presentations. The speed of delivery, voice levels, using silence, and getting the audience to participate are all techniques that you need to be familiar with and comfortable using (see Exhibit 6.16 for a checklist).

There are at least 25 rules for a good PowerPoint presentation:

1. Always prepare a paper for the audience covering detailed numbers and so forth so that you do not have to show detail in the slides (see rule 2).
2. Understand that the PowerPoint slide is not meant to be a document; if you have more than 35 words per slide, you are creating a report, not a presentation. Each point should be relatively cryptic and be understood only by those who have attended your presentation.
3. At least 10 to 20% of your slides should be high-quality photographs, some of which will not even require a caption.
4. A picture can replace many words; to understand this point you need to read *Presentation Zen: Simple Ideas on Presentation Design and Delivery* by Garr Reynolds,[3] and *Slide:ology: The Art and Science of Creating Great Presentations* by Nancy Duarte.[4]
5. Last-minute slide presentations are a career-limiting activity. You would not hang your dirty washing in front of a hundred people, so why would you want to show your audience sloppy slides? Only say "yes" to a presentation if you have the time, resources, and enthusiasm to do the job properly.
6. Create time so that you can be in a "thinking space" (e.g., work at home, go to the library, etc.).
7. Map the subject area out in a mind map and then create Post-It stickers for each point to help you organize your thoughts.[5]
8. Understand what is considered good use of color, photographs, and the "rule of thirds."
9. For key points, do not go less than 30-pt-size font. As Nancy Duarte says, "Look at the slides in the slide sorter view at 66% size. If you can read it on your computer, it is a good chance your audience can read it on the screen."
10. Where possible, if you are going to present on a regular basis, make sure you have a Exhibitt PC, which gives you the ability to draw when you are making points. This makes the presentation more interesting, no matter how bad you are at drawing.
11. Limit animation; it is far better that the audience is able to read all the points on the slide quickly rather than holding them back.
12. Use Guy Kawasaki's "10/20/30 rule." A sales-pitch PowerPoint presentation should have ten slides, last no more than 20 minutes, and contain no font smaller than 30 pt.
13. Bring theatrics into your presentation. Be active as a presenter, walking up the aisle so that those in the back see you close up, vary your voice, get down on one knee to emphasize an important point; have a bit of fun and your audience will, too. Very few things are unacceptable as a presenter. A colleague even commented to me that their

boring "Welcome to Uni" session was totally revolutionized by the junior lecturer giving the talk naked (that, however, may be a little over the top).

14. Be aware of being too cute and clever with your slides. The move to creating a lot of whitespace is all very well, provided your labels on the diagram do not have to be very small.

15. Never show numbers to a decimal place nor to the dollar if the number is greater than 10,000. If sales are $9,668,943.22, surely it is better to say, "approx. $10 million" or "$9.6 million." The precise number can be in the written document if it is deemed worthwhile.

16. Always tell stories to relate to the audience, bringing in humor that is relevant to them. A good presenter should be able to find plenty of humor in the subject without having to resort to telling jokes. No doubt, some of the audience have heard the jokes and would rather hear them from a professional comedian.

17. Make sure your opening words grab their attention.

18. Understand Stephen Few's work on data visualization if you are using graphs.

19. Have a simple remote mouse so that you can move the slides along independently of your computer.

20. Never use clipart; it sends shivers down the spine of the audience and you may lose them before you have a chance to present.

21. Practice your delivery. The shorter the presentation, the more you need to practice. For my father's eulogy, I must have read it through 20 to 30 times. Each time breaking down at a different point, I even had my brother as a backup in case I was unable to deliver it. He sat in fear throughout the whole service. However, on the day, all the practice paid off and I was able to deliver a worthy eulogy—one that has been commented on by many as the best they had ever heard. The point I am making is that the best speech I have ever delivered is the one I prepared the most for.

22. Always remember the audience does not know the whole content of your speech, particularly if you keep the details off the slides; if you do leave some point out, don't worry about it—they don't know or would not realize the error.

23. If there has been some issue relating to transportation, technology, and so forth that has delayed the start, avoid starting off with an apology. You can refer to this later on. Your first five minutes is the most important for the whole presentation and must therefore be strictly on the topic matter.

24. Greet as many members of the audience as you can before the presentation, as it will help calm your nerves, and it will also give you

the opportunity to clarify their knowledge and ask for their participation such as at question time. The other benefit is that it confirms that nobody in the audience would rather be doing your role, so why should you be nervous?

25. At the end of the presentation shake hands with as many of the audience as possible by positioning yourself by the door when the audience leaves. This develops further rapport between presenter and audience.

EXHIBIT 6.16 PowerPoint Presentations Checklist

The 25 key rules are embedded in this checklist in the appropriate area, with number and indent. The number refers to the rule stated earlier in this chapter.

The Planning Phase

1. Only say "yes" to a presentation if you have the time, resources, and enthusiasm to do the job properly (rule 5).	☐ Yes	☐ No
2. Create time so that you can be in a "thinking space" e.g., work at home, go to the library, etc. (rule 6).	☐ Yes	☐ No
3. Map the subject area out in a mind map and then create Post-It stickers for each point to help you organize your thoughts (rule 7).[i]	☐ Yes	☐ No
4. Develop a purpose of the presentation.	☐ Yes	☐ No
5. Have a goal for the number of slides you will need.	☐ Yes	☐ No
6. Perform research on the subject.	☐ Yes	☐ No
7. Do you know your audience?	☐ Yes	☐ No
8. Do you know why they are coming to the presentation?	☐ Yes	☐ No
9. Do you know what their emotional drivers, points of pain are?	☐ Yes	☐ No
10. Can you solve any of their problems?	☐ Yes	☐ No
11. Do you know what you want them to do?	☐ Yes	☐ No
12. Have you thought about why they might resist your suggestions?	☐ Yes	☐ No
13. Do you know how you can best reach them?	☐ Yes	☐ No

The Creative Phase

14. Always prepare a paper for the audience covering detailed numbers and so forth so that you do not have to show detail in the slides (rule 1).	☐ Yes	☐ No
15. Max of 35 words per slide, each point should be relatively cryptic and be understood only by those attending (rule 2).	☐ Yes	☐ No
16. At least 10 to 20% of your slides should be high-quality photographs, some will not even require a caption (rule 3).	☐ Yes	☐ No

(Continued)

EXHIBIT 6.16 (Continued)

The 25 key rules are embedded in this checklist in the appropriate area, with number and indent. The number refers to the rule stated earlier in this chapter.

17. Have your read *Presentation Zen: Simple Ideas on Presentation Design and Delivery* by Garr Reynolds,[ii] or *Slide:ology: The Art and Science of Creating Great Presentations* by Nancy Duarte (rule 4).[iii] ☐ Yes ☐ No

18. Understand what is considered good use of color, photographs, and the "rule of thirds (rule 8)." ☐ Yes ☐ No

19. For key points, do not go less than 30-pt-size font (rule 9). ☐ Yes ☐ No

20. Limit animation; let the audience read ahead (rule 11). ☐ Yes ☐ No

21. Apply the "10/20/30 rule for all sales pitches." Ten slides, 20 minutes, and contain no font smaller than 30pt (rule 12). ☐ Yes ☐ No

22. Be aware of being too clever with your slides (rule 14). ☐ Yes ☐ No

23. Round all numbers (rule 15). ☐ Yes ☐ No

24. Understand Stephen Few's work on dashboard design if you are using graphs (rule 18). ☐ Yes ☐ No

25. Never use clipart; it sends shivers down the spine of the audience (rule 20). ☐ Yes ☐ No

26. While you are creating avoid editing as you are going along—Do not mix editing with your creative side in other words, your first cut of a PowerPoint should never be edited as you are building it. Simply pour down your thoughts, leaving clues for your staff or peers to help in certain areas (see ahead for an example). ☐ Yes ☐ No

27. Review recent articles or recent seminars you have attended for clever and concise diagrams. ☐ Yes ☐ No

28. Find some diagrams that tell a story. ☐ Yes ☐ No

The Editing Phase

29. The person preparing the slides needs to have attended a course on PowerPoint. ☐ Yes ☐ No

30. Are you using the entire slide? (avoid using the portrait option for slides) ☐ Yes ☐ No

31. Do you create a progress icon to show the audience the progress being made through a presentation? ☐ Yes ☐ No

32. Portrait pictures can be moved to one side and the title and text to the other. ☐ Yes ☐ No

33. Are all detailed pictures expanded to use up the space of the whole slide? (ignore the need for a heading) ☐ Yes ☐ No

34. Repeat a good diagram if you are talking about a section of it at a time. ☐ Yes ☐ No

35. Have slides read through by someone who has good editing skills. ☐ Yes ☐ No

EXHIBIT 6.16 (Continued)

The 25 key rules are embedded in this checklist in the appropriate area, with number and indent. The number refers to the rule stated earlier in this chapter.

---

36. If you have pictures of people, do you ensure that they are looking toward the slide content? ☐ Yes ☐ No

First run Through of the Presentation

37. Once the slides have been edited go straight into a full practice run with one or two of your peers in attendance. ☐ Yes ☐ No
38. Time the length and avoid any interruptions; the audience are to note down improvements as they are spotted. ☐ Yes ☐ No
39. Practice your delivery. The shorter the presentation, the more you need to practice (rule 21). ☐ Yes ☐ No
40. Prepare the master copy of the slides so you can check all is clear, and courier to seminar organizer. ☐ Yes ☐ No
41. If workshop exercises are to be included, read through these carefully and get them checked for clarity by an independent person. ☐ Yes ☐ No
42. Print slides three to a page except for complex slides that should be shown on their own. ☐ Yes ☐ No
43. Test your laptop on at least two data shows as some custom settings that maximize your network can prevent your laptop linking to data projectors. ☐ Yes ☐ No

Night before

44. Avoid late changes; nothing annoys the audience more than the presentation being in a different order to the presentation handout. ☐ Yes ☐ No
45. Always test the data show projector the night before if you are required to run it. (you may find you have a missing cable) ☐ Yes ☐ No
46. Carry a spare power extension lead and the standard lap top to data projector cable with you. ☐ Yes ☐ No
47. Add some more story clues for you on the slides if necessary. ☐ Yes ☐ No
48. Travel up the night before. (plane travel deadens the senses, can effect hearing and you cannot trust the schedules) ☐ Yes ☐ No
49. If possible, bring a spare data show with you for extra protection. ☐ Yes ☐ No
50. Avoid excessive intake of alcohol the night before, it reduces performance the next morning. ☐ Yes ☐ No
51. Bring your own laptop to the presentation. ☐ Yes ☐ No
52. Practice the night before especially the first five minutes. You will need to grab the audience's attention. Be good at telling your lead story (you will need a story in the first five minutes). ☐ Yes ☐ No

(Continued)

EXHIBIT 6.16 (Continued)

The 25 key rules are embedded in this checklist in the appropriate area, with number and indent. The number refers to the rule stated earlier in this chapter.	🖺

On the day

53. Use a Tablet PC which gives you the ability to draw when you are making points (rule 10). □ Yes   □ No

54. Bring theatrics into your presentation (rule 13). □ Yes   □ No

55. Always tell stories to relate to the audience, bringing in humor that is relevant to them (rule 16). □ Yes   □ No

56. Make sure your opening words grab their attention (rule 17). □ Yes   □ No

57. Have a simple remote mouse so that you can move the slides along independently of your computer (rule 19). ⊔ Yes   □ No

58. Always remember the audience does not know the whole content of your speech, don't worry if you leave something out (rule 22). □ Yes   □ No

59. Avoid starting off with an apology. Your first five minutes is the most important for the whole presentation apologize later (rule 23). □ Yes   □ No

60. Greet as many members of the audience as you can before the presentation, as it will help calm your nerves, and it will also give you the opportunity to clarify their knowledge (rule 24). □ Yes   □ No

61. At the end of the presentation shake hands with as many of the audience as possible (rule 25). □ Yes   □ No

62. A brief run through the first one to five minutes at the proper speed before breakfast. □ Yes   □ No

63. Light exercise is a great idea to freshen the mind. (I usually go for a swim before I speak) □ Yes   □ No

64. At the first break meet with a sample of the audience and ask whether the material is of interest and about the pace of delivery. This will help pick up any problems and thus improve the assessment ratings. □ Yes   □ No

65. Run through an example of the workshop exercise to ensure every workshop group has the correct idea of what is required. □ Yes   □ No

66. Recap what has been covered to date and ask for questions. □ Yes   □ No

---

[i] Ibid., p. 28.

[ii] Garr Reynolds, *Presentation Zen: Simple Ideas on Presentation Design and Delivery*, New Riders, 2008.

[iii] Nancy Duarte, *Slide:ology: The Art and Science of Creating Great Presentations*, O'Riley, 2008.

Searching the Web Efficiently

Effectively searching the Web can be a very frustrating exercise. Exhibit 6.17 provides some tips that may make you more efficient.

EXHIBIT 6.17 Web Searching Checklist

---

1. Set a time limit but be patient; many people miss the good links because they expect a useful link on the first page of results but it may take five to ten pages to strike a good link even with a good search result! The order of the results is usually in "closest fit" but this does not necessarily mean useful links at the start!	☐ Yes	☐ No
2. If you find your search unhelpful, try another one (Lycos, Altavista, Google, Yahoo, Bing, etc.).	☐ Yes	☐ No
3. If you get more than 2,000 hits, refocus your search; ("topic + topic + topic") will ensure that all three pieces occur in each hit.	☐ Yes	☐ No
4. Remember that each search engine uses different cataloging techniques, so different engines/sites tend to be good at different types of searches.	☐ Yes	☐ No
5. If a direct word search does not work, use topic searches (e.g., Roald Amundsen, the famous polar explorer, can be found quicker by searching for "polar explorers'" than by searching by his surname).	☐ Yes	☐ No
6. Learn to use the advanced search capability (available on most search engines these days) and refine your search that way. The Lycos version uses "must have," "should have," "should not have," and preferred language options (which can weed out all the languages you do not know).	☐ Yes	☐ No
7. If the advanced search facility still does not track down the information you want, then try linking on from a simpler search (e.g., a site about polar explorers found by your search may not have a reference to Amundsen but it may have a link to a site that does). This sort of "springboarding" can be far more productive than simply querying a search site!	☐ Yes	☐ No
8. Try to get your searches down to about 200 results. But do not stress if a popular subject brings up thousands of results; that is the nature of the Web.	☐ Yes	☐ No
9. If you feel you are getting stuck in a mire of unrelated sites, it is not you; that is the nature of the chaos called the World Wide Web. It affects everyone that way sooner or later. Just relax, read a book for a few minutes, and try again when you have calmed down or had some inspiration.	☐ Yes	☐ No

Interview Techniques

Good interviewing is relatively simple. With about 15 to 20 minutes' preparation, you can look like a David Frost, a Michael Parkinson, or a Walter
Cronkite if you cover the material shown in Exhibit 6.18. Please see Chapter

EXHIBIT 6.18 Good Interview Checklist

1. Recheck venue of interview, especially if the venue is a meeting room that could be double-booked.	□ Yes	□ No
2. State the purpose of the interview and reconfirm the time available.	□ Yes	□ No
3. Prepare up to ten questions using the *who, what, why, when,* and *how* as guides to the type of questions.	□ Yes	□ No
4. Remember, perception is everything, so have a good-quality folder and a high-quality pen (I use a high-quality fountain pen but there are risks attached to this).	□ Yes	□ No
5. Position yourself at the interview to easily maintain eye contact with the interviewees and ensure the sun is not in anybody's eyes.	□ Yes	□ No
6. Allow the interviewee to cover topics slightly outside the question, but bring them back gently (an interview is like trout fishing; You need to give them line while they are running and bring it back efficiently and gently).	□ Yes	□ No
7. Fight the temptation to join in on a diversion; if you think of an idea or a new question note it down and come back to it when you have completed all the other questions. (I put ideas in square brackets so I know it was not said by the interviewee, and I put new questions in the top-left corner of the first page.)	□ Yes	□ No
8. If involved in a project to improve processes, ask "What are the three changes you would most like to make?"	□ Yes	□ No
9. Take neat, brief notes (they should not detract from the pace of the interview) as it meets a number of objectives: ▪ It helps maintain your concentration—remember an interviewee can detect immediately if you have mentally wandered off. ▪ It shows that you think what they are saying is important, and enables you to trap any good ideas that come to mind during the interview.	□ Yes	□ No
10. Avoid more than two back-to-back interviews so you are fresh for each one.	□ Yes	□ No
11. When ascertaining an opinion or a resolution during an interview, it is a good practice to summarize your understanding of what has been agreed.	□ Yes	□ No

Note: It is generally unnecessary to send your questions in advance to the interviewee.

I will never forget being taken to an interview by a partner in the London consultancy firm I worked for. He had prepared for the meeting meticulously, thinking about his questions. He asked the questions and then allowed the interviewee to cover topics slightly outside the question. He always brought him back gently to the question. He said that you will always be surprised by the gems you find. I now run interviews as I would land a hooked trout. I give them line while they are running and bring them back efficiently and gently.

Notes

1. A. Roger Merrill, Rebecca R. Merrill, and Stephen R. Covey, *First Things First*, Simon & Schuster, 1994.
2. Carl Honour, *In Praise of Slowness: Challenging the Cult of Speed*, HarperOne, 2005.
3. Garr Reynolds, *Presentation Zen: Simple Ideas on Presentation Design and Delivery*, New Riders, 2008.
4. Nancy Duarte, *Slide:ology: The Art and Science of Creating Great Presentations*, O'Riley, 2008.
5. Ibid., p. 28.

CHAPTER 7

Part Two Progress Checklist

If you have only a few minutes to skim over this chapter, this is what you should focus on:

> Lesson 3: When selecting a team make sure they are multi-skilled and have a sense of humor
> Lesson 5: Humility and drive are good bedfellows
> Lesson 8: Learn to know when you should seek help

Thirteen-Week Change Program

New methods and practices can be locked in if you perform the task each week for a 14-week period. The checklists in Exhibits 7.1 and 7.2 will help you make the changes that you chose to make relating to this section of the book.

Lessons from Sir Edmund Hillary's Expeditions

Sir Edmund Hillary has been credited with many things, yet few have realized what a great CEO he was. Having climbed Mount Everest, as a team member, he subsequently achieved everything else as a CEO. I have been fortunate enough to read *View from the Summit*[1] by Sir Edmund Hillary and *Hellbent for the Pole*[2] by Geoffrey Lee Martin. The lessons from these books, I believe, are ones we can apply in the business environment.

Lesson 1: If You Want to Be Picked for the Summit Team, Do Not Rely Just on Reputation

How often are we surprised when we are not chosen to lead a special project or are passed over for that management position when it was there for the taking?

EXHIBIT 7.1 Monitoring Behavioral Change Checklist

Activity demonstrated in weeks	The weeks in this quarter (Tick if trait was evident)												
	1	2	3	4	5	6	7	8	9	10	11	12	13
1. Demonstrated good anger management													
2. Made decisions													
3. Gave recognitions													
4. Kept nutrition up													
5. Kept fluids up													
6. Good mobile and email etiquette													
7. Helped boss summit													
8. Used neuro-linguistic programming techniques													
9. Attended courses to handle personal baggage													
10. Completed my own treasure map													

EXHIBIT 7.2 Getting Things Done Checklist

Action (P = planned, D = done)	Weeks												
	1	2	3	4	5	6	7	8	9	10	11	12	13
1. Found a mentor													
2. Attended a mind-mapping course													
3. Had a meeting wit mentor													
4. Made some progress with items on my treasure map													
5. Learned how to Post-It engineer a process													
6. Attending a management course confirmed													
7. Attending a course on a new computer application confirmed													
8. Contributed to the team intranet page													
9. Attending a course on better-practice PowerPoint presentations													
10. Used the 25 rules on PowerPoint presentations													
11. Applied some of the better-practice graph techniques													
12. At least 4 hours a day on service delivery activities													
13. Produced something innovative													
14. Used the work/home balance planner													
15. Completed the 4:00 P.M. Friday planner													

Hillary knew there were at least three pairs of climbers capable of making the summit in Sir John Hunt's successful expedition. He wanted to make sure that Sir John would not overlook the new team of Hillary and Tenzing, so he devised a test of stamina that would, without any shadow of a doubt, show they were the fittest team.

Hillary and Tenzing succeeded in ascending from base camp to advanced base and back in one day, a task previously carried out in two days. The test had, I understand, little purpose other than to be a thoroughly convincing demonstration.

In business, one has endless opportunity to highlight one's strengths and to demonstrate to the CEO and/or senior team that you are the *one*. If it worked for Hillary, it can work for you.

Lesson 2: Having the Best Team Does Not Necessarily Mean You Will Be Successful If You Have Ignored the Politics

Hillary had successfully climbed endless peaks with George Lowe in the 1952 and 1953 climbing seasons. They were clearly the best Himalayan climbing team based on current experience.

Having joined the Hunt expedition and already halfway to Everest, Hillary realized that Lowe and himself, two New Zealanders, would never be allowed to the summit first. A takeover by two Kiwis would never be allowed on a British-sponsored expedition.

Hillary changed his climbing partner, teaming up instead with Sherpa Tenzing Norgay, and together they succeeded in becoming the first to ever ascend to the summit of Everest.

You have hand-picked the best project team and yet it does not gain the support of the top team. In building a successful team, you need to take account of all the stakeholders. You may need to make alternative selections to take account of these. You will still get the job done, the team will still work; you just need to be flexible and cognizant of the stakeholders' needs and perceptions, and the "politics" they are answerable to. Only then will you be first to the summit.

Lesson 3: When Selecting a Team Make Sure They Are Multi-Skilled and Have a Sense of Humor

Hillary was very careful in his selection of staff. He recognized that in times of difficulty you want to have someone who can laugh at adversity, which Sir Hillary is famous for. The last thing he wanted was a team member going into a panic, or worse, a person who would rather look for a scapegoat. In addition Hillary looked for a collection of skills in an individual. He recognized that having more staff does not necessarily make the team stronger. The expedition's reporter also doubled as a tractor driver, the doctor took a dentistry training course, and the cook learned extra skills both to be able to cook for the masses and to deliver gourmet meals, the geologist was naturally a mountaineer, and the list goes on.

Why does a CEO appoint staff who are so one-dimensional? They can be excellent when the going is easy but the first to throw up their arms in alarm when the stormy weather arrives.

Lesson 4: Small Deeds of Kindness

Hillary is legendary for his small acts of kindness. One example was that on hearing that a two-year-old child was seriously ill in a hospital he immediately, wrote an inspirational note to him. Naturally it was inspirational both to the parents and to their now-teenage son.

CEOs should never forget the small details, for it is those small acts of kindness and consideration that will build a legend.

Lesson 5: Humility and Drive Are Good Bedfellows

Sir Edmund Hillary's obituaries, without fail, mention how little he sought for himself. He achieved at everything he participated in, yet never sought the limelight. As a legacy one would immediately recognize his contribution to Mother Earth. There are Sherpa pilots, doctors, nurses, and lawyers all of whom were taught to read and write through the facilitation of his schools. Like other children, my daughter, with a tear in her eye, once said, "He has taught me that anything is achievable."

Bill Gates is another great leader who is humble. While the press follows his every move, he seldom seeks the limelight. In a recent trip to New Zealand he was asked by a Kiwi who did not recognize him, "What do you do?" He replied, "I am in computers." The understatement of the year! Warren Buffett, the greatest investor alive today, always looks for a CEO who is a quiet achiever rather than a flash-in-the-pan "show pony."

As a CEO remind yourself every day that humility is a strength, not a weakness. Mount a picture of Hillary on your wall as a reminder and spend time making the world a better place.

It is worth noting that the meaning of life can be summed up in one word: *legacy*. Some of us leave a legacy through our children, some through our inspiration of others, and some through our own deeds.

Lesson 6: Dreaming of Your Eventual Goal

Hillary was an avid comic-book reader in his youth and on long walks would imagine himself as a hero. He read about and worshiped Shackleton and later on dreamed of being the first to climb Everest. Why, you may ask, was the first British team unsuccessful in 1953? Was equipment failure the excuse? Yet, would they have been able to invent a new way of climbing with oxygen bottles when they came up against the Hillary step? Hillary improvised a shuffle, using the oxygen bottles on the back pack and his feet as a pair of wedges, and inch by inch, in the thin air, using every bit of his legendary strength made it up the tight shaft. This route is now followed by thousands since.

It was the drive to succeed that pushed Hillary to "knock the bugger off." As a CEO you need to dream of your eventual goal—to smell, see, feel, touch, and hear what it would be like to succeed. You need to use the techniques of "neuro-linguistic programming" to make your dreams your reality.

Lesson 7: Sometimes "Giving It a Go" When Your Instincts Are Saying Otherwise Is Not Such a Great Idea

How often in business do we continue on a path when everything around us is sending signals to stop or change course? We are compelled, like lemmings, to complete the task rather than listen and change tactics.

It was interesting that Hillary suffered a similar fate on his Antarctic Expedition. I recall reading that twice he attempted to cross over, with his Fergusson tractors, ice bridges that he felt uneasy about. As was proved later, these two failed attempts could have proved costly to his successful South Pole journey. In each case he was able to later find a safer route, which no doubt would have been the better option in the first place.

When you find yourself about to say "Let's give it a go," stop and invest some time looking for an alternative route; you may well find the safe "ice bridge" you are looking for.

Lesson 8: Learn to Know When You Should Seek Help

For some of us seeking help is a sign of failure or weakness, whereas in reality it can offer that critical leap up the ladder of success.

Hillary sought the help of Admiral George Dufek on a number of occasions during his expedition to the South Pole. How significant that help proved to be and how rewarding it must have been for Admiral Dufek to see how useful it had been.

Admiral Dufek helped Hillary choose the site of Scott Base, which has been used continuously now for over 40 years. Admiral Dufek also helped Hillary at other critical stages of the expedition.

What is remembered today is that the expedition was successful and the gratitude Hillary had for Admiral George Dufek is clearly stated in *View from the Summit.*

In business, many costly failures could have been averted if advice had been sought from a trusted and wise mentor. The key is the selection (and use) of your mentor/advisor and to realize that just because you have asked once does not preclude a second or third request for help.

Find a mentor and seek advice on those major decisions; you will notice the difference it makes in your expeditions.

Lesson 9: In All Projects Other Goals Can Be Achieved If You Have Provisioned for Them

It is not uncommon to be halfway through a project and to come to the realization that more significant goals could have been achieved if some planning and provisioning had been done in the first place.

Hillary, when asked by Bunny Fuchs to provide a Kiwi support expedition to his grand traverse of the Antarctic, had in the back of his mind the possibility of Kiwis also getting to the South Pole.

Right from the start the provisions and planning did not preclude this as a possibility, albeit it was never on the official agenda. His successful South Pole expedition was not only a triumph of Kiwi ingenuity, but also a great vision (who would have put money on getting three converted tractors to the South Pole?).

Had Hillary kept strictly to his "project brief," the Kiwi involvement would have long been forgotten. So remember, look for these other possibilities when planning your next project expedition; you may find that in time the only evidence or memory of your efforts will be the *other goals* you achieved along the way.

Lesson 10: Do Not Start a Project If You Do Not Have the Ability to See It Through to the End

Whether ascending Mount Everest, driving tractors through the South Pole, jet boating up the Ganges, or building schools in Nepal, Hillary had a unique cluster of skills. In one person you have a great planner, a person who is focused, and one who completes the tasks that he sets out to do.

Often CEOs start projects with as little planning as possible and will be committed only until the next new interesting project comes up or when tying up the loose ends gets too boring. The result is that organizations are littered with projects that are stuck in limbo. These projects are of no value to the organization until someone refocuses on completing them.

Lesson 11: Get Your Base Camp Properly Set Up

Many projects fail not only because of lack of planning but through a failure to get the infrastructure, resources, training, and so on in place at the outset. There is a tendency to be more interested in measuring the speed of early progress rather than in the likelihood of completing the project on time and on budget.

If meticulous planning and testing of gear on the glaciers in South Island before the Antarctic Expedition worked for Hillary, then maybe we should invest more time, energy, and money in setting up a base camp from which a successful attempt is possible on our own projects.

For more on leadership, see Chapter 32.

Notes

1. Sir Edmund Hillary, *View from the Summit: The Remarkable Memoir by the First Person to Conquer Everest*, Gallery, 2000.
2. Geoffrey Lee Martin, *Hellbent for the Pole: An Insider's Account of the "Race to the South Pole" 1957–58*, Random House, 2007.

Being A Better Manager

CHAPTER 8

Improving Team Performance: The Basics

If you have only a few minutes to skim over this chapter, this is what you should focus on:

- Getting the induction process right
- Holding offsite meetings for your team at least twice a year
- Making work fun
- Maintaining levels of materiality

Attending Further Management Courses

By now you should have attended an in-house management course and the various day courses that are of interest to you. It would be wiser to be more strategic with your training at this point. Recognize that the occasional one-day training course creates little or no behavioral change in you. What is more important is continuous-learning training programs.

Here are some suggestions of continuous-learning training programs:

- Attend relevant, short, tertiary courses on management issues. These are offered by many business schools and can be a good alternative to an MBA.
- Look at local evening classes run by a professional association you may be a member of.
- Consider joining a group that meets to discuss management issues on a regular basis (e.g., you will find some local branches of professional bodies that may welcome nonmembers).
- Investigate institutions that promote better management through running training programs.
- Attend web-based courses on management issues.

Staff Debriefing at the End of the Day

Staff debriefings are a rare sight these days, and *if* they are scheduled, they are often the first meetings to be deferred or canceled. This is often because the debriefings are not handled in the appropriate way, and thus staff attending may consider them a waste of time. But these sessions can be very useful when attended by willing employees. One high-performance team has an open-ended debriefing every evening in the last 15 minutes of the working day. Normally, it only takes the allotted time but it can be extended should the team require it. In their debriefing sessions, the following issues can be discussed:

- How best to help a particular in-house client who is having difficulties
- Ways to improve operations
- Plans for the next day and next week
- Finishing off communications that due to the pressures of the day were not completed
- "Popping the balloon" on those difficult issues that may have grown out of proportion during the day

Another point worth noting is that this high-performance team could not operate if it chose to have meetings during its key service-delivery time. Yet that is the very thing we all tend to do.

Attracting the Best Staff to the Team

Attracting potential employees to the organization is the responsibility of all management. Great CEOs are constantly waving the flag, saying, "What a great company we are—why don't you come and join us?" Making your team a preferred team to join will attract high-performing people. You can make your team a more desirable place to work by:

- Establishing a relationship with your local universities, offering prizes to the best graduates, and delivering guest lectures.
- Offering internships to the top students—this will enable you to try before you buy!
- Writing articles in the relevant professional association and business journals.
- Delivering presentations to local branches of professional bodies where potential recruits may be in the audience.

Getting the Right Staff

See Chapter 10, "Effective Recruiting."

Getting the Induction Process Right

All good organizations put a lot of time and effort into a good induction process. There needs to be a high level of commitment to the induction process, not only by the team leader but by all other staff.

Far too often the induction process gets relegated to an item on the agenda. The new staff person arrives and is given the feeling that she is a burden.

An induction should include:

- Detailed handover with person leaving, or failing that, someone familiar with routines.
- Morning or afternoon coffee with some of the general managers or middle managers, depending on seniority of new recruit.
- Specified meeting times with the manager (e.g., 3:00 P.M. Wednesday and 3:00 P.M. Friday) to pick up any loose ends, give feedback, revise training program, and plan the week ahead.
- A selection of simple tasks where goals can be scored easily.
- Vetting of meetings so the new employee gets to go to meetings that are functioning well.
- Meeting with helpdesk and IT support to cover intranet, systems, email, hours of operation, remote access, security, and so on.
- Meeting with a representative from the Human Resources Team scheduled for three months after joining date.
- Visit to any production facilities.
- Phone number and email address of previous person who did the job, assuming permission has been sought and granted.

One government organization runs a two-day induction course on the first Tuesday and Wednesday of each month. The CEO is the major driver behind it and most managers turn up to present a session, as do corporate service managers. It is a very successful initiative and always gets good feedback.

Another core government organization runs an induction program that is set about one month after new employees start. The delay is

(Continued)

designed to ensure they have adequate knowledge of the organization and systems before being exposed to further learning opportunities. The new employees meet several senior government officials. They also go through a computer course that ensures they make maximum use of the computer systems.

One private-sector organization runs two different induction programs. One program is their "standard" induction course designed to help make the new employees feel comfortable with their new job. Run soon after they begin working in the organization, it focuses particularly on the specific job interfaces that the employees will encounter. The other program involves a "cultural orientation" of the organization. Every three months, all new recruits are flown to the Head Office for a one day visit. Here they are partnered off with their Home Office equivalent for the day. They are met by the CEO and spend some time with the senior managers discussing the company's culture and values. Staff response has been very positive.

Set Up Monthly One-on-One Progress Meetings with Direct Reports

Set up monthly progress meetings with your direct reports in the first week of the month and on the same day (e.g., Ted 2:00 P.M. first Tuesday of month; Sarah 3:00 P.M. first Tuesday of month) and give them performance feedback, which in most cases will be just verbal. In this meeting ask them to prepare a few PowerPoint slides rather than a written report and suggest a maximum of 30 minutes' preparation time.

These meetings will also replace the need for project report-back meetings. The content for PowerPoint would include:

- What I have done well last month
- What I have not done so well
- What I am planning to do this month
- The lessons I have learned
- The training I am going to organize

One manufacturing company performs monthly formal performance feedback. They hold weekly meetings that are supported by a more in-depth monthly meeting where monthly resource schedules are reviewed, expectations are spelled out, training needs are discussed, and performance evaluated. They also provide a monthly reward to staff based on revolving criteria including partner innovation, performance above and beyond, as well as customer service.

One manager of the Information Technology department of a public entity has developed a monthly performance feedback system for all his direct reports. The discussions cover not only team members' performance but also progress on projects. The manager finds it a useful tool for keeping in contact with his team members and now "could not imagine working without it." These monthly performance meetings are done on a Friday afternoon at a set time so that it is an automatic process (e.g., staff person A has the meeting on the first Friday of the month at 2:00 P.M. and staff person B at 3:00 P.M.).

Performance Reviews that Work

An annual performance review may exist in your organization but just because your organization is from the Cretaceous period you do not have to be. Establish a schedule where you give formal feedback more regularly.

As mentioned earlier, you should have one-on-one monthly meetings to discuss the month just gone and the month-end to come.

A core government department, which has a quarterly performance review process, has moved away from "rating" performance as they found managers were not providing fair assessments or addressing the real issues. Now commentary is required—the manager now evaluates whether performance was timely, accurate, achieved, and so on. The process also involves feedback from team members, and staff are asked to respond to the question, "How do you feel that your manager has performed?"

In addition, you should record the times when you have praised and reprimanded a staff member so that at the reviews you can refer back to factual events. The records do not need to be too onerous (see Exhibit 8.1). To make documentation easy, you can link to an icon on your desktop, password protected of course! See your IT helpdesk for help with setting up desktop shortcuts/icons.

EXHIBIT 8.1 Manager's Log Recording Feedback Given to Pat in the Past
Three Months

Date	Instances of good performance noted during the quarter include:
4/1/0x	Handled yourself well at the ____ meeting
4/8/0x	Good feedback from presentation
4/14/0x	Helped organize my work load, in particular when I am en route to client
4/19/0x	Good administration of process questionnaire
5/7/0x	Worked hard in a difficult time
5/22/0x	Satisfaction surveys done well
5/29/0x	Handled process survey well on the ____ job
6/5/0x	Handled yourself well on the ____ job
6/11/0x	Organizing the ____ job
6/27/0x	Documentation and invoicing prepared thoroughly

Date	Instances of below-average performance noted during the quarter include:
4/1/0x	Your spelling needs to improve and you are not learning from spelling errors you have made in the past. It is important to improve here as we cannot rely on spell check or the review process to pick up everything.
4/8/0x	Performance review delays and lack of follow-up
4/14/0x	Unnecessary precision in comments (e.g., referred to 82.1% increase in the xxxxx report, etc.)
5/7/0x	Errors with last month's letters sent out without xxxxx
5/22/0x	Did not follow up client calls (received an email of complaint)
5/29/0x	Error with comments, not enough self-review (e.g., 81 respondents on executive summary and it should have been 76)
6/5/0x	Poor use of calendar
6/11/0x	Temper shown
6/27/0x	Total lack of control over issuing reports (____ client annoyed)
6/27/0x	Poor quality assurance, wrong presentation given to me to present to the client

Many organizations are recognizing the power of doing *360-degree performance feedback*. This process needs to be handled carefully with Human Resources in full control.

One public entity has 360-degree feedback performed on all staff. Each person has feedback from about 12 to 15 people. While the exercise is very costly and time consuming, staff are providing thoughtful feedback to each other.

One financial institution makes universal use of 360-degree assessments for managers. For each position, the questionnaires went out to: up to five external peers; up to five peers within their function; all direct reports; and the manager. Approximately 5,500 questionnaires went out this year. At management level, the 360-degree assessment makes up 30% of their bonus (the balance being 40% on the managers' delivery in their key result areas and 30% from work in areas of managerial accountability, such as budgetary management and team training).

Exhibit 8.2 is a checklist to help you improve your performance reviews.

Hold Offsite Meetings for the Team at Least Twice a Year

Some teams hold a half-day offsite meeting every month, yet others hardly ever do this; they are too busy firefighting. One thing I know is which team I would rather work for and which team has the better team culture, higher productivity, and low staff turnover.

Exhibit 8.3 shows the agenda items of a typical offsite meeting of a finance team. One of the meetings will set the annual goals of the team. The CFO will prepare the first cut of the goals for the accounting team that support the organization's operating plan. During discussion these are broken down, developed, and taken on by individuals in the team. The benefits of this approach are that the team members are fully aware of each others' goals, and there is a greater degree of ownership to make it happen.

With cost-cutting exercises over the past 10 to 15 years, organized in-house courses are a rarity; individuals are often left to their own devices in selecting what they would consider to be a useful way to spend the training budget. The offsite meetings, if run frequently enough, are an ideal time to have the training session. One high-performance team has a training session in its every-third-month offsite team meeting. They invest considerable time planning the training workshop, which may include helping staff to revisit policies and procedures; looking at how to handle likely scenarios; what makes a supervisor excellent; client management; increasing knowledge about special processes, and so on. We can certainly learn from the commitment that this high-performance team makes to training and the positive team spirit that these in-house workshops generate.

EXHIBIT 8.2 Smart Performance Reviews Checklist

1. Do you undertake performance reviews frequently? The longer you leave them, the longer it takes to prepare them, the more reluctant both parties are, the less value they are (e.g., aim for quarterly or even better monthly feedback).	☐ Yes	☐ No
2. Have you set the dates in your calendar for the full year (e.g., first Tuesday of each quarter at 2:00 P.M., for Pat and 3:00 P.M. for Kim)?	☐ Yes	☐ No
3. Do you maintain a list covering all the reprimands and praise you have given? A pattern can be identified and you will also have the facts. This list should be linked to an icon on your desktop, password protected of course!	☐ Yes	☐ No
4. Do you hold performance reviews away from your office (i.e., on neutral territory)?	☐ Yes	☐ No
5. Have you covered:	☐ Yes	☐ No
■ Performance	☐ Yes	☐ No
■ Progress against agreed goals	☐ Yes	☐ No
■ Next quarter's goals	☐ Yes	☐ No
■ Training	☐ Yes	☐ No
■ Career aspirations	☐ Yes	☐ No
■ Mentorship	☐ Yes	☐ No
6. Do you maintain frequent eye contact and establish as much empathy as possible?	☐ Yes	☐ No
7. Have you practiced your opening comment to ensure that it is balanced and sets the scene appropriately?	☐ Yes	☐ No
8. Have you established the ground rules for the meeting (e.g., that you are going to provide feedback first and your staff member is encouraged to elaborate when the feedback is completed)?	☐ Yes	☐ No
9. Do you help the recipients understand how they can improve their performance in the eyes of others? Perceptions play an important part in performance reviews; these are never right or wrong.	☐ Yes	☐ No
10. Do your one-minute reprimands and commendations clearly indicate the nature of the performance during a period? The performance ratings should never be a surprise.	☐ Yes	☐ No

Make Work Fun

I believe putting fun into business stems right from the top. If the CEO and the senior management team are miserable to work with, my only suggestion is to start looking now to change your job. It is a tragedy to invest over 2,000 hours a year in a miserable, stressful, unfriendly work

EXHIBIT 8.3 Team Offsite Meeting Agenda Example

Agenda of the xxxxx Team Meeting

Location: xxxx Date: xxxx

Attendees: Entire accounting team with special guests xxxx xxxx xxxx

Requirements: **Session secretary (Pat Carruthers), laptops ×2, data show, whiteboards ×2**

8.30 A.M.	Welcome by manager, a summary of progress to date, an outline of the issues, feedback from in-house customer survey, and establishing the outcome for the workshop.
8.40	**Setting the scene.** A talk by a member of the senior management team (SMT). Topics covered include: • Importance of the _____ team • Future direction of _____ • Areas where the SMT is hoping to see improvements • Where can the accounting team score more goals for the SMT?
9.00	**Training session.** Topics covered could include: • Hermann's thinking preferences • Myers-Briggs team wheel, and others • Interpersonal skills • Looking at a new technology that could be of use for the team • Training in a new application that is now available to the team members
10.15	Morning break
10.30	**Workshop.** Post-It reengineering of a common process
12.15 P.M.	Lunch at venue
1 P.M.	Wrapup of workshop

environment; you simply deserve better. How often is your team work area a less-than-welcoming place? When colleagues arrive, is everybody's head down and the greeting, at best, a reluctant one? Your team needs to be perceived as a team that works hard and has fun doing this.

Some initiatives you can take to improve the working environment are:

- Buy ten movie tickets and give two tickets to members of staff who have gone beyond the call of duty. Besides the initial shock you will find it will create a small shift in the right direction.
- Hold a staff meeting in a café once a month and provide coffee and muffins.

- Set up a regime where birthdays are honored and celebrated. The staff person is actively encouraged to take that day off (out of their holiday allowance) and then celebrate it the next day in the office. The birthday staff member would be expected to bring in the cake and would receive a small gift from the team (to save time, do not bother with a collection; pay for it out of the department's budget).
- Take the team to a matinee at the movies with the staff investing their lunch hour in the process. (This is great for staff with young children, where a movie visit is a distant memory!)
- For festive season celebration, give your staff options; it is, after all, their celebration.
- During team meetings ensure that you find at least three team members to thank and recognize their achievements, some of which may have occurred outside work.

I had two young single mothers working for me and it was not surprising that my staff elected to go to the movies at lunchtime once a week for five weeks leading up to Christmas rather than having an evening dinner function.

In-House Satisfaction Survey

Initially once a year and then twice a year run a statistically based sample survey on your in-house customers. You could send them the survey set that is provided in Appendix A. The key features of the survey are:

- Ask two open-ended questions that will generate most of the benefit of the survey: "What are the three things we do well?" and "What are the three things we can improve on?" Never ask about the problems because half of them will not be fixable.
- Categorize all responses to the previous questions in a database and sort them by positive comments and suggestions for improvement (see Exhibit 8.4).
- Use a 5-point scale (5 = Very satisfied, 4 = Satisfied, 3 = Neither satisfied nor dissatisfied, 2 = Dissatisfied, 1 = Very dissatisfied, X = Not applicable/cannot rate).
- Separate the dramas caused by the IT system in your sphere of influence from the services your team provides by asking a series of system-related questions.

- Send the survey by email or use a web-based survey package such as SurveyMonkey.
- Never ask questions you will not act upon. As there is limited time to implement change, make the questionnaire simple and able to be completed within ten minutes.

Exhibit 8.4 is an example of how to analyze staff comments. I recommend that once you have sorted all comments into themes, which may take two or three iterations, you highlight the positive comments in bold text and put them first in each theme.

EXHIBIT 8.4 Extract from a Commentary Section Showing Identification of Comments

Judgment on Comment	Comment Used in Report
Customer focus (positive)	**Staff prepared to go the extra mile**
	Helpful (trying to be)
	Good personal assistant or executive assistant
	Good ability to respond to circumstances and needs that change rapidly
	Fairness and courtesy to all
	Staff willingness and very positive attitude
	Well-trained support staff
	Client focus and gives all parties more than reasonable time and attention
	If there are problems, there is usually immediate attention by senior staff
Customer focus (negative)	On occasion the staff have been a bit abrupt to me when they have been very busy.
Communication (positive)	**Initiatives to improve communication within the staff have been positively received and changes for the better have been made**
	Good communications
	Good liaison with the _____ and _____
Communication (negative)	My _____ were not told that this was not needed for June 1-3 case in New York when it was canceled
Database (positive)	No comments
Database (negative)	Improvement of the database operation is required
	The customer database is inadequate and some important fields are still missing

One CFO who has experience with running satisfaction surveys wanted to improve results. So he went around to every budget holder and member of the senior management team and asked, "What would my team need to do to get at least a very good rating from you on services our team provides?" To everyone's surprise, the team listened, acted on the suggestions, and in the next survey received the best results out of all teams.

Getting a Bigger "Bang" for Your Training Dollar

As a manager you need to maximize the value you get out of the training budget for you and your staff.

In-House Courses

Courses specifically tailored for an organization are without doubt the most cost-effective form of training. It provides the most control over the topic of training being given and ensures a common language. One large technology function holds a half-day training session every six weeks. An expert from the 40-strong team prepares a presentation on a topic, and the rest of the half-day can be taken up by a visiting lecturer or by presenters translating a successful external course to best meet the needs of the technology team.

One organization sends all managers to a project management course that is run in-house by a well-known expert. All of management are now on the same wavelength, draft project terms of reference in the same way, and so forth.

Another organization, which was going through restructuring, recognized that this was having a negative effect on the staff. The company organized an in-house stress workshop called "Stress, humor, and health" that was very successful.

One word of warning about having the training onsite: You need support from senior management that training is fundamental and that participants are expected to be there on time and for the full duration.

Funding Staff with Their University Education

While university education can offer very effective targeted training, there should be more than a tenuous link back to the organization's activities if this expenditure is to come out of the training budget. It is a good idea to track the level of "university support" expenditure.

Tapping into the Scholarship "Gold Mines"

Every year scholarship monies remain unallocated. Why not set yourself a target of ensuring at least one employee is helped to attend a major learning exercise, in part funded by a scholarship? It is a win-win solution and good publicity for the company: It stretches the training budget a bit further and makes a big difference to the individual.

As a start, track down the necessary websites and give assistance to staff members who are interested in applying.

Help Your Direct Reports Find a Suitable Mentor

Investing in mentors is the cheapest and most effective form of training. Often the only cost to the organization is the lunch or dinner that the mentor and staff member attend about three or four times a year, and a suitable holiday gift to acknowledge the mentor's contribution for the year.

Managing Staff on Sick Leave

The return of staff who are sick needs to be managed by you with the help of the Human Resources Team. If a staff member is allowed to be away for an extended period of time, he may find it difficult to return due to loss of confidence or even social changes that have quickly occurred within the family. The sick person's partner, who may have been the main caregiver for the children, could now have taken up a job as the children now have another caregiver, the 'sick/injured' parent. The household now has another income plus the sick pay coming in. Both partners may be enjoying the change and thus the sickness or injury may be extended indefinitely. It is thus important not to allow this home dynamic to happen by acting quickly and getting the sick/injured employee on a back to work program as soon as possible.

> A core government agency has made $1 million saving sick pay by cutting down the time staff spend away from work. An injured employee is immediately sent to see a medical practitioner and, if needed, to a specialist. Once there is a proper understanding of the injury the staff member's workload can be adjusted.

When dealing with a staff member with a long-term illness, managers show their true colors. Great managers make sure the sick employees are visited at least once a month by themselves or by a fellow team member. It is a gesture that will be respected by both the incumbent and those who witness it.

Stress Management

This is a major subject and I am sure the readers have suffered enough from stress to have found their own remedies. It is important that as a leader you are not the instigator of undue stress. Work stress (excluding that from one's own personal life) comes from a number of areas:

- Stress passed down by the manager
- Unreasonable deadlines (work overload)
- Poorly defined assignments (lost on assignment)
- Dysfunctional team dynamics
- Poor systems (slow systems, loss of work etc)
- Inadequate skills to undertake task
- Loss of productive time through attending superfluous meetings

Make sure that you, as a leader, are not contributing to these stress inducing situations and that you have made best endeavors to act as a buffer to your staff's stress. As a manager you can change people's roles to eliminate the stressful parts so the role best suits their skills and attributes. Much stress originates with anxious or unrealistic managers. Monitor your behavior.

Apply Pareto's 80/20 Principle in Your Work

Most of us are aware of Pareto's principle, but unfortunately seldom apply it. Why is it that we spend months on an annual planning process that we know is flawed? Why is it we spend days preparing a report that is informing management well and truly after the horse has bolted? Why do we regularly spend only 20% of our time on those strategic projects that are really going to make a difference?

Wilfred Pareto, an economist, published *Cours d'economie politique* (1896), which included his famous "law" of income distribution. It was a complicated mathematical formulation in which he attempted to prove that the distribution of incomes and wealth in society is not random and that a consistent pattern appears throughout history, in all parts of the world and in all societies. When he discovered the principle, it established that 80% of the land in Italy was owned by 20% of the population. Later, he discovered that his *Pareto principle* was valid in other parts of his life, such as gardening: 80% of his garden peas were produced by 20% of the peapods. It provides rough approximations and recognizes that effort and reward are not linearly related.

It applies in business, as rough approximations:

- Approximately 80% of process defects arise from no more than 20% of the process issues.
- Approximately 20% of your sales force is likely to produce 80% of your company revenues.
- Approximately 80% sales are likely to come from 20% of the product/ service range.
- Approximately 80% of your purchase invoices will be for small amounts, say under $2,000.
- Approximately 80% of work performed by your team members will be creating only 20% of the total added value your team creates.

> When a team loses sight of what is important, they cease to deliver effectively. As a corporate accountant I spent most of my time on month-end reporting, the annual accounts, and the annual planning process. None of these tasks were adding much value to the senior management team. My contribution to the organization and to the working lives of the management and staff was so minimal that when I left I had to organize my own leaving party! Had I focused on Pareto's 80/20 rule, it would have been obvious to me that I should have spent more time helping my internal clients who were working on the organization's *critical success factors (CSFs)*. That way I, too, would have been working indirectly on the CSFs.

Maintain a Focus on Materiality

As a manager you always need to see the forest for the trees. Far too often work is done checking items that are not material, whereas major items only get a cursory calculation. Your finance team members are experts with ascertaining materiality and they will tell you what amount is material to the organization.

As a guide you might set materiality as 1% of an organization's total expenditure (1% rule) or 5% of the average net profit for the past three years (e.g., for an organization with a total operating expenditure [salaries, wages, rent, power, telephone, etc.], of $5 million of the total expenditure, the 1% rule indicates that materiality for you might be $50,000).

If you are a manager in a small department, with a budget of $180,000, it is clear that it is not worth writing a monthly report on your financials as your monthly expenditure will be around $15,000–$18,000 a month. This is an immaterial amount for the organization in the example.

If a report is worth presenting to senior management, it contains material items (e.g., it concerns items over $50,000). Follow these rules:

- Have a separate reporting line for items over 10% of the total. All items below are consolidated until they become a category over the 10% threshold.
- Never show reports to the dollar or penny. This shows a total lack of common sense. Round to the nearest 1,000, 10,000, 100,000, $1 million, or whatever is appropriate. If $50,000 is material to a company, I would round my report numbers to $10,000.

Exhibit 8.5 illustrates what I am talking about. In this exhibit, by reducing the analysis to four figures and the total, we have been able to round the $182,243 to a more realistic number of $185,000, which is easier to remember and just as likely to occur as it is unlikely that actual costs can be predicted to less than an error factor of say $5,000.

EXHIBIT 8.5 Simplifying Reports by Showing Only the Material Numbers

Originally shown as		Now shown as	
Salaries and wages	123,456	Personnel costs	124,000
Levies	123		
Uniform allowances	234		
Other allowances	123		
Printing costs	9,807	Printing, consumables, etc.	16,000
Consumables	1,500		
Other miscellaneous	5,000		
Consultancy costs	25,000	Consultancy costs	25,000
Travel & accommodations	15,500	Travel & accommodations	17,000
Use of own car	650		
Overnight allowances	850		
Total project	182,243	Total project	182,000

CHAPTER 9

Improving Team Performance: The Cutting Edge

I f you have only a few minutes to skim over this chapter, this is what you should focus on:

- Implementing "action meetings" methods
- Baning morning meetings
- Learning how to negotiate
- Hidden costs of dismissing staff
- Team scorecard designed in Excel
- Lessons from a world-class coach

The following text discusses some of the cutting-edge winning habits of successful managers.

Implementing "Action Meetings" Methods

A majority of meetings are totally flawed. They are held because they were held last week, two weeks ago, last month. The actual fundamental purpose of the meeting has long been forgotten.

A large oil company in a major restructuring undertaken by the CEO found that there were layers of management whose sole purpose was to attend meetings. When the CEO initiated the move out of the head-quarters, he acquired a new premises that could house only a third of what the original headquarters previously held. He was quoted as saying, "Accommodate those whom you can and assist the others with their careers elsewhere."

Most managers have at some time received training in managing meetings, yet the level of frustration with meetings remains the same. The problem has been that the training has not looked at all the core reasons for failure.

Two management consultants, Mike Osborne and David McIntosh, have developed a methodology that is breathtaking in its simplicity yet profound in its impact. Action Meetings (www.actionmeetings.com) has attacked the core of dysfunctional meetings and the common features of unclear agendas, lack of engagement, rambling discussions, a total lack of understanding of "the space" the fellow attendees are in, and worst of all, poorly defined action points and follow through.

There are a number of key features to an *action meeting*. I will explore some of them here:

- **Get people properly into and out of the meeting.** The introduction of a first word (attendees indicate what state they are in) and last word (attendees give feedback). The first words could range from "I am very time challenged and this meeting is the last thing I need" to "I am excited to make progress with this assignment and to hear Bill's view on the XYZ development." The last words could include "This meeting once again promised little and delivered nothing" to "I look forward to receiving Pat's report and working with the project team." The key to the first and last word is that attendees can say anything about how they feel at that point in time and their comment is just that and is to remain unanswered.
- **An effective agenda is constructed as outcomes.** This is the introduction of precise wordings about *meeting outcomes* (see Exhibit 9.1). Outcomes provide focus and the ability to easily check whether an item has in fact been completed. One major benefit of establishing meeting outcomes worded in this way is that requested attendees can and should extract themselves from attending if they do not think they can add value or assist in achieving the outcomes.
- **Meetings are participant-owned, not chairperson-owned.** All attendees are trained in the new methodology and thus meetings are owned and policed by all the participants and so are less reliant on the capability of the chairperson.
- **Once an outcome is closed it remains closed.** During the meeting remind anyone who is opening closed items that the item has been closed.
- **Table nonrelated issues.** Any issues raised that are not related to the outcome under discussion are tabled for another future discussion.
- **Action steps.** Actions steps are written carefully on a special pad and then entered into a web-based application so all can see the progress.

EXHIBIT 9.1 Meeting-Outcomes-Based Agenda

Date:
Location:
Attendance record:

Pat Carruthers	4 out of 5
Sam Jones	2 out of 5
Melanie Maxie	5 out of 5
Dean Lorry etc	5 out of 5

Proposed meeting outcomes:
Project XYZ progress examined and **understood**
Monthly results **understood**
Next steps for project XYZ **agreed** and **assigned**
This month's key initiatives **agreed**
Responsibilities on the acquisition of ABC Limited
assigned

EXHIBIT 9.2 Layout of the Whiteboard in an Action Meeting

Outcomes	Hourly Cost of Meeting $2,500
To **understand** the issues surrounding the _____ To **agree** to the next steps in implementing _____ To **assign** the steps to be undertaken in the first phase of xxxxxxxxxxxx etc	

Agreed actions	Parking lot
1. Pat to write a brief project plan covering X, Y, and Z by Wednesday, October 12	1. Progress with project
2. Bob to prepare a presentation about the project and to incorporate PD's points, by Friday October 14	2. Training of staff

A layout of the whiteboard in an action meeting is shown in Exhibit 9.2, and a checklist can be found in Exhibit 9.3 and the write up of the agreed actions in Exhibit 9.4.

I will never forget working as a contractor and seeing, every Monday, the senior management team members attending their weekly meeting. At 12:30 P.M. they emerged, totally frustrated, seeing the meeting as a wasted exercise. The meeting could and should have been held on the previous Friday afternoon, lasting no more than an hour.

EXHIBIT 9.3 Action Meeting Checklist

Before the Meeting   □ Yes   □ No
1. Review previous meetings for agreed actions and find out
   progress; if little achieved, defer meeting and action a
   "shame and name."
2. Offer help to those "nonachievers" who are late on the   □ Yes   □ No
   material they have promised to deliver on.
3. Construct the draft outcomes of the meeting and send these   □ Yes   □ No
   as the agenda, asking only those who can help achieve
   these outcomes to attend.
4. Show the attendance record on the draft outcomes   □ Yes   □ No
   document; if the meeting is worthwhile, then all people
   designated should have attended.
5. Visit the most influential attendees before the meeting and   □ Yes   □ No
   seek their support on critical issues.

During Meeting
6. Ensure the minutes are limited to recording only the major   □ Yes   □ No
   agreements and issue them the same day after the meeting
   (a one-pager as opposed to four to five pages).
7. Remind everyone of the action meeting rules: □ Yes   □ No
   ▪ First word (attendees indicate what state they are in).
   ▪ Agreement on outcomes and the order in which they are
     to be discussed.
   ▪ Outcome once closed is to remain closed.
   ▪ Everybody has the right to challenge someone if the point
     being raised is not related to the current outcome.
   ▪ Be hard on the issue but soft on the person.
   ▪ Tasks cannot be assigned to anybody who is not at the
     meeting.
   ▪ All ideas are welcome as long as they relate to the
     outcome being discussed.
   ▪ All ideas not related to outcomes are put on hold and are
     discussed only when all other issues are completed and
     the attendees wish them to be aired.
   ▪ All agreed actions must have a person assigned to them
     and dates in which they will be completed.
   ▪ Last word (attendees give feedback on the meeting).
8. Write up the outcomes on a whiteboard and get agreement   □ Yes   □ No
   from everybody that the wording is correct.
9. Start off with the first word, ensuring everyone understands   □ Yes   □ No
   it is a statement about what space they are in, not about
   what they are doing at the present; give them an example.
10. Recap on agreements; check to see if deadlines are realistic. □ Yes   □ No
11. End with the last word.   □ Yes   □ No
12. Set up a reminder system to trigger follow-up calls to all   □ Yes   □ No
    those who have agreed to an action.

EXHIBIT 9.4 Agreed Actions

Agreed Actions	Responsibility	Deadline
To meet with ____ and obtain their commitment	PC	June 1
Update the project's intranet page	DL	June 7
Short-list three suppliers	FR	June 18
Canvas support from the senior management team	MK	June 19
Follow-up progress on these action points	ML	June 20

EXHIBIT 9.5 Hourly Cost of a Meeting Based on Number of Attendees and Average Salary of Those Attending

Average salary of attendees (estimate only required)	100,000
Factored by multiplier of 3 to cover all costs: salary, overheads associated with employee	300,000
Effective working hours (42 working weeks × 40 hours)*	1680
Average cost per member	180
Attendees	6
Cost per hour	1080

*Excludes holidays, sick leave, training. Based it on 40 hours as much time throughout the year is lost to traveling.

Hourly Meeting Cost

Stating the hourly meeting cost (HMC) may help focus the attendees. Here is how to work out the HMC. Exhibit 9.5 is based on the premise that staff only work on average 42 working weeks a year (i.e., taking out vacations, public holidays, training, sick leave, general staff function time, traveling time during office hours, etc.). This works out to be 1,680 hours a year based on 40 hours per week. Using an average salary of $100,000 of each manager attending, and a loading for indirect costs associated with each manager of 200% of salary, the total cost of $300,000 divided by 1,680 hours gives a chargeout rate of $180 per hour per attendee.

Check the Need for the Meeting

One successful manager assesses all meeting requests made on his team members. He reduces the need to hold them by either getting the staff to deliver the output so the meeting is unnecessary, or seeking agenda changes so that team members can leave after covering relevant matters.

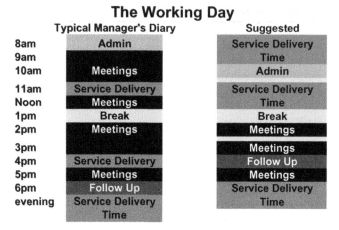

The Working Day

	Typical Manager's Diary	Suggested
8am	Admin	Service Delivery
9am		Time
10am	Meetings	Admin
11am	Service Delivery	Service Delivery
Noon	Meetings	Time
1pm	Break	Break
2pm	Meetings	Meetings
3pm		Meetings
4pm	Service Delivery	Follow Up
5pm	Meetings	Meetings
6pm	Follow Up	Service Delivery
evening	Service Delivery Time	Time

EXHIBIT 9.6 Before-and-After Working-Day Calendars

Ban Morning Meetings

This point was made earlier but it is so important it is worth reiterating. A good start to improving your efficiency is to avoid having meetings during your productive time (e.g., the mornings). I fail to see why, for example, a CEO feels the urge to have a senior management team (SMT) meeting at 9:00 A.M. on a Monday morning, and why the SMT members feel the need to follow it with a debriefing to their direct reports immediately after. This series of meetings hinders the morning's productivity. It is so bad in some organizations that SMT members do their utmost to avoid these meetings by deliberately scheduling important client meetings at this time.

Exhibit 9.6 explains how a manager's calendar often looks and how it could look.

The main changes are bigger chunks of service-delivery time, delaying email duties (see ahead), and meeting time rescheduled to the afternoons, allowing us to be more relaxed, having scored some early goals. Having rescheduled, we need to make the meetings more productive.

Learn How to Negotiate

The further your climb up the management mountain, the more your negotiating skills will be required. The guru of negotiation is Harry Mills, and a must-read is his book, *Negotiate: The Art of Winning*.[1] He has developed seven steps to agreement using the mnemonic **RESPECT**. The steps are:

Ready yourself.
Explore needs.
Signal for movement.
Probe with proposals.
Exchange concessions.
Close the deal.
Tie up the loose ends.

Mills says, "Never go into an agreement without a BATNA." In his book, he talks about the need for the "**b**est **a**lternative **t**o a **n**egotiated **a**greement." In other words, when going into a negotiation process always ensure you have carefully worked out the best fallback position. This does not mean we must be good at "poker;" if we cannot negotiate a win-win deal, it means working out what would be the next course of action. You will find that this gives you a sense of control and calmness. The evidence of the lack of this important step is littered right across the corporate world, where the SMTs are signing the most ridiculous deals—in some cases wiping out, within a few years of the deal, the annual gross domestic product of my country, New Zealand!

The Hidden Cost of Downsizing

Face it: Downsizing is the last thing you want to do. It is often very tempting to contract out this difficult process to the likes of George Clooney in the film *Up in the Air*. This, of course, is not the right thing to do. When faced with a situation where the business is contracting, there are at least three options you need to explore:

1. Can you re-deploy the staff and buy some time so staff members have time to seek further employment while employed? This is a managed staff reduction process and will save a huge amount of money on redundancies while at the same time giving your staff an opportunity to find employment. This, of course, does not work in a major recession.
2. Working with the Human Resources team, establish a voluntary redundancy program. This has some downside as you cannot directly target the staff with the lesser skill set.
3. Undertake a reorganization and have everybody reapply for their jobs. This is the coward's way and has huge hidden costs, including

the best staff leaving as they walk out the door with a golden hand-shake and straight into employment elsewhere. This leaves you with the also-rans, and the piranhas, who are those nasty individuals busily burying hatchets in all those around them. Thus organizations that have had reorganizations tend to end up with dysfunctional management teams.

You should never underestimate the long-term impact on downsizing staff and wherever possible you should fund the shortfall out of retained earnings. The cost of firing and rehiring when added to the public relations disaster it creates often is much higher than the alternative.

By my calculations (see Exhibit 9.7), an organization with 500 full-time employees that is contemplating dismissing between 50 and 70 staff would be no worse off if the staff were kept on and redeployed elsewhere in the organization for up to 2.2 to 2.5 years. In reality, through clever use of new initiatives implemented by these staff, some revenue would be generated, further supporting their payroll costs and thus stretching out this timeframe even further.

I hope that if you are involved in orchestrating a massive downsizing you will cost out all the options. If you manage to redeploy staff with the help of the Human Resources team, you may well have created a career-lasting achievement.

Dismissing a Poor-Performing Employee

A soon as any underperformance is noted, it is imperative that you commence some early discussions with Human Resources as to the next steps. Right from the early signs of nonperformance, evidence needs to be gathered that could be used in an employment court situation because invariably a dismissed employee will be discussing his options with an employment lawyer.

Reflect back: Was it a poor recruitment? Or was it that the employee has not had a chance to flourish? If the latter, often a shift to another department more suited to this person's skill base will sort out the issue, providing suitable support is available, because the employee's confidence will be dented.

If it was a poor recruitment decision, learn your lesson and pay more attention to the recruiting process. This is the most important activity any manager performs. Good recruitment practices are like a series of fences at the top of a cliff that prevent casualties. Recruiting well is much less time consuming than dealing with the casualty at the bottom of the cliff—an unfair dismissal case. You have been warned.

EXHIBIT 9.7 Hidden Costs of Dismissing Staff

Based on 500 FTE organization

	General Managers Time	Managers Time Organizing	Staff to Stay On	Staff Laid Off
Staff involved	4 to 6	90 to 100	340 to 350	50 to 70
		No. of Weeks Worked		
Unproductive time due to uncertainty	6 to 8	2 to 3	4 to 5	4 to 5
Time spent reapplying for own job	n/a	1 to 2	1 to 2	1 to 2
Interviews	2 to 3	2 to 3	0.50	0.50
Redundancy payments	n/a	n/a	n/a	10 to 16
No. of weeks worked per person	8 to 11	5 to 8	5.5 to 7.5	15.5 to 23.5
Total weeks for category	32 to 66	450 to 800	1870 to 2625	775 to 1645

	Cost
Total salary cost	$4.8m to 7.8m
Redundancy support	)
Cost of rehiring	) 1.7m to 2.8m
Cost of training	)
Unproductive time (new staff)	)
Total cost	$6.5m to 10.6m
Period it would have supported laid-off staff	Between 2.2 and 2.5 years

The Overnight Challenge

I recently met a coach of a national soccer team who had taken his team to two consecutive World Cup Finals and won. One of his team-building exercises was to ensure that the team went to an outdoor adventure center where there were basic accommodation amenities. He ensured there was no television because he wanted the team to always be together and learning more about each other.

I have also met a senior partner in an accounting firm who recalled that one weekend a group of staff got together and went on a hike. It turned out to be more of an adventure than most had anticipated. Swollen rivers meant crossing them was hazardous and everybody had an important role in the safety of others. The team dynamics post-hike were truly amazing. Those who went on the hike became known as the "A-framers," named after the A-frame huts they stayed in. To this day they still have reunions with members flying in from overseas.

Use the One-Minute-Manager Techniques

The *One Minute Manager*[2] was published over 25 years ago. It is as relevant today as it was then. This book will help you develop simple techniques to improve your management. It is written as a story about a student trying to find out how to be a good manager. One day he comes across "the one-minute manager," who tells him his "secret." This format makes it easy to read. The book covers three key techniques: the one-minute goal setting, the one-minute praising, and the one-minute reprimand. It should be reread from time to time to lock in the good behaviors.

Introduce a Team Balanced Scorecard

Organizations who have adopted the balanced scorecard reporting have introduced team scorecards. These help the team score goals in a balanced way and increase the alignment of the individual team members' work to their team and organization goals.

Even if the organization has not adopted the balance scorecard, you can introduce one for your team. Exhibit 9.8 shows a team scorecard designed in Excel. Excel is an excellent tool for designing a template and testing over a couple of months, after which it should be put into a proper balanced scorecard system.

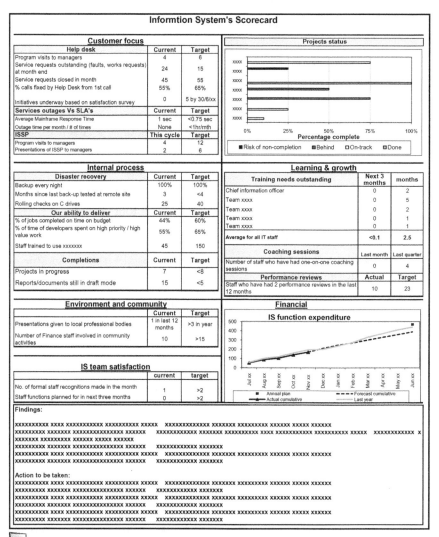

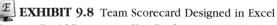 **EXHIBIT 9.8** Team Scorecard Designed in Excel

Source: David Parmenter, *Key Performance Indicators: Developing, Implementing, and Using Winning KPIs, 2nd Edition.* Copyright © 2010 by David Parmenter. Reprinted with the permission of John Wiley & Sons, Inc.

Lessons from a World-Class Coach

How many coaches can say they have coached the side that won two world championships in a row in a sport where major powers compete, such as Japan, Canada, and the United States? Don Tricker, former coach of the New Zealand Black Sox Softball team, is a gifted leader. I believe his methods would take any team to glory.

The following are some of the tips about building a "team to win" gleaned from conversations with Tricker:

Lesson 1: Strategy

In Tricker's world, strategy can be boiled down to four things:

1. What do we want? [What is the performance goal?]
2. Which athletes will deliver the performance goal? [What are our critical success factors (CSFs)?]
3. What will the athletes need to deliver the performance goal? [What do we need to do to constantly perform well in our CSFs?]
4. What could mess it all up? [What are the obstacles/constraints to realizing the performance goal?]

We can apply this simple view to the business model (see restated points in brackets above) and I am sure it would make strategy a lot clearer to staff and management.

Lesson 2: Leadership

Tricker suggests that CEOs who do not share or who are not open to change are typically those who are underperformers. Successful CEOs want their staff to stand up and say what they think.

He believes that senior players do not equal leadership. In the business world, how many times do we see this mistake being made? Leadership needs to run right through the team. Leadership means team members challenging the way things have been done in the past.

If we look at the trends in professional sports, it could be argued that athletes are conditioned not to think, with assistants telling them what to wear and where to be and organizing their daily routines. It is important in any team that has to function well under pressure that team members are making daily decisions and thus are equipped to function well when the pressure is on.

Tricker further believes that it is all right to leapfrog yesterday's heroes and select young talent that has a gift for leadership.

Lesson 3: Empowerment

We need to ask ourselves: Why do we want empowerment in organizations? Surely we want a group of individuals who can coach themselves. In the sporting sense, we want athletes to be the architects of what they do. This leaves the coach with the simple task of asking the right questions. A coach, therefore, is in the *self-esteem* business. A coach's tasks are to raise awareness and then transfer responsibility—with the deliverable being self-belief.

Tricker told me this story about his daughter:

One day, his daughter came up to him and said, "I'm really hopeless at doing handstands. My handstands really suck. Can you teach me how to do one?"

Tricker asked her to do a handstand, and when his daughter collapsed in a heap on the floor, he said, "Okay, let's do another one, but this time, tell me what part of your body feels 'sucky.'" After the second attempt she replied, "My arms."

So Tricker said, "Do another one, but this time I want you to focus on your arms and tell me, out of ten, how sucky they are, with one being really sucky and ten being not sucky at all."

With his daughter concentrating on her arms, she proceeded to do a much better handstand, and popped up saying her arms were "a five." "Let's do another one," said Tricker. This time, the daughter completed the handstand. "Nine and a half!" she exclaimed. Then she said, "I did it all by myself!" and marched off.

Let us analyze what happened here. It is easy as a manager/coach to refer to your own extensive knowledge and spend a lot of time talking about what you know. Instead of Tricker reverting to his days as a teenager and remembering all the techniques he used when doing a handstand, he transferred responsibility and raised awareness in his daughter as to what part of her body was failing her. Using her language, he got her to concentrate on this point of weakness, with the result that she left the room smiling with the belief that she did it herself.

As a manager and leader, can you shut up enough to allow your staff to tell you what they want?

Lesson 4: Planning for a Three-Day Week

Over the years, Tricker has become increasingly frustrated with sporting organizations promising more than they can deliver. One day he made a simple observation. In reality you do not have five days a week to do tasks in sports; sports is about people and by default issues that emerge are typically people issues that take time to resolve. Therefore, when planning I make the assumption that I will have only three days in the week with the remaining two days being taken up by some form of firefighting or unplanned activity.

He now plans all projects on the basis that full-time means three days a week. He has found that projects now are completed on time and has given himself space to think strategically.

Lesson 5: Handling Specialists

Tricker points out the need to celebrate specialists and he notes that sports historically has been very good at this. Yet in the business world these individuals are often overloaded until they start underperforming and lose their credibility. Instead, with these specialists, businesses should ask, "Where are we going to get the best out of Pat Carruthers?" and then remove Pat from all other less important activities.

Lesson 6: Integrity to Honesty

Tricker points out that many organizations have the words *integrity* or *honesty* in their values and wonders whether they are applied in practice. He asks the question, as I will ask you, "When was the last time you had a challenging conversation that caused pain?"—in other words, giving a reprimand, a warning, or a dismissal.

In high-performance sports, as in the business world, there are winners and losers. We thus need to be more honest with nonperformers—in sports the one thing that we cannot afford to burn is time.

Lesson 7: Use Critics

Tricker believes you should find your greatest critics in your organization and get them involved in the planning process. These critics obviously see the world differently and may stop you from making the same mistakes you have made in the past.

Lesson 8: Organize a Team Overnight Activity at an Outdoor Adventure Center

One of Tricker's team-building exercises was to leverage off the New Zealand Army. His rationale is that the military has been in the business of building teams for generations. Therefore, their environment is conducive to building teams and not filled with antisocial devices such as television. As Tricker put it,

> *Put four men in a hotel room with Sky [television network] and the conversation will stop once they have sorted out who has the remote. . . . We wanted our players to talk to one another—to leverage off each other's knowledge and experience. We also wanted them to share experiences that they wouldn't normally have in the city.*

Lesson 9: Adopt a Winning Coaching Style

Tricker's coaching style includes the following:

- It is not about the coach—it is about delivering a quality service to every person; therefore, find out what makes each of your team members tick—view the world through their eyes.
- Keep your messages positive—emotional scarring can take a lifetime to heal.
- Ensure that each performance goal is owned by the team.
- Focus on shared leadership—be a facilitator, ensuring the right questions are asked.
- Team building is vital—take your team out of its comfort zone and get to a situation where no one cares who gets the credit.
- Be excellent at doing the basics—key tasks must be easy to understand and able to be performed when under pressure.
- Clarify role definitions of each team member—ask your team members individually, "What do you want from me?"
- Be accepting of mistakes and analyze the decision making that led to the mistake; both the coach and the team player will learn something.
- There's no room for excuses.
- Have fun and make sure you celebrate success!

Notes

1. Harry A. Mills, *Negotiate: The Art of Winning*, The Mills Group, 1990.
2. Kenneth H. Blanchard and Spencer Johnson, *The One Minute Manager*, Morrow, 1982.

CHAPTER 10

Effective Recruiting

If you have only a few minutes to skim over this chapter, this is what you should focus on:

- Understand that time spent recruiting is the most valuable time
- Use simulation exercises and psychometric testing on the short-listed candidates
- Ask your valuable employees for referrals
- Select an executive assistant to be your copilot

Understand That Time Spent Recruiting Is the Most Valuable Time

Far too often managers, when looking at their calendar, throw up their hands when they realize that they have another recruitment interview to do. It is the last thing they need at this point in time. Yet, recruitment should be seen as the most important thing a manager does, for the following reasons:

- Recruiting properly is like putting a fence on the top of a cliff—it prevents causalities. As Jim Collins, of *Good to Great* fame, says, "You need to get the right people on the bus."
- You can recruit for technical skills and through training improve skill levels, but you cannot change a person's values. If an individual's values are different from those of the organization, you will always have conflict.
- Better recruits will lead to more internal promotion, both saving costs and maintaining institutional knowledge.

To have a good team it is a good idea to start with the best resources available. There are still too many staff selections made via an antiquated interview process accompanied by some cursory reference checking; the result is a high failure rate among new staff. Greater effort needs to be put into the selection process through the adoption of better practice recruiting techniques.

> Management guru Peter Drucker once observed General Motors' top committee spending hours discussing the promotion of one employee. On questioning management about the effectiveness of this, the reply from the CEO was, "If we didn't spend four hours on placing a man and placing him right, we'd spend four hundred hours on cleaning up after our mistake."

Cathay Pacific Recruitment

Cathay Pacific constantly seeks frontline staff that were born with the desire to serve. They firmly believe you cannot *train* staff to be as good at serving as Cathay Pacific requires—"They have to be born that way."

In order to sort the wheat from the chaff, all frontline applicants have to go through an arduous five-interview recruitment process that often takes about three months. Only applicants who are committed to joining Cathay Pacific get over this hurdle. During these interviews management is looking for the traits they need. The investment in the front end pays off with a quicker and more successful training process and one of the lowest staff turnover ratios in the industry. See Chapter 20 for more details about Cathay Pacific.

Peter Drucker's Five-Step Process

Management guru Peter Drucker, on observing great leaders, noted that there were five steps to a sound recruitment:

1. Understand the job so you have a better chance of getting a good fit.
2. Consider three to five people to maximize your chances of getting the best fit.
3. Study candidates' performance records to find their strengths so that you can ascertain whether these strengths are right for the job.
4. Talk to candidates' previous bosses and colleagues about them.
5. Once the employment decision is made, make sure the appointee understands the assignment.

14 Great Questions to Help Get Select 'A' Players

Dr Richard Ford has written a good article on "how to hire the 'A' players."[1] The 14 great questions he has raised are:

1. Why did you leave your last job?
2. Of what achievements are you most proud?
3. What has been your biggest business failure to date?
4. What are your weaknesses?
5. What sorts of things irritate and frustrate you most, and how do you express your emotions when frustrated?
6. What is the biggest mistake of your career?
7. What will reference checks disclose about your personal and operating style and how will your style impact on other team members?
8. How do you plan to grow and stretch yourself in the next five years?
9. What would your colleagues say is the worst thing about you?
10. How did you compare with other people doing the same job?
11. Tell me about a time when you had to persuade people to do something they did not want to do? What happened?
12. When I call your last boss, how will he/she rate your performance on a 0-10 scale and why?
13. How would your colleagues describe your team-playing abilities?
14. Why do you want this job?

Using the Organization's Values in Recruiting

As we all know about our current or past partners, you can change yourself but can seldom change others. Likewise with recruiting, you need to recruit people who demonstrate the same values as your organisation has or aspires to have. Your questioning should ascertain the interviewee's values as demonstrated in the examples you have asked them to discuss.

Involve the Human Resources Team

One of the most disconcerting departures from better practice has been the demise of the Human Resources (HR) team's influence in organizations. Where recruitment is left to managers, chaos ensues.

Most readers can reflect back to a recruitment that they approved that did not work out. In most cases this would have been based on interviews and references. HR practitioners have found there are far more effective ways to recruit, starting by making an in-depth focus on the job requirements and followed by behavioral event interviews, simulated exercises, and assessment centers. All of this takes experienced in-house resources to manage and deliver. As we all know, the cost of appointing the wrong person can be much greater than just her salary costs. These methods are discussed in the following.

Use Simulation Exercises and Psychometric Testing

The basic interview is a totally flawed tool; we tend to warm to those candidates who are similar to us. Clever interviewees realize this and will mimic back to us what we want to hear. Situation, role-playing, or scenario exercises are thus becoming more common in the recruitment process in an effort to find out more about the candidates. It is now quite common for report writing and presentation exercises to be set during the final interview round for the more senior roles.

Many organizations that I have surveyed report that they have been burned by recruiting staff who describe themselves as competent on an important skill, only to find out otherwise.

Psychometric tests, especially arithmetical and verbal reasoning, are found to be valuable predictors and should be used when sorting out which of the short-listed candidates you will give the offer to. High scores in these two tests are seen as signs of a high performer.

One organization comments on the usefulness of a simple scenario exercise as part of the recruitment process, with the candidate and the panel playing their respective roles. The organization says that it is not hard to set up and yet helps significantly in the selection process. Candidates are given only 15 minutes notice of what the scenario is going to be.

Assessment Centers

First used in the British army, assessment centers have long been recognized as a thorough way to recruit staff. They work particularly well when you are recruiting a group of staff or when you are looking to select senior and middle-management internally.

One manufacturing organization has a substantial investment in assessment centers for graduate recruitment. At their initial expression of interest, the graduates complete a comprehensive self-assessment questionnaire. From these returns, preselection of possible candidates is made and interviews carried out at the universities. Up to 24 graduates are selected to take part in the assessment centers. Two assessment centers are then run, each one day in duration, with 12 graduates plus up to 24 managers from the organization. Activities include an impromptu oral presentation, group work exercises, plus rigorous interviews. Usually about 50% of the graduates assessed are chosen.

One finance organization has been using assessment centers successfully to identify their best staff candidates for branch manager positions. Two years on from the first assessments and placements, they have experienced 60% success in the selections made. The core competencies in these generic positions have been clearly identified and are reflected in the assessment center tasks and activities. They have continuously modified and refined their assessment centers with input from outside consultants.

Involve Your Team in the Final Selection Process

Far too often a new staff member is soon found to be deficient in a key process he claimed expertise in. This is a shame, as a brief exposure to the team during a casual walk could have exposed a potentially serious weakness in the candidate's skill base.

It is a good idea to have staff on the team somehow involved in the final selection from the short list of candidates. This need not be too complex. A meeting over an afternoon cup of coffee can give the staff a chance to subtly quiz candidates on their "expert knowledge."

One technology team had interviewed an impressive candidate and duly short-listed him. In the second round of interviews, they found that the candidate, albeit a certified Microsoft engineer, had little or no practical experience. This was discovered by the team members when they gave him a tour of the team's IT equipment.

Ask Your Top Employees for Referrals

One high-performance manager asks the team members if they know a person who would fit in the team before she advertises a position. Often this has proved successful in saving hours of sifting through the great unknown.

> Google is famous for its referral recruiting. Staff members who recommend candidates are rewarded for their efforts if and when their contact becomes an employee.

Reference Checks: The Do's and Don'ts

A reference check has little or no validity unless it is from a person known to your organization or a past employer whom you can rely on. Random references, especially if they are received attached to the resume, should be treated with caution. At the very least you should phone and ask questions about the candidate's skill base, such as:

- "Can you give me some instances where Pat has shown her ability to complete what she has started?"
- "Can you give me some instances where Pat has shown initiative?"
- "Can you give me some instances where Pat has shown her ability to handle pressure?"
- "Are there any special needs that this candidate has in order to perform well?"

Asking about any special needs may force the referees to be a little bit more honest about the baggage this individual is currently carrying. It may not change the appointment decision, but it could make a significant difference in the way you operate with that person in those critical first three months.

> One important government organization asks all short-listed candidates to find a referee who is known by the organization. If none can be found, they ignore this step. Naturally, this would count against an applicant. They believe a reference is worth getting only if it can be relied upon. They know that a referee who is aware of the organization, how it operates, and its values and staff would be unlikely to give an unreliable reference if he wants to retain his relationship with the organization.

A common mistake is not to verify the academic record. Papers are littered with cases where high-profile appointments have been made where the individual has claimed a masters or Ph.D. degree, only to be found out when poor performance brings his claims into question. Always check against the university records where the appointments are very important to the organization.

Selecting an Executive Assistant to Be Your Copilot

Behind all great managers and leaders is a great *executive assistant*. The question is, do you want to find one by chance or be proactive about it? Here are some steps to select one that will fit:

- Find an assistant with similar interests as you; you will spend a lot of time together, so it is important that you have something in common.
- Undertake simulation tests on the candidate's ability to take dictation, handle difficult callers, and write a few letters covering a visit to a branch or a staff announcement.
- A tertiary education is a must.
- Interview at least two previous bosses the assistant has worked for to find out about her interpersonal skills.
- Ensure you perform psychometric tests, especially for arithmetical and verbal reasoning, as high scores in these two tests are a good sign of a high performer.
- Find an assistant who has the same mental horsepower as the senior team members, exceptional organizational capability, and ability to grasp complex issues, and to work well under pressure, and who demonstrates a strategic focus, an eye for detail when required, and so forth.
- Ensure there has been adequate testing of spelling, grammar, and coherency of speech.
- Offer conditions of employment that are so good that the candidate will not be tempted by another position.

The passenger next to me on a flight happened to be an entrepreneurial CEO. Among the many things we discussed was the importance of the executive assistant. He stated that he has done whatever it takes to keep his even though she has a young family. He treats her as a member of the senior management team. She is paid a six-figure sum and has whatever time off she needs for her children.

They have worked together for over ten years and are the perfect team. He has the big ideas and she is the implementer! He said that even if she works two days a week she is worth the salary she is paid.

(Continued)

With his travels there is plenty of downtime potential for her to manage her children. He says they have an arrangement that assures her longevity with him. "The SMT [senior management team] can come and go, but losing my executive assistant would be catastrophic because she has much institutional knowledge as well as the ability to make the two of us work so effectively."

Notes

1. Dr. Richard G. Ford, *"How to Hire the 'A' Players,"* Finance & Management ICAEW, March 2010.

CHAPTER 11

Becoming More Financially Aware

If you have only a few minutes to skim over this chapter, this is what you should focus on:

- Understand internal controls
- Participate in an efficient budget process
- Help create an efficient month-end reporting process

Understand Your Financial Responsibilities as a Budget Holder

The fiscal responsibilities of a budget holder are vitally important. Good practices learned early on will hold you in good stead as you are given increasingly greater budget responsibilities. Having a good working relationship with the finance team will pay dividends; remember, they process your salary and expense claims. In addition, you will need timely and accurate reports to run the finances of your team. If you put garbage in, you will get garbage out! The fiscal responsibilities of a budget holder include:

- To prepare any expense claims on a timely basis
- To comply with purchase procedures (e.g., orders, delegations, and purchase invoices)
- To achieve results within budget
- To prepare monthly accruals
- To monitor the month-end report budget versus actual and comment on variances
- To prepare a thorough budget (this is prepared on a quarterly rolling basis, as opposed to an annual basis, in leading organizations)
- To prepare consistent and accurate forecasts
- To liaise effectively with the accounting team

The simple checklist in Exhibit 11.1 will assist you in this area.

𝔈 EXHIBIT 11.1 Fiscally Responsible Manager Checklist

1. Have you developed a simple yet effective control over your expenditure commitments?	☐ Yes	☐ No
2. Do you fully understand the purchasing procedures?	☐ Yes	☐ No
3. Do you provide approvals promptly to orders and invoices? (the purchase system is critical to accurate accounting)	☐ Yes	☐ No
4. Do you understand the importance of good internal controls, especially segregation of duties?	☐ Yes	☐ No
5. Do you have more than the basic understanding of accounting? (including accruals, how profit and loss statements and balance sheets relate to each other)	☐ Yes	☐ No
6. Have you learned how to interrogate the general ledger?	☐ Yes	☐ No
7. Do you prepare and submit accruals on the last working day of the month?	☐ Yes	☐ No
8. Can you prepare a brief report on the month's progress wthin 30 minutes?	☐ Yes	☐ No
9. Can you prepare your budget in less than two days?	☐ Yes	☐ No
10. Do you maintain regular liaisons with the accounting team?	☐ Yes	☐ No

Understanding Internal Controls

The importance of understanding and complying with better-practice internal controls cannot be underestimated. Most managers will have been exposed to situations where breaches will have led to material losses in their organizations. To understand what makes better-practice internal controls, it is advisable to go for training and seek training from your accounting team. The checklist in Exhibit 11.2 covers most, if not all, internal controls issues.

Understand Your Organization's Financial Statements

To help better understand how your current role fits into your organization it is desirable to know the major numbers on your organization's financial statements. The key is to redraft these statements into a form you better understand, rounding all the numbers (e.g., debts of $2,356,125 should be $2.3 million and fixed assets of $52,356,125 should be $52 million). Large rounded numbers are easy to remember and thus encourage you to think about the significance of work you do in relation to the financial statements. As already mentioned, attending a course on "finance for budget holders" is highly desirable. The content matter in the following will help you understand some of the basics.

𝓔 EXHIBIT 11.2 Internal Controls Checklist

1. Do you rotate your staff periodically, especially in high-risk areas such as cash, receipting, or purchasing officer?	□ Yes	□ No
2. Do you ensure staff take at least ten consecutive working days off a year? (This is particularly important if they are involved with handling checks or cash.)	□ Yes	□ No
3. Do you segregate ordering, processing of purchase invoice, receipting of goods and services, and payment approval duties?	□ Yes	□ No
4. Do you request internal audit reviews of your high-risk areas about every six months?	□ Yes	□ No
5. Do you perform random checks on transactions? (This is also useful to pick up on those meaningless procedures that are being carried out solely because they have been carried out in the past.)	□ Yes	□ No
6. Have you attended a training course on internal controls?	□ Yes	□ No
7. Do you conduct unannounced checks on petty cash and other cash accounts?	□ Yes	□ No

Balance Sheet or the Statement of Financial Position

The balance sheet can be expressed in a number of ways as set out in Exhibits 11.3 and 11.4.

The key points include:

- It describes what an organization owns and what it owes.
- It is a snapshot in time. You will always see an exact date given (the balance date).
- It always balances; in other words, **assets** equals **liabilities + debt + owner's equity**.
- **Assets** equals fixed assets + stock + debtors + cash in bank + investments.
- **Liabilities** equals creditors + accruals.
- **Debt** equals bank overdraft + loans + debenture stock.
- **Owner's equity** equals share capital + retained profits (profits or surpluses that have not been paid as dividends).
- There is more than one way to show a balance sheet.
- In many balance sheets, assets and liabilities that will be turned over in the next 12 months are set off against each other to come up with a term called *working capital*. Working capital is like the oil in a car engine. You want it neither too high nor too low.
- "Notes to the Accounts" describe important accounting policies where these affect the way the accounts look.

EXHIBIT 11.3 Balance Sheet

Statement of Financial Position as at 30 April 20XX

	Month-End Actual	Last Month Actual
Bank and Cash	4,000	5,800
Debtors	2,000	1,800
Stock	2,000	1,800
Fixed Assets	9,000	8,800
Other Assets	1,000	800
Total Assets	18,000	19,000
Accounts Payable	(3,500)	(2,500)
Other Liabilities	(1,000)	(800)
Net Assets	13,500	15,700
Funded by		
Current Year Profit	2,700	2,500
Share Capital and	10,800	13,200
Accumulated Funds		
Total Equity	13,500	15,700

EXHIBIT 11.4 Balance Sheet from Exhibit 11.3 Expressed in Another Way

Statement of Financial Position as at 30 April 20XX

	Month-End Actual	Last Month Actual
Bank and Cash	4,000	5,800
Debtors	2,000	1,800
Stock	2,000	1,800
Accounts Payable	(3,500)	(2,500)
Other Liabilities	(1,000)	(800)
Working Capital	3,500	6,100
Fixed Assets	9,000	8,800
Other Assets	1,000	800
Net Assets	13,500	15,700
Funded by		
Current-Year Profit	2,700	2,500
Share Capital and	10,800	13,200
Accumulated Funds		
Total Equity	13,500	15,700

Statement of Profit and Loss

The key points of a profit and loss statement, as shown in Exhibit 11.5, include:

- It describes the performance of a company over a period of time (e.g., "For the year ended December 31").
- Revenues less expenses incurred to get those revenues = profit or surplus.
- It surprises many when they realize that the final profit or surplus is not a black-and-white area; in fact it is very much like a sculpture. Two identical organizations, with the same transactions will report a different result, albeit in the same ballpark, because they would be adopting different accounting policies.
- The high-profile company collapse of WorldCom was where expenses were treated as assets, thus artificially inflating profit.
- In all organizations, including not-for-profit organizations, there is need to make a profit or surplus in order to have enough reserves to acquire operating assets and act as a buffer in difficult times.
- "Notes to the Accounts" describe important accounting policies where these affect the way the accounts look.

Statement of Financial Performance for the period ending 31 December 20XX

Act	Bud	Var		Act	Bud	Var		Budget	Forecast
Month $000s				**Year-To-Date $000s**				**Full Year $000s**	
			Revenue						
920	1200	-280 ✗	Revenue 1	6150	5630	520 ⇔		10000	8800
220	200	20 ✓	Revenue 2	2770	2900	-130 ⇔		5000	3800
220	220	0	Revenue 3	1750	1630	120 ⇔		3500	2300
190	170	20 ✓	Other Revenue	1330	1280	50 ⇔		1500	1400
1,550	1,790	-240 ✗	**Total Revenue**	12,000	11,440	560 ⇔		20,000	16,300
250	270	20	Head Office Expenditure	1370	1480	110 ⇔		1700	1500
			Divisional Costs						
250	230	-20 ⇔	Division 1	2710	2420	-290 ✗		3000	3400
230	210	-20 ⇔	Division 2	2090	2180	90 ⇔		2800	2700
75	70	-5	Division 3	1530	1460	-70 ⇔		1900	1900
100	80	-20 ✗	Division 4	1050	1090	40		1200	1100
75	70	-5	Division 5	1660	1700	40		1900	1900
65	50	-15	Division 6	1470	1500	30		1600	1600
85	50	-35 ✗	Other Divisions	990	450	-540 ✗		700	1400
880	760	-120 ✗	**Total Divisional Costs**	11,500	10,800	-700 ⇔		13,100	14,000
420	760	-340 ✗	**Surplus/(Deficit)**	-870	-840	-30		5,200	800

Key
all variances greater than 10,000 are marked with
⇔ within +/- 10% of budget
✗ unfavourable variance
✓ favourable variance

EXHIBIT 11.5 Profit and Loss Statement

Management Report

Actual Source & Disposition of Funds

Current Month				Year To Date		
Actual	Budget	Variance	$000s	Actual	Budget	Variance
			Operating Cashflow:			
16,000	16,000	0	Operational Revenue	151,000	151,000	0
(8,000)	(9,000)	1,000	Operational Costs	(74,000)	(84,000)	10,000 ✓
1,000	1,000	0	Interest Received	1,000	1,000	0
(200)	0	(200)	xxx	(8,000)	(9,000)	1,000
1,000	1,000	0	xxx	(5,000)	(6,500)	1,500
9,800	9,000	800	OPERATING CASHFLOW	65,000	52,500	12,500 ✓
			Investing Cashflow:			
-14,000	-14,000	0	Capital Expenditure	(151,000)	(169,000)	18,000 ✓
-900	0	(900)	xxx	(9,000)	(9,000)	0
-14,900	-14,000	(900)	INVESTING CASHFLOW	-160,000	-178,000	18,000 ✓
-5,100	-5,000	-100	NET CASH FLOW	-95,000	-125,500	30,500
			Financing Cashflow:			
1,000	1,000	0	Borrowing	61,000	41,000	20,000 ✓
28,000	29,000	(1,000)	xxx	66,000	61,000	5,000
(23,900)	(25,000)	1,100	xxx	(32,000)	23,500	(55,500) ✗
5,100	5,000	100	FINANCING CASHFLOW	95,000	125,500	-30,500 ✗

EXHIBIT 11.6 Source and Application of Funds Statement

Source and Disposition of Funds

Otherwise known as a *cash flow statement*, this statement shows where the cash has been generated and where it has been spent or saved

The key points of a source and application of funds, as shown in Exhibit 11.6, include:

- No matter how profitable it is, a company that runs out of cash to pay its bills is in trouble. The statement of source and application of funds identifies how the company has sourced cash (from sales, borrowing, share floats, etc.) to meet its needs to repay debt, distribute dividends, reinvest in plant and equipment, and so forth.
- One reason for including this statement in the accounts is that the statement of profit and loss does not make any distinction between whether sales generated or expenses incurred were paid in cash or put "on account." If all your expenses were cash expenses and all your sales offered 90-day terms to your customers, you would run out of cash quickly (whether those sales were profitable or not).
- It describes the real cash flows in the business excluding all accounting adjustments—in other words what cash came in and what cash went out.
- It is for a period of time, the same period of time as the profit and loss statement (e.g., "For the year ended December 31"). It is a

snapshot in time. You will always see an exact date given (the "balance date").

- It always balances.
- Cash flows from **operating** activities equals **investing** cash flows + **financing** cash flows.
- **Operating** activities (±)—for example, cash flow from turning over your debtors and creditors, along with any cash transactions.
- **Investing** activities (±)—for example, buying or selling fixed assets.
- **Financing** activities (±)—for example, increase or decrease in debt and changes in owners' equity.

CHAPTER **12**

Developing Your Selling Skills

I f you have only a few minutes to skim over this chapter, this is what you should focus on:

- Selling a new process through "emotional drivers"
- Selling by emotional drivers: how a car is sold
- Always pre-sell your proposals

Selling a New Process through "Emotional Drivers"

Remember, nothing was ever sold by logic! You sell through *emotional drivers*. Remember your last car purchase? Many initiatives fail at this hurdle because we attempt to change the culture through selling logic, writing reports, and issuing commands via email! It does not work.

We need to radically alter the way we pitch a sale to the senior management team (SMT) and the board. We first have to make sure we have a good proposal with a sound focus on the emotional drivers that matter to them. In addition, all major projects need a public relations (PR) machine behind them. No presentation, email, memo, or paper related to a major change should go out unless it has been vetted by your PR expert. All your presentations should be road-tested in front of the PR expert. Your PR strategy should include selling to staff, budget holders, SMT, and the board.

Selling by Emotional Drivers: How a Car Is Sold

Let us look at how a second-hand car salesperson sells cars using emotional drivers. Three customers arrive on the same day to look at the "car of the week" that has been featured in the local paper.

The first person is a young information technology guru, generation Y, with the latest designer gear, baggy trousers partway down exposing a designer label on his shorts. The salesperson slowly walks up, all the time assessing the emotional drivers of this potential buyer, looking for clues, such as clothing, the car he arrived in, and so on. The opening line could be, "I hope you have a clean license, as I will not let you out in this beast if you don't. This car has 180 BHP, a twin turbo, and corners like it's on railway tracks." SOLD.

The second person could be me, with my gray hair. The salesperson would say, "This car is five-star rated for safety, with eight air bags, enough power to get you out of trouble, unbelievable braking when you have to avoid the idiots on the road, and tires that will never fail you." SOLD.

The third person, with designer clothing and bag, is addressed with "This car has won many awards for its design. Sit in the driver's seat and feel the quality of the finish. Everything is in the right place. I assure you that every time you drive this car you will feel like a million dollars!" SOLD.

Always Pre-Sell Your Proposals

We then need to focus on selling to the "thought leader" on the SMT and board before we present the proposal. This may take months of informal meetings, sending copies of appropriate articles, telling better-practice stories, and so forth to awaken their interest.

It is worth noting that the thought leader of the SMT and the board may *not* be the CEO or chairperson, respectively. Having pre-sold the change to the thought leader, watch, after delivering your presentation, how the meeting turns to listen to the thought leader's speech of support. Your proposal now has the best possible chance of a positive vote.

Risking a proposal on the whims of the decision makers on the day of the presentation is far too risky. If the proposal has been worth all the time you have put into it, make sure it has the maximum chance of success by pre-selling to the thought leader attending the meeting

One CFO explained in a course how he always pre-sold an idea to a board member before presenting the idea to the board for their approval. The pre-selling ensured that the relevant board member would be first to speak after his presentation and would make supportive comments, thus ensuring a positive reception to the concept.

Selling Your Team to Your Peers

Why is it that many hardworking managers, who are dedicated to the organization, are ostracized by their fellow colleagues? Why is it that some hardworking teams are not understood and do not get the respect their efforts deserve? Reasons include that the team and their manager do not bother spending time selling their services and benefits to the rest of the organization, or that the team seldom takes time out to network within the organization.

If you are a manager of a team with these issues, there is time to change before it is too late. I suggest the following:

- Limit working hours of team members to no more than 50 hours a week so you all have to change your work habits.
- Ensure all staff in the team network with at least two of their peers and in-house clients, over a coffee each week for the next 12 weeks.
- Before embarking on a major project, speak to your mentor as you may well be going in the wrong direction.
- Have a makeover so you look and feel a million dollars.
- Ensure you talk positively to others (keep negative thoughts to yourself).
- Cut down the length of your reports; nothing was ever changed by a report—it was the follow-up action that made the change.
- No matter how much pressure there is, learn to smile every time someone comes to your desk (this needs plenty of practice).
- Learn to give recognitions more freely (see "Creating Winning Personal Habits," Chapter 5).
- Reread Part One of this book and implement as much as you can.

CHAPTER **13**

Working Smart with the Outside World

If you have only a few minutes to skim over this chapter, this is what you should focus on:

"A prince who is not himself wise cannot be wisely advised"
Consulting assignment checklist

Supplier Relationships

Probably the greatest improvement a budget holder can make is improving efficiencies through greater integration with key suppliers. It is important to eliminate the paper flow between you and your major suppliers and eliminate the need for the accounts payable team to process low value transactions. Remember that it costs the same to process a $2 million transaction as it does a $20 transaction and these costs can be as much as $30 per transaction.

Some of the improvements you can make quite easily as a budget holder are:

- Use your purchase card/procurement card, if you have been issued one, for all small-dollar invoices; your accounts payable team will have issued guidelines.
- Help the finance team to create more national contracts that give your organization the ability to streamline the processing of the transactions as well as the ability to negotiate cost savings through economies of scale.
- Invest in liaison time with all the major suppliers you deal with to organize electronic feeds of the invoices that will include the general

ledger account codes—this requires liaison between the information technology teams, yours and each major supplier's!

- Obtain consolidated invoices.

One finance sector organization has had a number of successes with business reengineering. They have made significant inroads by using preferred suppliers and eliminating paperwork or passing the paperwork to their suppliers. Continuous improvement is now part of their culture. Previously they had to process 9,000 window screen insurance claims and make 9,000 check payments. They now make 12 payments a year. A window screen provider now has the national contract. They run the toll-free call center, check whether the claim is valid (via linkage through access to the finance company's extranet), organize replacement, and electronically provide a weekly schedule with the sum to be paid. At the end of the month, the total sum is directly debited from the finance organization's bank account.

One day, the owner of a famous fish restaurant in Brisbane, Australia, pointed out to me a serviceman delivering the linen tablecloths. He was a burly man dressed in a yellow T-shirt and shorts (it could have been somebody's idea of a corporate uniform, someone mad). The owner pointed out that this person is critical to the business and a friend of the staff and does a valuable duty. He ensures the tablecloths are always accounted for and those used each day are taken by him and cleaned. The supplier is thus part of the team, to such an extent that the supplier is invited to the holiday staff function as are the cleaners. How is that for vertical integration of the supplier into the organization!

One finance team I know invites their bank to their organization's annual awards. Naturally the bank's staff are encouraged to sponsor a prize and come, as do all the other guests, in fancy dress. The night is a "taxi home event" so that it can be enjoyed by all and the night is talked about for months later. Naturally enough, the organization always has a smooth run when seeking a loan—another example of working with an important supplier, your bank!

EXHIBIT 13.1 Developing Strategic Relationships with Key Suppliers Checklist

1. Before sending a tender document out, have you short-listed suppliers? (much information can be gathered via the intranet)	□ Yes	□ No
2. Do you meet with their system staff so you can assess the synergies of linking systems? (see stories ahead)	□ Yes	□ No
3. Do you use workshops with local suppliers to see where more win/wins can be achieved?	□ Yes	□ No
4. Have you considered an intensive one-day think-tank at your consultant's offices to kickstart a project?	□ Yes	□ No
5. Do you seek fortnightly invoices from the consultants in busy periods so you can be tightly control costs?	□ Yes	□ No
6. Do you avoid seeking lengthy consultant reports? (you will not read them and they absorb a lot of fees—best to get brief updates in PowerPoint format)	□ Yes	□ No
7. Have you organized functions where all relevant staff from the supplier and your organization get together?	□ Yes	□ No

Exhibit 13.1 is a checklist of the points you should consider.

Seeking Publicity

All great leaders manage the public relations (PR) machine well. Franklin Roosevelt, Sir Ernest Shackleton, and Sir Winston Churchill were all masters at creating stories that the media immediately warmed to. They treated the press as their friends, not their enemies. Early on you need to be familiar with how to become a celebrity in your field. A very good reference book for this is *Get Slightly Famous.*[1]

Using Outside Consultants Effectively

Behind most successful managers are the successful projects where they have been able to obtain leverage from using consultants properly. You have a choice: Learn to achieve through hiring third-party expertise or set yourself up for failed projects. From my observations there are some lessons to be learned.

Lesson 1: Understanding Consultants' Chargeout Rates

Some organizations have an anti-consultants culture. This commonly starts from the top and seeps insidiously all through the organization, possibly

EXHIBIT 13.2 Consultants' Chargeout Rate Calculation

A consultant year may look like this;	Weeks
Vacation/holidays	6
Sick leave	2
Training and updating	2
Marketing (visits, delivering presentations, phone calls)	5
Unsuccessful proposal time (nonrecoverable)	5
Time written off (consultancy time that is not billable)	3
Balance being consultancy time	29
At 45 hours a week this comes to just over	1300 hours a year
Budget revenue is typically at least 2.5 times the salary to cover the costs of running the firm and to contribute to the profit. Thus if a consultant's salary is $150,000, the revenue target would be $375,000.	$375,000
Chargeout rate	$290 per hour

based on previous bad experiences or misconceptions about the chargeout rates. Exhibit 13.2 looks at how chargeout rates are calculated.

If a consultant had attracted a salary of say $150,000 in a senior management role she needs to be getting at least that in a major consultancy firm. A major consultancy firm needs a factor of 2.5 to 3 times salary to cover overhead, such as training, administration support, accommodation, equipment costs, nonrecoverable flights, recruitment costs, and so on.

Lesson 2: Invest in a Comprehensive Selection Process

It is imperative that you invest as much time as possible in the preselection process, before you are in dialogue with short-listed consulting firms. Your first point of call is to short-list three to five consultants based on reputation. Where possible, interview previous clients. As a guide, spend at least one day for every $50,000 of project budget, short-listing consultants who have achieved similar results to those you seek.

If you have to resort to an open tendering process, ensure that interested suppliers need to provide references of clients where they have performed the same assignment that is required in the tender; this will reduce the number of firms submitting expressions of interest/proposals (depending on how involved you want the selection process to be). These references should be checked prior to any short-listing.

Having made the selection, it is worth reinterviewing a couple of their previous clients to better understand how the consultants work best (they may not realize it themselves).

On a large assignment it may be necessary to "hire a thief to catch a thief" (no offense intended). I remember being asked to quote on a major proposal when all the signs were bad. I instead offered our services as part of the quality selection process behind the scenes, to help with the short list, evaluate the proposed teams, and suggest lines of questioning. One of the interesting parts was ensuring that a staff member mentioned in the proposal was elevated to a higher role in the team. It meant revenue moving within the consulting firm, from one office to another; hence, the office in charge of the proposal had selected their staff at the expense of the strongest team.

The advantage of preselection work is that it creates a win-win for you and the consultants. You are asking only those firms that can do the job and have a successful track record to invest time in proposals. At the same time, you will be more confident in the consultants and hence more likely to actively promote them in-house, to give them the freedom to get on with the job, and last, but not least, to listen to them. Remember, if you are not careful you will be creating the same amount of consulting time in the selection process as in the whole assignment. So help keep things in perspective.

Lesson 3: Market the Consultants In-House

The right consultants, in the right place, at the right time offer many benefits and these need to be actively marketed in-house. Here are just some of the reasons why you may wish to use consultants:

- To mentor the project staff
- To enable the organization to undertake projects it does not have the in-house capability to do
- To bring a wealth of knowledge of better practices
- To hone the in-house project management skills
- Because they are not corrupted by in-house culture or thinking
- Because they have done it all before (unless you are asking them to venture into the great unknown)

If your consultants have been employed for these reasons, then the senior management team (SMT) needs to actively market them in-house, prior to the project starting. One manager commented that if the SMT does not market the reasons for the consulting assignment and the benefits of the particular consultants (their success stories, etc.), then it is no surprise that management and staff resent the consultants being foisted on them.

Downstream effects of poor marketing of consultants are that meetings with the consultants are treated as negotiable, promised deliveries are not met, and so forth. It is no surprise that consultants work better in a receptive environment where they can blossom; even a cactus needs water.

Lesson 4: "A Prince Who Is Not Himself Wise Cannot Be Wisely Advised"

Regrettably, many managers do not have the skills to manage large complex projects, let alone handling the additional requirements when adding consultants to the mix. That is, if you do not have strong in-house project management skills, contracting them in will not solve the problem. Project management skills must reside within the project manager, the project sponsor, and the SMT. Where skills in project management are lacking in any of these three areas, chaos often reigns. The SMT needs to fully understand project management techniques so they can be forewarned and take the necessary actions when their large projects are going off-track. Many of the large failed projects that I am aware of have been screaming for help during much of their life and in many cases the SMT was helpless due to the huge gap in the team's knowledge and experience.

It is not uncommon for young enthusiastic managers to be given the headroom to extend beyond their level of competence on large projects. The common symptom in these cases is that the management team up to and including the SMT could do no better or were no wiser.

My suggestion is to play to your skills. Do not have big projects if you are not a big-project organization. It is as simple as that. Then you will not need to keep the 12-gauge loaded shotgun ready to shoot the messenger.

Lesson 5: Some Projects Should Never Have Been Started

All consultants, when being frank, will admit to the odd self-inflicted disaster. The responsibility of many failed projects rests fair-and-square with the initiators. They create projects or new starts with utter abandonment, overlooking the commitments each require. Like children, projects need to have plenty of affection, attention, and nurturing. The consequences for projects when these three traits are not present are equally dire. Here is a list of projects that are high risk from the start:

- Projects where management does not have a clue of what is involved.
- Complex projects that are highly technical and have not been done before; in other words, management and the consultants do not have a clue (these projects make landing on the Moon look easy!).
- Project teams that respect only their own capabilities (in other words, they are difficult to work for!).
- Projects in organizations where the whole SMT has a serious case of attention deficit disorder.

- Projects that are run by egos rather than project management expertise (the projects then take on a life of their own, invariably in the wrong direction, following the laws of gravity).
- Projects that never had economic rationale behind them—the only linkage was to politics rather than strategy.
- Any takeover, merger, or reorganization project, as most are doomed to failure by their very nature (see Chapter 30, "Avoiding a Rotten Takeover or Merger").
- Projects in organizations that have a history of failed projects (even though each one has been blamed on the consultants).

Sometimes consultants have "forward" books that are as bare as 'Old Mother Hubbard's cupboard.' With high overhead and a month or so of expensive employees milling around in the office, any job—I mean *any assignment*—begins to look and smell like roses. Never assume because the consultants look keen that the assignment has any merit, they might just be desperate for work.

Lesson 6: Relate the Size of the Contract of Engagement to the Risks Involved

Relate the size of the contract to the risks involved. Contracts for minor assignments (less than $30,000) should be at most a two-page document. In most cases it would be an email confirmation or a simple signature with the words "agreed as outlined above" written on the consultant's proposal or scoping document.

Lesson 7: Start Off with a Think-Tank Session

The secret of a good briefing is access to enough SMT time at the beginning. I advocate a think-tank session at the start. Recently, a CEO flew in to be part of a one-day workshop with me at my offices to ensure that I was capable of delivering on the assignment, at the same time giving me a thorough briefing on the assignment. This visit was beneficial for both parties. The SMT members were much more supportive due to the CEO's commitment to and confidence in the chosen consultant. Another by-product was a much clearer understanding of the terms of reference than any document could convey. The message is to give the consultants a good induction or suffer the consequences. The meeting has more chance of being successful in the consultants' office, where interruptions will be minimized.

In this meeting establish the foundation stones of the project. Just like building a house, the project, during its life, should never be allowed to be built away from these foundation stones!

Lesson 8: Create Leverage to Maximize the Value for Money

On all projects, ensure you use in-house staff in the project team. In most cases where a client has said "We do not have the resources" I have been able to prove otherwise. Nowadays, graduates are available for all types of occupations, so it is often easy to find bright, quick, and insightful minds. All you need to do is search the employee database. Ensure you have assigned at least two young staff members to the project. You will have rescued them from some meaningless task.

These young graduates will reduce the time spent by the consultants, and at the same time make the project more interesting for the consultants. There are few experienced consultants who do not get a thrill out of working with some young and motivated staff.

Lesson 9: Heed the Warning Signs Early

Not all consultancy relationships are going to work. The key is to recognize early on that the relationship is off the rails and to investigate the breakdown.

Warning signs of a project going off track include:

- In-house project staff are too busy with other duties.
- The project has been simmering for a long time before consultants were involved.
- Only one or two of the SMT members know of the project.
- Project team members talk in jargon.
- The project team produces prestigious reports (a reporting machine, rather than an action team).
- You are writing letters to the consultants.
- Terms of reference creep are beginning to become an epidemic.
- You see the consultants as contractors performing a task you could do better if you had the time.

Beware of managers who suddenly fall out with the consultant; the best action in the first instance is to organize some conflict resolution. Often a perception rather than facts may be the root cause of the problem.

Lesson 10: Sacking the Consultants Is the Start of a Bigger Problem

As Francis Urquhart, the prime minister in the British TV series, *House of Cards*, would say, "Some may think that sacking the consultants has solved the problem, others may say that the problem has just begun as the new consultants are awash with details and are unable to field the ball cleanly. You may think that; I cannot possibly comment."

Changing consultants midstream is no different than bringing in a new surgical team halfway through a complex operation. It is a last resort that will be prone to failure and cost you more in the process.

The business world is a very small place; it pays to terminate a relationship equitably and fairly. Always have a termination clause stating that you can terminate the contract and take over without penalty as long as adequate notice is given and fees are paid up to date. This can and sometimes should be seen as a compliment to the consultant for transferring knowledge quicker than expected.

Talk rather than send letters; they can follow, and should come out of the meetings so there are no surprises.

If the relationship is beyond repair, treat the closeout as a negotiation. Look to give the consultant concessions that do not cost you much. Look to end it in a win-win solution. I can recommend Harry Mills's book, *Negotiate: The Seven Step Master Plan.*[2]

See Exhibit 13.3 for a consulting assignment checklist.

EXHIBIT 13.3 Consulting Assignment Checklist

Pre-assignment Check

1. Do we have the resources to implement the project? □ Yes □ No
2. Do we have a receptive environment assisting consultants □ Yes □ No
   with their delivery?
3. Have we a successful track record in projects this size? □ Yes □ No
4. Does the SMT have a serious condition of attention deficit □ Yes □ No
   disorder?
5. Is the project one of these high-risk ones:
   a. A project where management does not have a clue of □ Yes □ No
      what is involved?
   b. A complex project where management and the □ Yes □ No
      consultants do not have a clue?
   c. A project that is run by egos rather than project □ Yes □ No
      management expertise?
   d. A project involving a takeover or merger? □ Yes □ No
   e. A reorganization project? □ Yes □ No
6. Have we organized training for the SMT to cover any lack □ Yes □ No
   of understanding of the project?
7. Does the SMT have adequate project management expertise? □ Yes □ No

Consultant Selection

8. Have we invested one day for every $50,000 on the □ Yes □ No
   selection process?
9. Have we hired a consultant to help in the selection process? □ Yes □ No

(Continued)

EXHIBIT 13.3 (Continued)

10. Is there a personality fit between the consultants and the in-house team?	☐ Yes	☐ No
11. Have you locked in the best selection for the consulting team—local staff may be promoted ahead of a national expert from another office?	☐ Yes	☐ No
12. Have we created a short list of consultants based on reputation?	☐ Yes	☐ No
13. Have we reference checked all short-listed consultants?	☐ Yes	☐ No

Set Up of Assignment

14. Having made the selection, have you reinterviewed a couple of previous clients to better understand how the consultants work best? (they may not realize it themselves)	☐ Yes	☐ No
15. Have we organized the "think-tank" project start at the consultant's offices? (one-to two-day workshop where the consultants have the chance to impress and start the project running)	☐ Yes	☐ No
16. Have we organized decent facilities for the project team?	☐ Yes	☐ No
17. Have we got the SMT behind the project? (maybe more selling is required)	☐ Yes	☐ No
18. Have we agreed on the project format? (it can be a very costly and low-value part of the assignment)	☐ Yes	☐ No
19. Have we locked in their experts so they cannot be sold on other assignments? (we expect Pat will spend xx days on this assignment)	☐ Yes	☐ No
20. Have we got full control of the project in-house?	☐ Yes	☐ No
21. Do we have a ratio of two in-house staff to one of theirs?	☐ Yes	☐ No
22. Are we able to create a win-win? (make it known from the start you are happy to be a reference site)	☐ Yes	☐ No

Use of Technology

23. Does the technology to be used on the project have a long expected shelf-life with the organization?	☐ Yes	☐ No
24. Are we maximizing the applications that are available via the information technology team?	☐ Yes	☐ No

Meeting Etiquette and Progress Reporting

25. Have we asked for biweekly or weekly invoices so we can keep track of costs?	☐ Yes	☐ No
26. Are we getting regular presentations on progress? (via PowerPoint and keep them informal so the consultants do not burn too much time here)	☐ Yes	☐ No
27. Have we checked to ensure that progress reporting is only taking less than 5% of project time in any given period?	☐ Yes	☐ No
28. Have we kept to the original term of reference unchanged?	☐ Yes	☐ No

EXHIBIT 13.3 (Continued)

29. Have we considered bringing in an independent consultant to evaluate progress? (recommended on all those complex assignments)	☐ Yes	☐ No
30. Are we controlling the project by quadrants?	☐ Yes	☐ No
31. Are we marketing success stories of the project to staff? (via the intranet)	☐ Yes	☐ No
32. Are we ensuring that the in-house team do all the presenting? (keep consultants in the background unless they are figureheads whom the project needs to obtain credibility)	☐ Yes	☐ No

End of Assignment

33. Have we invited all parties to the celebration?		
▪ Consultants	☐ Yes	☐ No
▪ Project staff	☐ Yes	☐ No
▪ SMT	☐ Yes	☐ No
▪ Relevant in-house staff	☐ Yes	☐ No
34. Have we sent a thank-you note to the consultants?	☐ Yes	☐ No
35. Have we sent a copy of the post-project review to the consultants?	☐ Yes	☐ No

> On one major financial accounting consulting project, instead of quoting for the assignment I decided to seek being part of the selection panel. When I explained the risks to the organization that they faced, they were eager to proceed. I then had the opportunity to see all the competitors' proposals. One thing surprised me: One of the best proposals had a key person from another office in only a support position. I proposed to the client that they seek that person as a full-time member of the team. It appeared that the local office of the firm did not want to share the spoils with another office!

Notes

1. Steven Van Yoder, *Get Slightly Famous*, Bay Tree Publishing, 2007.
2. Harry Mills, *Negotiate: The Seven Step Master Plan*, The Mills Group, 1997.

CHAPTER 14

Part Three Progress Checklist

If you have only a few minutes to skim over this chapter, this is what you should focus on:

Lesson 2: Have a good hobby so in times of crisis you have a refuge

Lesson 4: Have a sanctuary where you can escape the maddening crowd

Lesson 5: The written word is mightier than the sword

Lesson 7: Learn to be a great orator

Lesson 9: Personal contact with key decision makers is vital

New methods and practices can be locked in if you perform the task each week for a 13-week period. The checklist in Exhibit 14.1 will help you lock in good managerial habits.

A Bulldog Who Never Gave Up: Churchill's Leadership Lessons

Winston Churchill is so iconic that his statute facing the Houses of Parliament simply says "Churchill." What is fascinating is that Churchill's success came after many calamities that would have floored a mere mortal. His lessons in leadership are quite profound and are different from those of many other leaders. I believe they are lessons we can apply to leadership in a business environment.

Lesson 1: Always Believe You Have a Legacy to Leave the Human Race

Andy Warhol famously said that everybody could be famous for 15 minutes. We all have a unique mix of attributes, skills, and experiences that can be put to use, leaving a lasting legacy. The trick is to find it. It is not always obvious.

EXHIBIT 14.1 Being a Better Manager Checklist

Action (P = planned, D = done)	Weeks												
	1	2	3	4	5	6	7	8	9	10	11	12	13
Organized training on "action meetings"													
Held action meeting in week													
Removed some morning meetings this week													
Held one-on-one progress meeting with direct reports													
Recorded reprimands and commendations in week													
Overnight team-building activity at outdoor pursuit center confirmed													
Team balanced scorecard introduced													
Held at least one team debrief at the end of the day													
Completed induction program for new staff													
Offsite training meeting organized for the team to occur within next six weeks													
Organized some team celebrations													
Action points from in-house team satisfaction survey													
Maximized training opportunities for staff													
Manage dissues relating to staff on sick leave													
Completed the 4:00 P.M. Friday planner													
Developed a motivation the mission statement													
Work organized so it is consistent with the team mission statement													

	Weeks		
Workload spread fairly between team members in week			
Advertised new positions internally to staff members			
Next in-house training session no more than three months in the future			
Sought feedback from in-house clients			
Some innovation has been embraced this week			
Have given recognition to staff in week			
All reports in week focused on the big picture			
Service culture was evident in week			
Had effective control over expenditure commitments in week			
Approved all orders and purchase invoices promptly in week			
All major purchases entered in the purchase order system			
Reviewed department's account in the general ledger in the week			
Administration procedures up to date			
Proposals sold to management through their emotional drivers			
Pre-sold proposal to thought leader before presentation			
Carried out some initiatives to promote myself in the organization			
Met supplier to increase transaction efficiency			
Maximized consultants' contribution			

Churchill failed during his time at Eaton in style. In fact you could say he refused to learn. It was only in the army, with time on his hands, that he discovered his love of reading. It was his need to finance his cavalry horses that led Churchill to earn some money as a war correspondent.

Churchill knew he had war in his blood. He was a descendent of the famous warrior, the First Duke of Marlborough, and was, by accident, born at Blenheim Palace, the palace gifted to the first Duke by a grateful nation. His parents were attending a dance at the palace, held by the current Duke, when his mother went into premature labor. Over a five-year period from 1895 to 1900, he sought action in India, the North West frontier, Sudan, South Africa, and Cuba. Every time it got a bit quiet, he wanted to get in the thick of it elsewhere. He achieved this in collusion with his mother and using all the contacts that the name of Churchill granted.

Churchill performed a rare feat in the early 20th century. He "crossed the floor" and joined the opposition in a move he calculated carefully. He realized that he would get nowhere in the Conservative Party, and they would definitely be losing the election. Churchill left the sinking ship. While this alienation from the Conservative Party caused many problems later on, he achieved his objective, a ministerial post in the new government, within 19 months of his crossing the floor.

If you were to make a one-paragraph statement as to what your legacy is to be, what would it say? Helping form this legacy in your mind gives meaning to life and helps put up a guiding star in the sky that will shine brightly no matter what dark clouds are over you.

Lesson 2: Have a Good Hobby So in Times of Crisis You Have a Refuge

Churchill had three major career crises: the calamity of the Dardanelles (World War I), the wilderness years of 1930–1939 when he was consigned to the backbenches of the opposition, and the disastrous defeat at the polls just months after Victory Day in 1945.

Lesser mortals would have consigned themselves to depression. Churchill turned to his love of writing and painting and the landscaping of his beloved Chartwell property. These hobbies kept him afloat and enabled him to build up his resolve to fight again.

Have you a passion that absorbs your time that can be a "safe house" when times are tough? If not, you need to establish one as soon as possible.

Lesson 3: When You Foul Up, It Is Better to Fall on Your Sword, as You Will Surely Rise Again Soon

Churchill was blamed for the botched Gallipoli expedition. As First Lord of the Admiralty, he was dismissed and he resigned from Parliament to enlist back in the army. He became a must-visit curiosity in the trenches of Flanders.

It was, however, only six months later that he was recalled to take up a role in Parliament.

By falling on his sword early on, Churchill did not waste his energy on a hopeless cause. He thereby gave less ammunition to his enemies in the Houses of Parliament.

When you have made a mistake, know that it will not define you or your contribution. Know that you will recover to fight another day. With this assurance, take the blame and move on.

Lesson 4: Have a Sanctuary Where You Can Escape the Maddening Crowd

When Churchill first saw Chartwell he immediately realized its potential. I can assure you that if you were to visit Chartwell you would want to swap houses immediately. The setting, the ambience, and the design all make for an almost-perfect sanctuary.

Churchill once said, "Every day away from Chartwell is a day wasted." It was in this creative environment that he would dictate his books starting in the afternoons and working long into the night.

His wife was given free range to modernize, decorate, and extend Chartwell to fit the needs of the family. Churchill understood the importance of having a supportive partner, giving her the freedom to pursue her own goals. Lady Churchill was honored by Britain and Russia, the latter for her efforts as Chairwoman of the Red Cross Aid to Russia.

Having a grand house does not in itself create a sanctuary. The difference is subtle. Do you feel that a day away from your house is a day wasted? If not, maybe your sanctuary is yet to be created.

Lesson 5: The Written Word Is Mightier Than the Sword

Churchill's first stint of fame came as a war correspondent. He wrote in a style that was user friendly and a blend of fact, autobiography, and descriptive text. He was blunt, to the point, and did not hold back from saying what others feared to say. He would be critical of his superiors' handling of the army, their organization, tactics—nothing was sacred. He went where angels feared to tread and his dispatches became the must-read in high society back in London.

Time and time again he came back to writing and was awarded the Nobel Prize for Literature in 1953. While it could be said he was not the most knowledgeable historian, he wrote in a style that made history interesting. It was his writing *History of the English Speaking Peoples* that at last made him financially secure. He was so destitute after losing the premiership that a fund was established and Chartwell was purchased from the Churchills and then leased back to them for the rest of their lives.

Far too many leaders today do not pay enough attention to the power of the written word in helping build one's profile. This important point did not escape President Obama, who wrote his memoirs, *Dreams From My Father*, four years before he ran for president.

Maybe it is about time you started to make your views, thoughts, and experiences more public.

Lesson 6: Never Let the Lack of a Degree or a Sound Education Hold You Back

Churchill was a total failure at school. He never went to college. He hated the establishment. He was whipped but never succumbed to the mindless mediocrity of learning for the sake of learning.

He won his "tertiary spurs" later on in life when university after university gave him honorary degrees. He had in fact put himself through his own university. He studied and became an expert in many areas such as navy, army, aviation, and history.

While tertiary education is a valuable asset, never let the lack of it hold you back. If you succeed in life you will end up getting an honorary doctorate in any case.

Lesson 7: Learn to Be a Great Orator

Churchill is remembered most for his great speeches. These were very carefully constructed in his great study at Chartwell. He would rehearse the words until he was sure they flowed—that they sent a clear message to "the common man." He used words that a 14-year-old would understand.

His delivery was legendary: slow, deliberate, and repetitive. He was an actor delivering a performance to his audience—the people of Britain, the Commonwealth, and importantly, the United States.

Leaders need to realize that being a good orator is a vital part of leadership. Time and effort need to be devoted to delivering a meaningful message. Special coaching and endless practice should be seen as an important investment rather than a chore.

Lesson 8: Manage Public Relations

Churchill understood the power of public relations. He never missed an opportunity to present his ideas in the best light. The pictures of him with his "V-for-victory" sign, or holding a Tommy gun in his business suit while standing over rubble, are iconic.

His wartime speeches, so carefully prepared, were avidly listened to by all who could get to a radio.

While the press had often written ruinous headings about Churchill during his fall from grace, he realized their importance and worked closely with them to promote the image of the bulldog who would never surrender. His use of radio and the newspapers is unparalleled among modern-day leaders. Given the media options that now exist, one could only speculate as to the dramatic use Churchill would apply today's technology and show up many of current international politician's as rank amateurs.

Start befriending the press, issue them useful copy, be available for comment, and do not be afraid to speak out on issues you feel passionate about. Find yourself a leader who manages public relations professionals well and uses their experience.

Lesson 9: Personal Contact with Key Decision Makers Is Vital

When you walk through Chartwell, Blenheim Palace, or Churchill's warrooms in Westminster, you are struck by the amount of personal letters he wrote. These were not correspondence dictated to his secretaries but handwritten letters and notes. Churchill knew who the important decision makers were and maintained regular contact. In fact, he devoted as much time to writing to President Roosevelt as drafting major speeches to Parliament. Churchill's correspondence bypassed the cabinet and helped forge the alliance with the United States.

With whom are you in regular contact? Make the time this week to dust off some of your contacts with decision makers.

Lesson 10: See and Own the Future

Like all great leaders, Churchill spent a lot of time thinking about what the future had in store. He was the first to see the rise of Hitler as a major menace. He understood the importance of a united Europe to prevent further wars. After World War II, Churchill supported a practical rebuilding of Germany in order to avoid the kind of harsh retribution that had been levied against Germany following World War I.

Last, but not least, he saw the need to end the Cold War because the atomic bomb made any form of warfare impossible between the superpowers.

The key was that Churchill created an environment where he could think deeply, uninterrupted by what was going to happen next. He tried as much as possible to own the future.

Have you planned your workweek to allow for some "blue-ocean" time? How about a Friday morning when you stay at your home office until lunchtime, where you spend time making all those strategic calls, finishing off the strategic reports, and thinking about the future. Once you start doing this you will find it addictive.

Lesson 11: Keep up with Technology Advancements

Churchill had an unfailing regard for scientists and engineers, he stayed close to them so he was aware of all relevant new technologies. He gave them free license to create new methods of warfare. They came up with many inventions, including the floating Mulberry harbors (key to the Normandy offensive), the bouncing bomb, and modifications to the spitfire Merlin engine that enabled the planes to keep up with Germany's V1 flying bombs.

He was conversant with technology, he understood it, and he was able to communicate effectively with the scientists and move them to greater heights.

How close are you to the creative techs in your organization? How about taking one or two of them out for a great coffee?

Lesson 12: Understand Your Body Rhythms and Work Patterns

Churchill worked late and rose late. He was not a morning person. He knew what made him efficient and kept to that regime, never allowing events to disorganize him. Even during the war, he was woken only if the matter was urgent.

While working to 2:00 A.M. and rising for breakfast at 11:00 A.M may not be your style, it is important to develop a routine and keep to it, fighting off the need to conform to the organizational requirements wherever you can.

Churchill does not rate as high as a serving leader, as Sir Ernest Shackleton, the Antarctic Explorer clearly did, see chapter 32. He was reckless with his life and with those he was in charge of. Yet through the many leadership traits he did have he left a legacy that will be remembered for all time. While we might not be able to leave such a legacy, we can and should leave a legacy that says we were here, we added up to something, we had something to say, and we changed people's lives for the better. Winston Churchill shows us a way forward if we choose to learn.

Being a Leader Who Makes a Difference

CHAPTER 15

Learning Must Never Stop

If you have only a few minutes to skim over this chapter, this is what you should focus on:

- The thinking of Jeremy Hope
- The thinking of Harry Mills

A Constant Thirst for Knowledge

Far too often CEOs exhibit an air of "I do not need to know this information—talk to Pat." In other words, it is very common today for U.S. CEOs to stop learning, which is the opposite of their counterparts in South East Asia. As a CEO, when did you last:

- Talk with your mentor? (If you do not have one, you need to see Part One of this book.)
- Undertake some personal development work, attempt to understand your thinking preferences, review your Enneagram profile, and so on? (See Part One of this book.)
- Read about the movement to replace the archaic annual planning process? (As a CEO, it is your role to think through old and outdated processes.)
- Study the new thinking on key performance indicators (KPIs)?
- Attend a residential strategic management course designed for CEOs?

Delivering workshops in a number of countries I have noticed the same thing occurring all the time. Seeing the senior management at these sessions is very rare. Yet I once delivered a presentation to 450 CEOs, all of whom had signed up for one day of mentoring every month. That is what

I call a commitment to learning. All of these CEOs were part of the Malaysian TEC, a group of CEOs who are mentored by wiser ex-CEOs. So it can be done. It is just a matter of a state of mind—a *commitment* to continuous learning.

There are many admirable writers of business books. I would like to point out two whom I have met and who I believe have something profound to say.

The Thinking of Jeremy Hope

One of the greatest management thinkers of this decade is Jeremy Hope[1] of *Beyond Budgeting* fame. He will in his lifetime see the dismantling of the annual planning cycle all over the Western world—a massive legacy saving organizations millions of dollars of wasted effort.

Hope also writes on many subjects challenging the status quo, and it is appropriate for all managers to keep up to date on his thinking.

- Beware of the promises of new systems such as customer relationship management (CRM) and activity-based management (ABM).
- Never tie a remuneration scheme to a fixed annual performance target. It will never be right; it will be too soft or too hard.
- Understand the damage created by centralized command-and-control—large, head-office command-and-control departments should be challenged.
- Replace the annual plan with a more adaptive dynamic process—quarterly rolling planning—which is outlined in a later section.

The Thinking of Harry Mills

I first met Harry Mills when I attended a course on negotiation. The story he told me about the negotiation process of a trapper and a trader has remained with me ever since. He explains the process of a win/win negotiation.

"Consider the problems an Eskimo trapper faces when he emerges from the Arctic darkness to trade his fox furs at the one and only trading post for hundreds of miles around. If ever a buyer enjoys a monopoly, it has to be the Arctic fur buyer. Yet the Eskimo knows just how to limit the power of the trader." Harry Mills[2]

In fact, Mills was the first person to make clear to me the benefit of teaching lessons through storytelling. All the great teachers through time have done it.

Mills has written a number of books. He has developed some extremely useful tools in negotiation and selling services. He has pointed out that:

- In some service organizations, 20% of the customers are generating 120% of the net profit. In other words, you are paying to service 80% of the customers. Many of these customers are the ones who complain, pay late, reject perfectly good services, ask for uneconomical quantities, and so on. This rule has a profound impact on the way one can look at such businesses. It will impact many procedures and KPIs at the workplace as we should be performing special procedures, and monitoring these 24/7 for these special customers, and removing costly procedures for those customers where these are not so important. Why should we monitor customer satisfaction on the 80%? Logic would say we should monitor satisfaction frequently with our key customers, as no doubt many readers' organizations are doing.
- Never go into an negotiation without a *BATNA* (the "best alternative to a negotiated agreement"). In other words, when going into a negotiation process always be sure you have carefully worked out the best fallback position.
- Mills has developed a brilliant concept for orientating the business around its customers in his book, *The Rainmaker's Toolkit.*[3] He breaks customers into four groups remembered by the mnemonic DROP:
  - **D**iamonds are the top 1% of customers.
  - **R**ubies are the next 4% of customers.
  - **O**pals are the next 15% of customers.
  - **P**earls are the balancing 80% of customers.

This process helps the sales, production, and dispatch staff get their priorities correct. Otherwise, an uneconomical order from a "pearl" can very easily hold up the delivery and adversely affect the quality of a large order going to a "diamond" customer. The airlines have been using this *tiered* approach to servicing their customers for years. Why aren't we?

Notes

1. Jeremy Hope and Robin Fraser, *Beyond Budgeting: How Managers Can Break Free from the Annual Performance Trap*, Harvard Business School Press, 2003.
2. Harry Mills website and blog http://blog.millsonline.com/2008/05/15/power-is-often-a-state-of-mind-a-tale-from-the-arctic-wilderness/
3. Harry Mills, *The Rainmaker's Toolkit*, AMACOM, 2004.

CHAPTER 16

Key Performance Indicators Can Transform Your Organization

If you have only a few minutes to skim over this chapter, this is what you should focus on:

- KPI story—late planes
- Characteristics of a KPI
- Journey from a mission and vision to performance measures that work (Exhibit 16.2)
- Winning KPIs are the only thing that directly link day-to-day activities with strategy

In this chapter I have extracted some of the key points CFOs need to learn about performance measures from my book "Key Performance Indicators"[1]. At some point it would be worth reading the other issues that I have had to omit due to space constraints.

The Great KPI Misunderstanding

Many companies are working with the wrong measures, many of which are incorrectly termed *key performance indicators (KPIs)*. From my research, very few organizations really monitor their true KPIs. The reason is very few organizations, business leaders, writers, accountants, or consultants have explored what actually is a KPI. From the extensive research I have performed and as a by-product of the years I spent writing a book on implementing winning KPIs,[2] I have come to the conclusion that there are four types of performance measures:

1. The key result indicator shows how you have done in a critical success factor or balanced scorecard perspective.

2. Result indicators are summary measures that tell you what teams have achieved together.

3. Performance indicators tell you what an individual team has done.

4. KPIs tell you *what to do* to increase performance dramatically.

Many performance measures used by organizations are an inappropriate mix of these four types.

I use the onion analogy to describe the relationship of these three measures as shown in Exhibit 16.1. The outside skin describes the overall condition of the onion: how much sun, water, and nutrients it has received, and how it has been handled from harvest to supermarket shelf. However, as we peel the layers off the onion, we find out more information. The layers represent the various performance indicators, and the core represents the key performance indicators.

The 10/80/10 Rule

Kaplan and Norton[3] recommend no more than 20 KPIs, and Jeremy Hope[4] of *Beyond Budgeting* fame suggests fewer than ten. To aid those involved in performance measurement, I have developed the *10/80/10 rule*. This means an organization should have about ten *key result indicators (KRIs)*, up to 80 *performance indicators (PIs)* and *result indicators (RIs)*, and ten KPIs. Very seldom does there need to be more measures than these numbers, and in many cases less can be used.

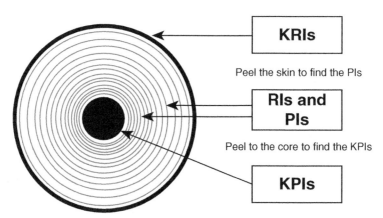

EXHIBIT 16.1 Four Types of Performance Measures
Source: David Parmenter, *Key Performance Indicators: Developing,
Implementing, and Using Winning KPIs, 2nd Edition.* Copyright © 2010 by
David Parmenter. Reprinted with the permission of John Wiley & Sons, Inc.

So what are key result indicators (KRIs)? KRIs are measures that have often been mistaken for KPIs, including:

- Customer satisfaction
- Net profit before tax
- Profitability of customers
- Employee satisfaction
- Return on capital employed

The common characteristic of these measures is that they are the result of many actions. They give a clear picture of whether you are traveling in the right direction. They do not, however, tell you what you need to do to *improve* these results. Thus KRIs provide information that is ideal for the board (i.e., those not involved in day-to-day management).

A car's speedometer provides a useful analogy. The board will simply want to know the speed the car is traveling. However, management needs to know more information since the traveling speed is a combination of what gear the car is in and what revs the engine is doing. Management might even be concentrating on completely different measures, such as how economically the car is performing (miles per gallon) or how hot the engine is running. These two completely different gauges are performance indicators or may even be KPIs.

KRIs cover a longer period of time than KPIs. They are reviewed on monthly/quarterly cycles and not on a daily/weekly basis. These measures also link back to the strategies and are called by some *strategic KPIs*. This title is misleading. I believe there should be only one type of KPI, as defined in the following.

Separating KRIs has a profound impact on reporting, resulting in a separation of performance measures into those impacting governance and those impacting management. In other words, an organization should have a governance report (ideally in a dashboard format) composed of up to ten measures providing high-level KRIs for the board, and a *balanced scorecard (BSC)* comprising up to 20 measures (a mix of performance indicators and result indicators) for management. It is important to note now that KPIs will be reported separately to management via the intranet, see Chapter 17.

The more numerous performance and result indicators are shown in a cascading suite of the organization, division, department, and team scorecards.

Result indicators that lie beneath KRIs could include:

- Sales made in a day
- Profitability of the top 10% of customers

■ Net profit on key product lines

Performance indicators that lie beneath KRIs could include:

■ Late deliveries (a KPI would be more focussed—late deliveries to key customers)
■ Percentage increase in sales with top 10% of customers
■ Number of employees participating in the suggestion scheme

Key performance indicators represent a set of measures focusing on those aspects of organizational performance that are the most critical for the current and future success of the organization. They have certain characteristics.

My favorite key performance indicator (KPI) story is about Lord King, who set about turning British Airways (BA) around in the 1980s by reportedly concentrating on one KPI. He was notified, wherever he was in the world, if a BA plane was delayed. The senior BA official at the relevant airport knew that if a plane was delayed beyond a certain threshold, they would receive a personal call from the chairman. It was not long before BA planes had a reputation for leaving on time. This KPI affected all six of the balanced scorecard perspectives.

The late-planes KPI also linked to many critical success factors for the airline. It linked to the "delivery in full and on time" critical success factor—namely the *timely arrival and departure of airplanes*. The importance of this critical success factor can be seen by its impact on all six perspectives of a modified balanced scorecard.

These late planes:

■ Increased cost in many ways, including additional airport sur- charges, and the cost of accommodating passengers overnight as a result of late planes being curfewed due to noise restrictions late at night.
■ Increased customer dissatisfaction, and alienation also of those people meeting passengers at their destination (possible future customers).
■ Contributed more to ozone depletion (environmental impact) as additional fuel was used as a result of the pilot using full boost to make up time.
■ Had a negative impact on staff, particularly in their development, as staff would replicate the bad habits that had created the late-

planes problem. They also adversely affected supplier relationships and servicing schedules, resulting in poor service quality.

■ Increased employee dissatisfaction because they had to deal both with frustrated customers and the extra stress each late plane created.

The CEO of a distribution company realized that a critical success factor for the business was trucks departing filled as close to capacity as possible. Large train trucks capable of carrying more than 40 tons were being sent out with small loads as dispatch managers were focusing on "delivery in full and on time" to customers.

Each day by 9:00 A.M., the CEO received a report of those trailers that had been sent out underweight. The CEO called the dispatch manager and asked whether any action had taken place to see if the customer could have accepted the delivery on a different date and thus enable better utilization of the trucks. In most cases the customer could have received it earlier or later, fitting in with the schedule of a past or future truck going in that direction. The impact on profitability was significant. Just as with the airline example, staff did their utmost to avoid a career-limiting phone call from their CEO.

Characteristics of a KPI

From a number of years of study I have come up with the following characteristics of a KPI:

■ Nonfinancial measures (not expressed in dollars, yen, pounds, euros, etc.).
■ Measured frequently (e.g., daily, or 24/7 and sometimes weekly).
■ Acted upon by CEO and senior management team.
■ All staff understand the measure and what corrective action is required.
■ Responsibility can be tied down to a team.
■ Significant impact (e.g., impacts most of the critical success factors and more than one balanced scorecard perspective).
■ Has a positive impact (e.g., affects all other performance measures in a positive way).

When you put a dollar sign on a measure, you have already converted it into a *result* indicator (e.g., daily sales is a result of activities that have taken place to create the sales). The KPI lies deeper down. It may be the number of visits to/contacts with the key customers who make up most of the profitable business.

KPIs should be monitored 24/7, daily, and a few maybe weekly. A monthly, quarterly, or annual measure cannot be a KPI as it cannot be *key* to your business if you are monitoring it well after the horse has bolted. KPIs are therefore *current* or *future*-orientated measures as opposed to past measures (e.g., number of key customer visits planned for next month, or a list by key customers of the dates of next planned visits). When you look at most organizational measures, they are very much *past* indicators measuring events of the past month or quarter. These indicators cannot be, and never were, KPIs.

All good KPIs that I have come across, that have made a difference, had the CEO's constant attention, with daily calls to the relevant staff. Having a career-limiting discussion with the CEO is not something staff members want to repeat, and in the airline's case, innovative and productive processes were put in place to prevent a reoccurrence.

A KPI should tell you about what action needs to take place. The British Airways late-plane KPI communicated immediately to everybody that there needed to be a focus on recovering the lost time. Cleaners, caterers, ground crew, flight attendants, and liaison officers with traffic controllers would all need to work some magic to save a minute here, a minute there, while maintaining or improving service standards.

A KPI is deep enough in the organization that it can be tied down to an individual. In other words, the CEO can ring someone and ask "Why?" Return on capital employed has never been a KPI as it cannot be tied down to a manager; it is the result of many activities under different managers.

A good KPI will affect more than one core critical success factors and more than one balanced scorecard perspective. In other words, when the CEO, management, and staff focus on the KPI, the organization scores goals in all directions.

A good KPI has a flow-on effect. An improvement in a key measure within the critical success factor (CSF) of customer satisfaction would have a positive impact on many other measures. Timely arrival and departure of planes give rise to improved service by ground staff because there is less fire fighting to distract them from a quality and caring customer contact.

KPIs could include:

- Late projects, reported each week to the senior management team (SMT)
- Planes in flight that are two or more hours late

- Trucks sent on a delivery run less than 75% full
- Deliveries not made in full or on time to *key customers*

Importance of Identifying the Critical Success Factors

Many performance measurement initiatives fail because management has not worked out which are the organization's top five to eight CSFs. How to find these is discussed in Chapter 19. The relationship between CSFs (also referred to as *key result areas*) and KPIs is critical, as illustrated in Exhibit 16.2. Once you have found the CSFs, it is very easy to locate the KPIs! In the airline case, once the consultants had determined on "timely arrival and departure of airplanes," it was easy to the find the winning KPI: late planes over, say, two hours late.

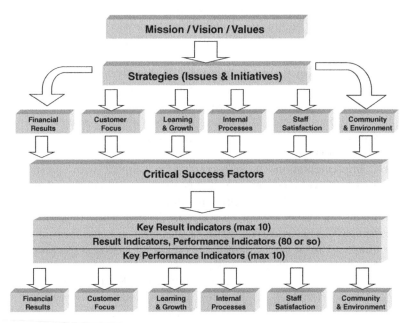

EXHIBIT 16.2 Journey from a Mission and Vision to Performance Measures that Work

Source: David Parmenter, *Key Performance Indicators: Developing, Implementing, and Using Winning KPIs, 2nd Edition.* Copyright © 2010 by David Parmenter. Reprinted with the permission of John Wiley & Sons, Inc.

The Balanced Scorecard

The balanced scorecard was first developed in Japan, as Hoshin Kanri, it was brought to the western world Kaplan and Norton[5] who saw it as a way to ensure strategy was both balanced and implemented.

The focus by many organizations on the financials had left the key areas of the business at risk. For example, you can increase profitability in the short term by cutting back on training, client servicing, and internal control processes. The long-term impact is immense.

Many balanced scorecard implementations have failed. After years of looking into this area I have made the following observations:

- The primary role of performance measures is to help the work force focus on the **critical success factors** of the business, day-in day-out. Whereas Kaplan and Norton see the primary purpose of performance measures is to translate and help execute strategy.
- You need to know your organisations critical success factors as these are the key to finding the KPIs. Whereas most organizations, implementing BSC projects, develop measures without knowing their critical success factors.
- KPIs are all non financial, measured frequently and have five other characteristics and are thus rare, with less than ten in a business. Measures that are not KPIs are either result indicators, key result indicators, or performance indicators. Most BSCs are littered with meaningless measures, which are "key" to the business, yet they are all called Key performance indicators.
- BSC implementations have become too complex with questionable processes developed by consultants to ensure a continued growing revenue stream. The strategic mapping process is flawed because strategic objectives and success factors do not neatly fit into the BSC perspective. The cascading down of measures in some form of matrix, common to most applications, can only lead to chaos. Measure must spring from the critical success factors.
- The four BSC perspectives, reflect the Hosni Kanri perspectives and need two additional perspectives. Environment and community and employee satisfaction, as illustrated in Exhibit 16.2.
- The BSC perspectives are incorrectly used in most implementations. The perspectives are a guiding force ensuring you have balance to your strategy and strategic initiates'. The minute you try to make everything fit into the perspectives things fall apart. The "timely arrival and departure of planes" and the "planes two hours late in the sky" KPI impacts, I argue all six perspectives.

■ The process of finding the right performance measures needs careful consideration and training, yet in most BSC implementations, little or no thought goes into this area. Managers are asked to fill out their boxes in the application, and as Russell Crow would say "lets give them Hell."

Winning KPIs Link Day-to-Day Activities to Strategy

Over the past few hundred years management has had the belief that if they are on target for the month, they are on target with their strategy. The logic goes something like this: The monthly budget is part of the annual plan, and the annual plan is the first year of the five-year medium-term plan, which in turn is linked to the long-term strategy. In reality, as we all know, the *strategy* is an *all-encompassing view*, drawn appropriately as a horizontal bar in Exhibit 16.2, covering the six perspectives of the balanced scorecard, whereas the *annual plan* (as Exhibit 16.3 shows) is a *series of silos*. How much does the operations department need for the year? How much does the finance team need for the year? The annual plan is then divided into 12—one of the greatest mistakes ever made by management. Thus, creating a monthly target has no linkage at all to the organization's strategy.

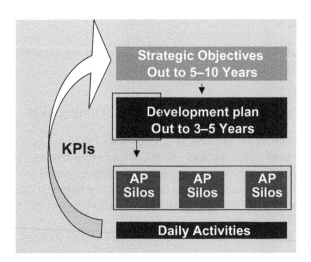

EXHIBIT 16.3 Linking Daily Activities to Strategy
Source: David Parmenter, *Key Performance Indicators: Developing, Implementing, and Using Winning KPIs, 2nd Edition.* Copyright © 2010 by David Parmenter. Reprinted with the permission of John Wiley & Sons, Inc.

KPIs, if monitored and managed 24/7 or daily, link daily activities to the strategic objectives. In the late-planes case, staff were focused on getting planes to arrive and depart on time. In the freight case, staff were focused on maximizing the freight a truck was carrying.

Winning KPIs are in fact the missing link. They are the tool to link daily activity at the workplace to the organization's strategy.

Implementing Winning KPIs

To assist you with implementation of winning KPIs, you can access for free the "Winning KPIs" webcasts on www.Davidparmenter.Com/Webcasts. The webcasts listed below are the most important ones, at the time this book was going to print.

- Introduction to winning KPIs (Aug 09)
- Implementing KPIs: a 12-step process
- Implementing KPIs in smaller orgs (<200 staff)
- Finding your organization's critical success factors
- Balanced scorecard in 16 weeks, not 16 months
- Getting started or restarted with winning KPIs
- Revitalizing a floundering balanced scorecard with winning KPIs
- Winning KPIs: two question-and-answer sessions
- Sorting the wheat from the chaff: finding your wining KPIs
- Reporting KPIs to improve performance

I have provided a checklist to help get your implementation started, see Exhibit 16.4.

Use the Emotional Drivers When Selling Winning KPIs

As already mentioned, nothing was ever sold by logic! You sell through *emotional drivers*. This project needs a public relations (PR) machine behind it. No presentation, email, memo, or paper should go out unless it has been vetted by your PR expert. All your presentations should be road-tested in front of the PR expert. Your PR strategy should include selling to staff, budget holders, SMT, and the board.

These are some of the emotional drivers that will help sell the KPI process in your organization. In the current situation you may have:

- A lack of linkage of daily activities to strategy
- Endless performance management meetings that are not improving the performance, yet are adversely affecting job satisfaction

EXHIBIT 16.4 Checklist for Starting Your Implemention of Winning KPIs

1. Have you obtained adequate SMT commitment to the scorecard?	☐ Yes	☐ No
2. Is the CEO committed to daily follow-up of the winning KPIs?	☐ Yes	☐ No
3. Have you focused enough on the critical success factors?	☐ Yes	☐ No
4. Do you separate governance and management reporting?	☐ Yes	☐ No
5. Are the KPI project staff committed full time, and does your service team have a liaison person?	☐ Yes	☐ No
6. Has the SMT and balanced scorecard project team ensured that the balanced scorecard project culture is a "just do it" culture?	☐ Yes	☐ No
7. For the first 12 months, are you avoiding the purchase of a balanced scorecard application?	☐ Yes	☐ No
8. Have you adequately tested your KPIs against the seven characteristics of KPIs?	☐ Yes	☐ No
9. Is the project team entrusted with designing the final balanced scorecard templates?	☐ Yes	☐ No
10. Have you reviewed www.davidparmenter.com/webcasts for the free webcasts?	☐ Yes	☐ No
11. Have you accessed *Key Performance Indicators— developing, implementing, and using winning KPIs*, 2nd Edition by David Parmenter (John Wiley & Sons 2010) to assess whether it will be useful?	☐ Yes	☐ No

- Many lost weekends away from your family producing performance reports that are meaningless
- A lack of linkage between the CEO and key staff in the organization
- A lack of focus in key processes and procedures as the critical success factors have not been identified and communicated to staff
- Staff not sharing the same vision as the management team due to a lack of clarity in communications

The project team needs to focus on the marketing of a new concept as much as it does on the training. Budget holders will need to understand how this process is going to help them manage their business. Providing success stories throughout the implementation is therefore a must.

If Your KPIs Are Not Working, Throw Them Out and Start Again

If the KPIs you currently have are not creating change, throw them out. There is a good chance that they are wrong. They are probably measures that were thrown together without the in-depth research and investigation KPIs truly deserve. KPIs that have not been based on the CSFs of the organization will serve very little purpose other than measuring for the sake of measuring.

Importance of Daily CEO Follow-Up

The CEO follows up every single shortfall with a personal phone call. After their first phone call from the CEO about nonperformance, branch managers, store supervisors, or the sales reps will move heaven and earth to avoid another career-limiting phone call from the CEO. Performance will change quickly! Behavioral scientists would say the change will come within a 12-week period.

These career-limiting phone calls should be balanced with publicly congratulating high-performance teams. Otherwise, KPIs will be seen as a negative tool. As one flight attendant said to me, "Our bosses monitor performance in real time. We are contacted immediately when there is a problem, but we never hear from them when we deliver timely planes day-in and day-out."

Notes

1. David Parmenter, *Key Performance Indicators: Developing, Implementing, and Using Winning KPIs*, 2nd Edition John Wiley & Sons, 2010.
2. David Parmenter, op. cit.
3. Robert S. Kaplan and David P. Norton, *Translating Strategy into Action: The Balanced Scorecard*, Harvard Business School Press, 1996.
4. Jeremy Hope and Robin Fraser, *Beyond Budgeting: How Managers Can Break Free from the Annual Performance Trap*, Harvard Business School Press, 2003.
5. Kaplan and Norton, op. cit.

CHAPTER 17

Reporting Performance Measures in a Balanced Way

If you have only a few minutes to skim over this chapter, this is what you should focus on:

Information systems team scorecard designed in Excel (Exhibit 17.4)

Progress report for staff (Exhibit 17.5)

The frequency of reporting of performance measures depends on what type they are: KPI, PI, RI, or KRI (see Chapter 16). Your understanding of this concept is important.

Reporting Measures Daily, Weekly, Monthly

Reporting KPIs 24/7 or Daily to Management[1]

Reporting KPIs to management needs to be timely. As mentioned, KPIs need to be reported 24/7, daily, or at least weekly. Other performance measures can be reported less frequently, say monthly and quarterly.

The main KPIs are reported 24/7 or daily via the intranet. Exhibit 17.1 shows how they should be reported, giving the senior management team (SMT) contact details, the problem, and some history so a meaningful phone call can be made.

Another benefit of providing senior management with daily/weekly information on the critical success factors (CSFs) is that the month-end becomes less important. In other words, if organizations report their KPIs on a 24/7 or daily basis, management know intuitively whether the organization is having a good or bad month.

EXHIBIT 17.1 Intranet-Based KPI Exception Report

Time:

Late planes over 2 hours

	Statistics of last stop					Contact details			No. of late planes over 1 hour		
Flight Number	Arrial late by	Departure late by	Time added	Region manager's name	Current time at location	Work	Mobile	Home	Last 30 days	30-day ave. of last 3 months	30-day ave. of last 6 months
BA1243	1:40	2:33	0:53	Pat Carruthers	18:45	xxxxx	xxxxx	xxxx	4	3	4
BA1598	1:45	2:30	0:45	xxxxxxx	19:45	xxxxx	xxxxx	xxxx	2	3	4
BA12	1:45	2:27	0:42	xxxxxxx	20:45	xxxxx	xxxxx	xxxx	4	4	5
BA146	1:45	2:24	0:39	xxxxxxx	21:45	xxxxx	xxxxx	xxxx	5	4	4
BA177	1:45	2:21	0:36	xxxxxxx	22:45	xxxxx	xxxxx	xxxx	2	4	3
BA256	1:45	2:18	0:33	xxxxxxx	23:45	xxxxx	xxxxx	xxxx	5	4	5
BA1249	1:45	2:15	0:30	xxxxxxx	0:45	xxxxx	xxxxx	xxxx	2	4	3
Total	7 planes										

Source: David Parmenter, *Key Performance Indicators: Developing, Implementing, and Using Winning KPIs, 2nd Edition.* Copyright © 2010 by David Parmenter. Reprinted with the permission of John Wiley & Sons, Inc.

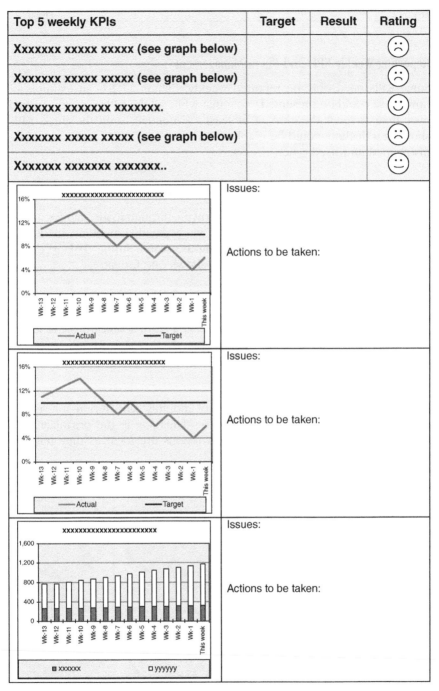

Top 5 weekly KPIs	Target	Result	Rating
Xxxxxxx xxxxx xxxxx (see graph below)			☹
Xxxxxxx xxxxx xxxxx (see graph below)			☹
Xxxxxxx xxxxxxx xxxxxxx.			☺
Xxxxxxx xxxxx xxxxx (see graph below)			☹
Xxxxxxx xxxxxxx xxxxxxx..			☺

EXHIBIT 17.2 Top-Five KPIs Weekly Report: xxxx xx, 20xx

Source: David Parmenter, *Key Performance Indicators: Developing, Implementing, and Using Winning KPIs, 2nd Edition.* Copyright © 2010 by David Parmenter. Reprinted with the permission of John Wiley & Sons, Inc.

Reporting Weekly KPIs and PIs to Management

Some KPIs need only be reported weekly. Exhibit 17.2 is an example of how these could be presented. Note that while all the KPIs will be graphed over time (over a duration of at least 15 months), only the three KPIs showing a decline would be graphed. The other two KPI graphs would be maintained and used when necessary.

Reporting Weekly and Monthly RIs and PIs to Management

There are endless ways these can be shown—through icons, gauges, traffic lights, and so on. It is best to visit the www.davidparmenter.com site for good examples or search the Web using the search string: "balanced scor ecard+formats+templates". Exhibit 17.3 shows one format.

Reporting Monthly Progress to Teams

Exhibit 9.4, Chapter 9 is an example of a team scorecard using Excel. Use Excel until a more robust and integrated solution is found.

Reporting Monthly Progress to Staff

It is a good idea to have some form of monthly icon report for staff, a report that if left on a bus would not be damaging to the organization if it found its way to a competitor. Icon reports are ideal as they tell you

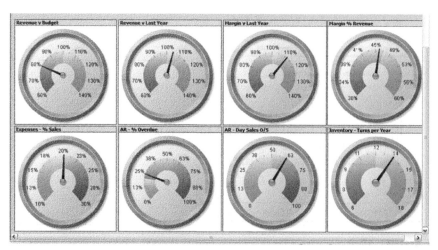

EXHIBIT 17.3 Scorecard from Qlikview
Source: Inside Info see www.insideinfo.com.au

Progress Report to Staff - For our Operations Throughout September 20XX

Our mission	**To provide energy at the right price at the right time**
Our vision for next five years	**To be the preferred energy provider in the xxx**
Our Strategies (what we are doing to achieve our vision)	**1. Acquiring profitable customers** **2. Increase cost efficiencies** **3. Innovation through our people** **4. Using best business practices**

Amber (acceptable)
Red (poor)
Green (good)

What we have to do well every day - our Critical Success Factors (CSFs)	Our performance measures in the CSFs		Actual	Target
Delivery in full on time to key customers (KC)	On time deliveries to key customers (KC)		98%	99%
	Goods rejected by KC due to quality defects		3%	4%
We are warriors against waste	Wastage reduction programs started in month		0	2
	Waste reduced from existing programs		9%	10%
We finish what we start	Number of late projects		5	15
	Number of project finishes in month by due date		9	10
We are a learning organisation	Staff training hours this month		150	220
	Staff with mentors		35	80
We grow leaders	Leaders appointed from within last month		4	2
	Managers in leadership programs		8	10
Attracting new profitable customers	Orders from new customers		3	10
	Positive feedback from new customers		3	2
Innovation is a daily activity	Ideas adopted last month		9	20
	Ideas for implementation within 3 months		20	50
We are respected in the communities we work in	Community participation by employees in month		30	20
	New initiatives planned for community, next 3 months		3	2
Increase in repeat business from key customers (KC)	Order book from key customers		$320,000	$400,000
	Number of product developments in progress		3	2

EXHIBIT 17.4 Progress Report for Staff

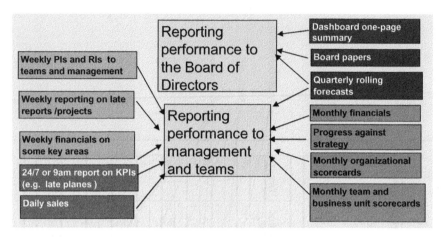

EXHIBIT 17.5 Performance Management Framework

what is good, what is adequate, and what needs to be improved without disclosing sensitive data. Exhibit 17.4 is a particularly good example as it shows icons and reminds staff about the strategies.

How KPIs and Financial Reporting Fit Together

Exhibit 17.5 shows how the components of performance management fit together. The reporting framework has to accommodate the requirements of different levels in the organization and the reporting frequency that supports timely decision making.

Note

1. Adapted from David Parmenter, *Key Performance Indicators: Developing, Implementing, and Using Winning KPIs,* John Wiley & Sons, 2007.

CHAPTER 18

Making a Difference in the Senior Management Team

If you have only a few minutes to skim over this chapter, this is what you should focus on:

- Map of a thriving intranet portal (Exhibit 18.1)
- Walkabout
- Work is meant to be enjoyed

Your Involvement with the Organization's Intranet

Many organizations are failing to make the big leap forward in their use of the intranet because the senior management team (SMT) has failed to recognize its significance to the company's universe. One child, I understand, described a home page as the center of a solar system with information revolving around it. That kid will go far. That is exactly what it is for your organization, even though you may not have a very big solar system yet.

Nature teaches us many lessons. It is a shame we are so slow to learn. An organization, to excel, needs to model its intranet on the garden spider's web. The SMT can learn much from the garden spider. Let me explain.

The spider knows that the web must let the wind through, yet catch all passing insects. Your intranet must trap all meaningful data, yet let the flotsam pass through.

When building its web, the spider connects to all available support structures. Your intranet needs to capture all aspects of your organization in order to be the one-stop-shop for all your employees.

Spiders are constantly rebuilding their webs throughout the night. Your intranet likewise should be repaired, and linkages improved, on a daily basis.

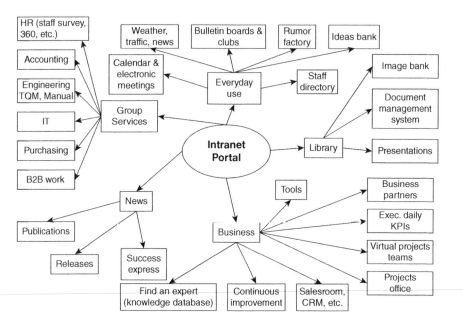

EXHIBIT 18.1 Map of a Thriving Intranet Portal

The spider's web operates 24/7 just like your intranet should. Staff should be able to access their work so they can finish off that report at 1:00 A.M. from their home office.

Spider webs are sticky, and your intranet likewise needs to be designed to ensure employees are constantly in contact with it throughout the day. Eventually the intranet will become a fundamental part of their working life.

The Intranet Is One of the Best Business Tools Your Organization Has

The intranet is simply the best business tool a company has. When used correctly the intranet will enhance performance, job satisfaction, communication, and knowledge transfer between teams and individuals. The intranet is far too important to leave solely in the hands of the technology team. In order to extract full competitive advantage, your intranet needs to be driven and supported by all teams within the company.

Show me an organization that has a vibrant and sticky intranet web with its connections reaching everywhere, and I will show you an organization that is going places. The intranet web should reach everywhere and should be the fountain of all knowledge within the company and the gateway to all business applications.

Organizations are constantly moving toward this state. One publicly owned entity, for example, has a good mapping system covering all staff in the organization. Besides the standard photos, title, short career summary and contact details (the basis of a good intranet section on staff), it includes a section on skills and knowledge. Imagine you are in the middle of a complex problem and you need an expert on statistics or discounted cash flow. All you need to do is search this area. The section on "skills and knowledge" is updated by the staff themselves, albeit their managers have the opportunity to add their comments on the intranet site.

Exhibit 18.1 of an intranet portal gives a simplistic view of what an intranet can cover. It could be said that the senior management team has two options: either embrace the company intranet and fully support it, or fiddle while Rome is burning. See Appendix C for an intranet content checklist.

The IT Staff Might Not Be Communication Experts

IT staff will be the first to agree that they are not communication experts. Their strength lies elsewhere.

It is imperative that the good communicators within the company are actively involved in publishing material and helping others who may be less skilled. The SMT can make a significant contribution here. Remember that we are communicating to staff and key stakeholders, such as major suppliers and customers (via the extranet).

Ensuring That Each Service Team Has a Home Page

Each team should have an informative intranet page including success stories and the photos and short-form CVs of all the team members. Exhibit 18.2 is an example of an accounting finance team's home page.

I have included a checklist in Exhibit 18.3.

Some teams are very progressive with what they put on their intranet sites, with team photos, forms, access to systems, and so forth. The key is to make sure everybody on the team can update the team pages and also that this task is spread around. You should update your team's intranet pages at least once every two weeks.

Your Ability to Lead

The whole subject of leadership is addressed in Chapter 32.

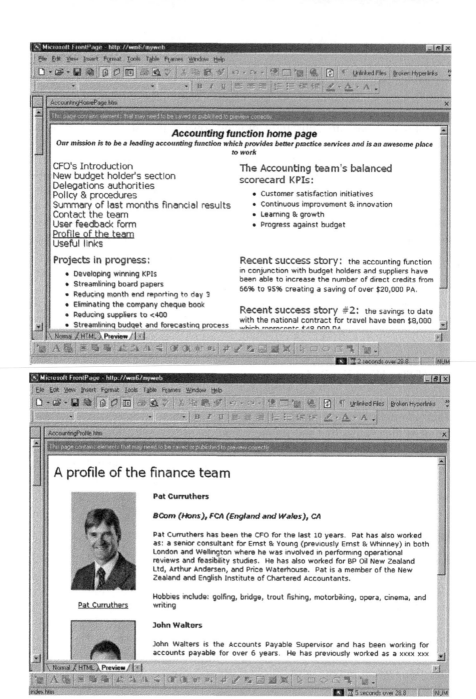

EXHIBIT 18.2 Finance Team's Home Page

Source: David Parmenter, *Pareto's 80/20 Rule for Corporate Accountants.*
Copyright ©2007 by John Wiley & Sons. Reprinted with permission of John Wiley
& Sons.

190

EXHIBIT 18.3 Intranet Checklist

Intranet Checklist

1. Does the SMT recognize how important the Intranet is to the company?	☐ Yes	☐ No
2. Does your organization model its intranet on the garden spider's web?	☐ Yes	☐ No
3. Does your intranet trap all meaningful data yet let the flotsam pass through?	☐ Yes	☐ No
4. Does your intranet capture all aspects of your organization in order to be the one-stop-shop for all your employees?	☐ Yes	☐ No
5. Is your intranet repaired and linkages improved on a daily basis?	☐ Yes	☐ No
6. Are staff able to access their work so they can finish off reports from their home office?	☐ Yes	☐ No
7. Is your intranet designed to ensure employees are constantly in contact with it throughout the day?	☐ Yes	☐ No

Your Competency with Technology

It is not uncommon to see technological dinosaurs roaming around in the SMT. Yet the required skills and the level of technological literacy needed are well within the reach of anyone on the SMT. Witness the number of senior people who on retirement discover the Web. How does an organization allow these minor barriers to remain un-hurdled by the SMT?

Being a technological dinosaur has other costs. A lack of technological literacy results in projects not being effectively led or understood by the senior team, often leading to expensive U-turns or involvement in inappropriate projects.

The answer is quite simple: Invest in personal trainers for the senior team until the team members are completely up to speed with using email, accessing the executive management system (which was built for them, after all), working with electronic board papers, and editing their own PowerPoint presentations. They will be forever grateful.

Your Ability to Work in the "Not Urgent and Important" Quadrant

How many members of the senior team are "adrenaline junkies"—addicted to postponing tasks or asking for major changes at the last minute? Management writers have for some time talked about analyzing time in *sectors*.

Quadrant 1: Urgent and important	Quadrant 3: Urgent and not important
Quadrant 2: Not urgent & important	Quadrant 4: Not urgent and not important

EXHIBIT 18.4 Four-Quadrant Approach to Time Management

One such approach is the *four quadrants*, illustrated in Exhibit 18.4. The aim is to spend quality time in quadrant 2, and minimize, if possible, quadrant 1 (urgent and important), to avoid rushed decisions and unnecessary pressure.

Smaller organizations can cope better with high levels of quadrant 1 activity, but larger ones with staff of over, say, 400 full-time employees (FTEs) are severely handicapped as whole departments are sent into a spin. It is sobering to analyze those last-minute, rushed quadrant 1 activities. How many, when the dust has settled, have turned out to be quadrant 4 activities!

The senior team should set the example. Before you ask for the next senior management meeting, it might be worth thinking what quadrant your concerns fall into. How much is this meeting costing the organization per hour?

Your Ability to Finish

It is no good running the first 1,000 yards in three minutes if you do not finish the remaining 760 yards. Among the greatest management time wasters are unfinished projects or discontinued initiatives.

If senior management do not have the discipline to see initiatives through, then they should not expect a high finishing rate from their teams. "Moving on to more interesting pastures" is a very contagious virus and does not respond well to short-term treatments.

If your organization has a history of unfinished or discontinued initiatives, here are some suggestions:

- Log all initiatives in a project office so you know how many are in progress so as to avoid reinventing the wheel.
- Develop a culture that celebrates completion.
- Support new initiatives with regular training programs aimed at getting buy-in from new middle and senior managers.

■ Recognize that companies need *oracles*—those long-serving employees who remember everything. Turn them into mentors and watch the performance of your younger staff take off!

Your Commitment to Human Resources Management Techniques

If senior management are not aware of modern human resources (HR) techniques, they will have a tendency to undervalue them.

Disenfranchise the HR function at your peril. The possible consequences of such action include:

■ A trend toward purchasing rather than growing trained staff and thus becoming over-reliant on the training provided by past employers
■ Remuneration out of kilter, especially at the senior levels
■ Organization culture being talked about with nothing really done about it
■ New recruits not performing as anticipated
■ Staff turnover and absenteeism rising
■ Young, talented staff never learning good management skills
■ Poorly targeted training

Read Chapter 28 for more information on how important the HR team is.

CHAPTER **19**

Finding Your Organization's Critical Success Factors

I f you have only a few minutes to skim over this chapter, this is what
you should focus on:

- Few organizations know their critical success factors
- Definition of critical success factors
- Workshop to determine your organization's critical success factors

In this chapter I have extracted some of the key points CFOs need to learn
about how to find your organization's critical success factors from my book
"Key Performance Indicators"[1]. At some point it would be worth reading
Chapter 7 from that book for a full account of this important process.

 Few Organizations Know Their Critical Success Factors

Most organizations know their success factors; however, few organizations
have done the following:

- Worded their success factors appropriately
- Segregated out success factors from their strategic objectives
- Sifted through the success factors to find their critical success factors
  (CSFs)
- Communicated the CSFs to staff

Finding an organization's CSFs is a relatively simple step and is the
focus of this section. I want to show you a process that can be run in-house
without the assistance of complex methodologies that only a brain surgeon
can operate.

If your organization has not completed a thorough exercise to know its CSFs, *performance measurement* will be a random process, creating an army of measurers producing numerous numbing reports and who often measure progress in a direction very remote from the strategic direction of the organization.

This chaos needs to stop now! I will show you a process that over a couple of weeks will crystallize and communicate your organization's CSFs. This exercise may well leave a legacy in the organization that will be greater than everything you have done in the past.

You will have created CSFs that help to link daily activities into the organization's strategies—the El Dorado of management.

Definition of *Critical Success Factors*

I first came across this definition in the late 1990s, and it is as good now as it was then:

> *Critical success factors are a list of issues or aspects of organizational performance that determine ongoing health, vitality, and well-being.[2]*

Identifying Organization-wide Critical Success Factors

CSF selection is very subjective. Anybody who says different is misleading you. Any two groups of management within the same organization would come up with different ingredients, albeit the flavor and texture would be similar.

In addition, the effectiveness and usefulness of the CSFs chosen are highly dependent on the degree of analytical skill of those involved. Active leadership by senior management in this step is essential.

The relationship between CSFs (also referred to as *key result areas*) and the four types of performance measure (KRIs, RIs, PIs, and KPIs), which were discussed in Chapter 16, are very important. If you get the CSFs right, it is very easy to find your winning KPIs (e.g., in the late-planes scenario, once the "timely arrival and departure of planes" CSF was identified, it was relatively easy to find the KPI "planes over two hours late").

When you first investigate CSFs, you may come up with 30 or so issues that it can be argued are critical for the continued health of the organization. The second phase of thinning them down is key to the success of the KPI project. There are a number of characteristics of CSFs worth dwelling on:

- They will come as no surprise to management and the board; they will have talked about them as success factors.
- The influence of CSFs cuts across a number of balanced scorecard (BSC) perspectives (e.g., the timely arrival and departure of planes impacts nearly all the BSC perspectives of an airline; see the following).
- CSFs have a positive influence on the organization.
- CSFs have a great influence on other success factors.
- They are focused in a precise area, rather than being a bland statement so often characterized by strategic objectives (e.g., "increased profitability," "cost reduction," "maximizing the use of our most important resource—our people").

Better practice suggests that organizational CSFs should be limited to between five and eight regardless of the organization's size. However, for a conglomerate, the CSFs will be largely industry specific (e.g., the CSFs for an airline are different from those of a retail clothing chain store). Thus

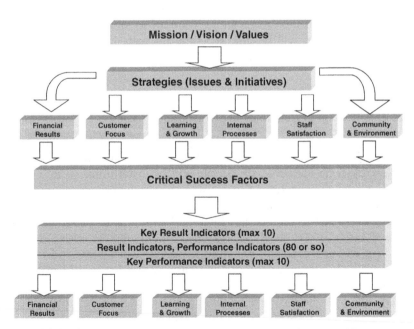

EXHIBIT 19.1 Journey from a Mission and Vision to Performance Measures that Work

Source: David Parmenter, *Key Performance Indicators: Developing, Implementing, and Using Winning KPIs, 2nd Edition.* Copyright © 2010 by David Parmenter. Reprinted with the permission of John Wiley & Sons, Inc.

there would be a greater number of CSFs in the conglomerate than the suggested five to eight.

Identifying Organization-wide CSFs: A Three-Stage Process

To help organizations around the world find their CSFs, I have developed a three-stage process. (This process is explained in detail in a whitepaper[3] and on webcasts that can be accessed via www.davidparmenter.com.)

Stage 1: Gathering the success factors we already know about
Stage 2: Workshop to determine the CSFs
Stage 3: Presenting the CSFs to the senior management team

Stage 1: Gathering the Success Factors We Already Know About

Review all the strategic documents in your organization covering the past ten years. Then draw and develop SFs from these documents. Interview as many of the organization's oracles as you can as well as the SMT. From this information you will be able to come up with a list. To ensure you have covered all bases in your search for the existing success factors, see Appendix B.

Stage 2: Workshop to Determine the Organization's CSFs

Invite members of the focus group, along with others who have shown an aptitude in this area, to a two-day workshop. There are breakout sessions where workgroups of up to six people will brainstorm this issue. Use the workshop timetable as set out in www.davidparmenter.com.

To find your five-to-eight CSFs, a good technique is to draw all your critical success factors on a large whiteboard and draw in all the linkages— which SF factor affects which SF. Take care in drawing the arrows the right way. In a recent workshop, we were handling over 40 SFs and thus the arrows were shown as leaving and entering, with a letter to identify them by (see Exhibit 19.2).

The SFs with the most arrows *out* are the ones with the greatest influence and are thus most likely to be the critical ones, the CSFs!

If you have the strategy mapping software, you can use this to support the output from this workshop.

After Day 1 is completed, the KPI project team tests the list of the top-five-to-eight CSFs against the six BSC perspectives and the organization's strategic objectives. See Exhibits 19.3 and 19.4.

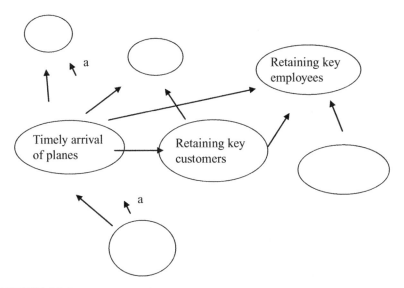

EXHIBIT 19.2 CSF Relationship Mapping
Source: David Parmenter, *Key Performance Indicators: Developing,
Implementing, and Using Winning KPIs, 2nd Edition.* Copyright © 2010 by
David Parmenter. Reprinted with the permission of John Wiley & Sons, Inc.

In Exhibit 19.5 the CSFs are not impacting strategic objective 4, and
thus we need to ask whether we have all the CSFs. Could one be reworded,
or is strategic objective 4 correct in the first place?

Stage 3: Presenting the CSFs to the Senior Management Team

The KPI team prepares a 40-minute presentation selling the short-listed
CSFs to facilitate discussion and agreement by the SMT.

The presentation will cover:

- Top-five-to-eight CSFs
- Discussing these CSFs with employee representatives
- Conveying these CSFs to staff
- Ramifications for performance measurement
- What 24/7, daily, weekly performance measures, if any, are currently
  being collected in these CSFs
- Permission to proceed to next stage (selection of the team and orga-
  nizational measures)

EXHIBIT 19.3 How Do Your CSFs Cover the Six Perspectives of Performance?

Critical success factor	Perspectives					
	Financial	Customer Satisfaction	Staff Satisfaction	Learning & Growth	Internal Process	Environment & Community
e.g., timely arrival and departure of planes	√	√	√	√	√	possible
e.g., delivery in full and on time to key customers	√	√	possible	√	√	
1. xxxxxx		√			√	√
2. xxxxx	√					
3. xxxxx		√	√			
4. xxxxx		√		√	√	√
5. xxxxx	√		√			
6. xxxx		√		√	√	
7. xxx	√	√		√	√	√

EXHIBIT 19.4 Testing How Your CSFs Link to Your Strategic Objectives

Critical Success Factor	Strategic Objectives					
	SO#1	SO#2	SO#3	SO#4	SO#5	SO#6
e.g., timely arrival and departure of planes	√		√			possible
e.g., delivery in full and on time to key customers	√		possible			
1. xxxxx		√			√	√
2. xxx	√					
3. xxxxx			√			
4. xxx	√	√			√	
5. xxxxx			√			√
6. xxxx			√			
7. xxxx	√		√		√	

EXHIBIT 19.5 Checklist for Identifying the Organization's Critical Success Factors

1. In your search for the organization's SFs, have you reviewed the following:
   - Vision statement? □ Yes □ No
   - Mission statement? □ Yes □ No
   - Values statement? □ Yes □ No
   - Strategic plans over the last five to ten years? □ Yes □ No
2. In your search for the organization's SFs, have you covered the following:
   - An analysis of economic, social, political, environmental, and technological trends that will shape the general context in which the organization operates (i.e., an environmental scan)? □ Yes □ No
   - Analysis of the markets in which the organization operates and identification of future trends and developments? □ Yes □ No
   - Review of current expectations and satisfaction levels of the organization's *key* customers? □ Yes □ No
   - Analysis of likely *future* customer expectations and requirements? □ Yes □ No
   - Review of current supplier performance and likely future requirements and the status of those relationships or partnerships? □ Yes □ No
   - Analysis of the financial status of the organization and the available capacity to meet future requirements? □ Yes □ No

(Continued)

EXHIBIT 19.5 (Continued)

■ Review of the human resource capabilities of the organization, taking into account the future requirements identified?	☐ Yes	☐ No
■ Review of the existing organizational culture and its appropriateness for meeting the anticipated challenges?	☐ Yes	☐ No
3. Have you checked to ensure that the wording of each SF is as specific as possible?	☐ Yes	☐ No
4. Have you looked for missing SFs?	☐ Yes	☐ No
5. Have you short-listed to between five and eight CSFs?	☐ Yes	☐ No
6. Have you used the workshop processes suggested?	☐ Yes	☐ No
7. Do the CSFs address all six of the perspectives?	☐ Yes	☐ No
8. Have you tested the short-listed CSFs to ensure that, between them, they link back to *all* the organization's strategic objectives?	☐ Yes	☐ No
9. During the process, have you consulted with:		
■ Employee representatives?	☐ Yes	☐ No
■ Key customers?	☐ Yes	☐ No
■ Key suppliers?	☐ Yes	☐ No
■ Board?	☐ Yes	☐ No

Source: David Parmenter, *Key Performance Indicators: Developing, Implementing, and Using Winning KPIs, 2nd Edition.* Copyright © 2010 by David Parmenter. Reprinted with the permission of John Wiley & Sons, Inc.

If CSFs are not going to be discussed with employee representatives, or conveyed to the staff, the performance measure development process needs to be put on hold. In effect, there is no agreement as to the direction in which the organization is going. It is also likely that there is not sufficient agreement on the holistic strategy for achieving best practice.

Without this agreement the foundation stone of partnership has been undermined. The only option is to consult further to secure agreement. See the checklist in Exhibit 19.5.

Notes

1. David Parmenter, *Key Performance Indicators: Developing, Implementing, and Using Winning KPIs*, 2nd Edition John Wiley & Sons, 2011.
2. *Key Performance Indicators Manual: A Practical Guide for the Best Practice Development, Implementation and Use of KPIs* (AusIndustries, 1996). Now out of print.
3. David Parmenter, *Finding Your Organization's Critical Success Factors*, www.davidparmenter.com, 2010.

CHAPTER 20

Special Organizations

If you have only a few minutes to skim over this chapter, this is what you should focus on:

Recruiting frontline staff born with the ability to serve: Cathay Pacific's story
"Love thy neighbor as thyself" (the fourth dimension): SMASH
Toyota's 15-year advantage
Toyota culture change checklist

Cathay Pacific Recruiting Frontline Staff Born with the Ability to Serve

I am sitting in the cattle (economy) class of Cathay Pacific, en route to New Zealand. The difference is I do not feel like I should *moo*. Why? Service: The staff are exceptional. Studying them I have come to the conclusion that service is not something you can simply teach. Your recruits first have to have the basics.

I feel that you can class airline staff into 2-, 4-, 6-, 8-, 10-, and 12-hour airlines. By that I mean that for the first 2 hours you can hardly distinguish them apart. They are gushing over you, even in economy class. After 2 hours of working in a cooped-up space with nowhere to run, the staff start showing their true colors. Some airlines are what I call 2-hour airlines—anything more than a short internal flight exposes you to appalling service.

I called the Cathay Pacific chief steward across to speak to her. She asked if I had a problem. During the discussion I asked, "Can you train staff to be this good or do they have to be born that way?" She said immediately that their staff were born with the desire to serve. This made immediate sense to me. How would you expect a person who is not innately service oriented to remain so for 12 hours?

As a CEO you need to establish a recruiting strategy for your front-line staff that is based on the Cathay Pacific model. The Cathay Pacific frontline staff had to have all of the following traits:

- The fortitude to commit to a five-tier/five-month recruitment journey.
- A love for the "common man."
- An eye for detail.
- The ability to deal with the proverbial "sick bag."
- The ability to look like a million dollars when the batteries are empty.
- The desire to be a team player. (Many flight attendants have never worked together before. They meet at the crew debrief an hour before boarding commences.)
- The ability to smile at both customers and team members.

Fortitude to Commit to a Five-Tier/Five-Month Recruitment Journey

The chief steward told me that the staff who applied for a job had to go through an arduous five-month process. Only the applicants who are committed to joining Cathay Pacific get over this hurdle. During these interviews management are looking for the traits they need. The investment in the front end pays off with a quicker and more successful training process and one of the lowest staff-turnover ratios in the industry.

Love for the "Common Man"

The image is one of a man sleeping, hugging a pillow, with a wife and child all connected through love and proximity. How do you get staff to care at the same level as this scene of domestic bliss? The staff have to be born with a love of caring for the so-called "common man," to observe their needs and offer Rolls Royce–level service, or as I will say from now on, a *Cathay Pacific service*.

An Eye for Detail

I noted that even the smallest thing out of place was rectified with a smile. Each flight attendant would pick up paper, no matter how small, rectify the tangled headsets, and straighten up blankets overhanging into the aisle as a matter of course.

The Ability to Deal with the Proverbial "Sick Bag"

In all jobs there are tasks one would rather not do. The key to service is for staff to undertake these tasks willingly, realizing that they have to be done. I observed this trait on a number of occasions on the flight. It goes without saying that the toilets were the cleanest I have ever used.

To Look a Like Million Dollars When the Batteries Are Empty

After serving people in cramped conditions for over 12 hours, being able to look like a million dollars when the batteries must be empty is truly exceptional. All staff when we departed were immaculate, smiling and looking ready to do another 12-hour shift rather than a 12-hour sleep!

The Desire to Be a Team Player

One fascinating thing about the flight crews is that they first meet each other an hour or so before the flight. Airlines use a pool system and flight crew are rostered onto flights ensuring only that they have the necessary experience to serve the various different classes. So within an hour these individuals need to develop a rapport so that the customer thinks they have been together for years. In fact they have; they are part of a brotherhood and sisterhood that is strongly connected to the ethics of the airline. They can only achieve this seamless service by training all staff, no matter where in the world they are based, in the same way. To achieve this, I'll wager that Cathay Pacific has a centralized training school that *all* frontline staff, around the world, must attend.

The Ability to Smile at Both Customers and Team Members

Smiling seems to be a lost art. So often when working under stress the furrowed lines appear on the forehead and the scowl develops, hopefully warning all away as we are too busy for any sort of interaction. This trait is deadly in a service-oriented enterprise. We need to recruit staff who can maintain that air of friendliness and humor even under pressure.

Building an Organization That Works in the Fourth Dimension: SMASH

It's 5.45 P.M. and I am running late, as usual, to pick up my two children from their after-school care, called *SMASH* (to be defined later). I arrive there trying to look calm and collected after a stressful drive from town, to see a strange sight—my children sitting quietly, reading books (they don't manage this at home!). The staff, while keeping an eye on the children whose parents are late, are having their daily team debrief. When was the last time you had a team brief?

I noticed other strange things happening and I began to wonder that maybe I had discovered something. As David Attenborough, the naturalist and filmmaker, would say, "This is a rare sight not often caught on camera." I subsequently interviewed the manager and found that the SMASH team works on many levels, including the fourth dimension.

Develop a Team Mission Statement

The SMASH mission statement includes the words "to be awesome" in it and it is no surprise that staff are passionate about their work, because they live and breathe the mission statement. The word *awesome* is particularly powerful. It suggests that many staff members and managers would need to change the way they look at their working life, as they themselves are preventing others from being awesome.

When you look at a company's mission statement, one thing that is often lacking is any sense of passion, or the word *awesome*. If individually we all want to be awesome at home and at work, why does the word not appear in our corporate mission statement? Every single individual is passionate about something; what we as managers have got to do is try and dig into those reserves and spread them across their work activities, if only thinly at first, until they themselves buy into the mission.

Based on Spiritual Belief of "Love Thy Neighbor as Thyself" (Fourth Dimension)

SMASH is based on many spiritual beliefs, including "Love thy neighbor as thyself." Maybe the problem is that many of us in the corporate world do not love ourselves enough, and that is why we quite happily create conflict in our working environment.

Based on Spiritual Belief That Prayer Works Both at Work and at Home (Fourth Dimension)

Prayer is an important part of the SMASH manager's life and the guidance received is feedback as to the way the staff (and children) work together. The children at SMASH, for example, have a prayer wall, where they stick their current prayers.

I was fortunate enough to hear a testimonial, recently, where the speaker pointed out how he learned to pray both at work and at home. He has found an amazing clarity of thought and improved working relationships when he has sought guidance from his God.

Debriefing of Staff at the End of the Day

At SMASH they have an open-ended debriefing every night. On a difficult day this debriefing may take over an hour and a half; the length of the debrief is very much up to staff and runs largely into their own time. In their debriefing sessions they cover the following issues:

- How best to help a particular child who is having difficulties
- Ways to improve the program
- Plans for the next day and next week
- Finishing off communications, which due to the pressures of 40 to 50 children traveling in different directions, is difficult
- Popping the balloon on those difficult issues that may be growing out of proportion during the day

Another point worth noting is that SMASH could not operate if it chose to have meetings during its key service-delivery time. Yet that is the very thing we all tend to do. (See Time Management-The Basics in Chapter 6.)

Careful Staff Selection

SMASH always likes to recruit people who are previously known to them. They have a high occurrence of staff rejoining when they are back in town, and if they do have to advertise, they go through a careful interview and selection process to ensure the person will fit.

Systematic and Organized Team Training Session

SMASH has a training evening each term and they invest considerable time planning the training workshop, which may include: helping staff to revisit policies and procedures; looking at likely scenarios; what makes a supervisor excellent; triggers of children's bad behavior; increasing knowledge about special needs, and so on. We can certainly learn from the commitment that SMASH makes to training and the positive team spirit that these in-house workshops generate.

Resolving Conflict Effectively and Efficiently

The SMASH team has a three-step process for resolving conflict between the children:

Step 1. Both parties have an opportunity to speak and give their views of the situation.

Step 2. It is then explained to both parties that the dispute is wasting time that they could better invest elsewhere.

Step 3. The options are explained, and repeated until the idea sinks in.

This procedure works successfully in resolving conflicts. Maybe it would also work well in the office environment, where typically conflicts are allowed to fester for months on end—including the sending of unsavory emails.

It is important at the very least to have a conflict-resolution policy and that it is communicated to all staff, making clear what is expected to occur when a dispute arises.

Getting the Induction Process Right

Like all good organizations, SMASH puts a lot of time and effort into a good orientation process, which is committed to, not only by the Team Leader, but by all other staff. In addition to the orientation process, the staff meet together offsite once a quarter to go back to basics and once again build on their understanding of SMASH, starting off from the mission statement. They also have an orientation program for their clients (the children). How many customer relationships would be improved if we had an orientation program with them so that they could maximize the benefits of working with us?

Creating a Service Culture

When you walk through the door at SMASH you are greeted with a smile by all staff, who make eye contact with you. As adults we cart around a lot of baggage, which makes life difficult. One of those crippling behaviors is the inability to maintain eye contact. There must be many reasons why this occurs, but it is a very damaging and career-limiting behavior trait. Organizations need to support their managers and staff in casting this trait away and thus making "summiting" much easier.

At SMASH, making eye contact is part of the staff's training and part of their job. This is no mean achievement as they are under minute-by-minute pressures and dramas as 30 young children are racing around all at once. In business we are often less welcoming. You arrive into an entity and everybody is so busy and stress pervades the air. How you move from this to the SMASH atmosphere I do not know; all I can say is that it is obviously worthwhile. Perhaps you need a charismatic leader, which SMASH clearly has.

EXHIBIT 20.1 Message on the Whiteboard to the Parents

Dear Parent/Caregiver!

SMASH is looking to employ a:
* full-time,
* long-term,
* second in command

Please list below what you consider to be the important attributes when caring for your children:

_____

_____

_____

Please get involved in this process.

Obtaining Buy-in from Staff and Clients

Recently SMASH was looking to set up a new position, so they cleverly put a notice board up so that parents were encouraged to write down their thoughts as to what was important. (See Exhibit 20.1).

It was simple and effective. We, too, can seek feedback in such simple ways. Often companies dither around when it comes to producing surveys, many of which can be set up really quickly if you *just do it.*

Accommodating Special Needs

At SMASH, some children need more care and attention than others. The staff achieve this by ensuring there is appropriate disclosure from parents and then putting in action a partnership between the home and SMASH. Staff are trained to know what the warning signs are and what support action is required.

Continuous Innovation

At SMASH, innovation is discussed every day during the debrief. The staff want to know what they can do differently tomorrow, next week, next month. In many organizations that I have worked in and visited, this is not the case. Innovation needs to be on every agenda—it needs to be pushed so that staff know what is expected. Otherwise, we are simply standing still.

Bringing Passion into the Workplace

SMASH is exhibiting *servant* leadership. As the words suggest, this is leadership by serving the people:

When servant leadership is demonstrated in organizations it quickly builds trust and relationships. Furthermore, applying the principles of being slow to anger and quick to forgive also builds relationships. Being greeted by a smile comes from the heart and a genuine love of the people they [the staff] serve.

So what does SMASH stand for? St. Mary's After School House.

Toyota's 15-Year Advantage

In the book, *The Toyota Way*,[1] it is clear how different the company is. Here are some examples:

- Staff on the production line have the authority to stop production if a unit has a fault that cannot be fixed in time.
- They do not merely test for quality at the end; they ensure it is in every step.
- They introduce staff-suggested innovations at an alarming rate.
- They take a long time over a decision and then implement it quickly.
- They tackle all the areas where money is lost, such as downtime, and now can change the production line from one model to another in less than three hours where other manufacturers take days.

Barring the recent problems Toyota has had, show me a car manufacturer who has not had a recall. I believe they are one of the best companies in the world. To replicate Toyota's success would take a 15- to 20-year timeframe, and although a daunting period, it is a worthwhile journey. To succeed, an organization needs to have the top three layers of management having experienced the change process. The checklist in Exhibit 20.2 sets out the journey you will need to undertake.

The *culture change process* will take at least 15 to 20 years because all of your executive team will need to give way to the new breed of senior managers who can cope with the new culture. The "old guard" will never be able to cope with the new culture it will be too difficult to modify the 20 or 30 years of programming. The existing senior management's role is to enjoy the last of the summer wine while preparing the young guns in the new environment. This is a case of the senior management saying "Do as I preach, rather than do as I do." All new senior managers will come from existing ranks. There will be no place for outsiders, unless they themselves come from exceptional organizations (e.g., ex-Toyota).

The *recruiting and training* change will take the longest. You will have arrived only when managers in the organization have worked their entire career in the new way. In other words, the senior management team was trained in the new ways when they joined at the lowest management level. If your senior management team is in their fifties, they have already had a working life spanning 30 years.

The move to a truly *innovative organization* will take around ten years to perfect. We need at least two layers of management who were "born" into the new way. That innovation is part of the daily life cycle.

The change to *strategies* will also take time as senior management and the stock market need to fully understand that the organization will never be a prisoner to short-term thinking. Longevity of trading results is required before the organization can free itself from the stock market's shackles.

Changes to the *processes* can be relatively quick—ten years! The change in culture will be achieved when two layers of management have been fed this "food" all their working life.

The *customer loyalty* change can be locked in within the ten-year period. New products will need about seven years to prove that they are market leaders in all key characteristics.

The approach to *new markets* is achievable within the ten-year time-frame. This allows enough time to unwind existing approaches that will not work in this new environment.

The checklist in Exhibit 20.2 analyses the steps you will need to cover. It was designed from the content of *How Toyota Became #1: Leadership Lessons from the World's Greatest Car Company*,[2] by David Magee.

EXHIBIT 20.2 Toyota Culture-Change Checklist

Culture Change (15-year horizon to make change)	Is it Covered?	
1. Removal of all executive perks that separate the senior management team from the workforce (e.g., executive parking spots, excessive offices)	☐ Yes	☐ No
2. A removal of all performance-related pay schemes that can be influenced by market conditions rather than actual efforts	☐ Yes	☐ No
3. A management style that "manages like you have no power"	☐ Yes	☐ No
4. Daily connect between the SMT and the workforce	☐ Yes	☐ No
5. Executive pay linked by a relationship to the workers' pay	☐ Yes	☐ No
6. Humility and "to serve" being a major driver of leaders	☐ Yes	☐ No
	(Continued)	

EXHIBIT 20.2 (Continued)

Culture Change (15-year horizon to make change)	Is it Covered?	
7. Honesty about performance	☐ Yes	☐ No
8. Devolve decision making authority to frontline teams	☐ Yes	☐ No
9. Things that are running smoothly should not be subject to any control	☐ Yes	☐ No
10. Immediate sharing of problems and mistakes	☐ Yes	☐ No
11. See for yourself (walkabout)	☐ Yes	☐ No
Recruitment and training (5-year horizon to make change)		
12. Recruited based on attitude and fit rather than achievements to date	☐ Yes	☐ No
13. One-year induction program	☐ Yes	☐ No
14. Mentoring program for all	☐ Yes	☐ No
15. Team players rather than individuals	☐ Yes	☐ No
16. Integrity and honesty evidenced	☐ Yes	☐ No
Innovation (5–10-year horizon to make change)		
17. Systematic thinking (*kaizen*)	☐ Yes	☐ No
18. Nonblaming (*kaizen*)	☐ Yes	☐ No
19. Innovations adopted every day (ten innovations per employee per year being the benchmark)	☐ Yes	☐ No
20. Barriers to change removed	☐ Yes	☐ No
21. Constantly looking for improvement (never business as usual)	☐ Yes	☐ No
Strategy (15-year horizon to make change)		
22. Long-term view always over short-term view	☐ Yes	☐ No
23. Vigorously challenge plans	☐ Yes	☐ No
24. Implementation carried out quickly	☐ Yes	☐ No
25. All implementations checked and amended	☐ Yes	☐ No
26. Profits made in most trading conditions	☐ Yes	☐ No
27. Isolate yourself from short-term stock market forces	☐ Yes	☐ No
Processes (10-year horizon to make change)		
28. Produce to order ("pull" system)	☐ Yes	☐ No
29. Plan-Do-Check-Act philosophy	☐ Yes	☐ No
30. Build new products, ground up, rather than acquire products	☐ Yes	☐ No
31. Continuous flow (*takt time*) with a pace that never varies	☐ Yes	☐ No
32. Work processes are a controlled scientific experiment	☐ Yes	☐ No
33. Just in time	☐ Yes	☐ No
34. Stopping production lines delegated to staff on the shop floor (*jidoka*)	☐ Yes	☐ No
35. Cost reduction through design	☐ Yes	☐ No
36. The leveling sequencing of production (*heijunka*)	☐ Yes	☐ No

EXHIBIT 20.2 (Continued)

Culture Change (15-year horizon to make change)	Is it Covered?	
37. Cost reduction through working closely with key suppliers	□ Yes	□ No
38. Zero landfill waste—Recycling all packaging with suppliers	□ Yes	□ No
39. Annual planning replaced with rolling planning and producing what is sold	□ Yes	□ No
40. Performance monitored against key ratios, exceptions on a 24/7 basis rather than monthly variance analysis	□ Yes	□ No
41. Zero clutter in all operations	□ Yes	□ No
Customer Loyalty (10-year horizon to make change)		
42. Live like your customers to fully understand them	□ Yes	□ No
43. Understand who your customers really are	□ Yes	□ No
44. Focus of everything on improving customer outcomes	□ Yes	□ No
45. Overdeliver, underpromise	□ Yes	□ No
46. Be market leader for "quality-for-price"	□ Yes	□ No
47. Let brand loyalty be your marketing edge	□ Yes	□ No
48. Commitment to the long-term changes in consumer demand rather than the current flavor	□ Yes	□ No
New Markets (10-year horizon to make change)		
49. Pilot manufacture in new country to test workforce and culture	□ Yes	□ No
50. Understand local community	□ Yes	□ No
51. Total commitment to being local	□ Yes	□ No
52. Local products for local market	□ Yes	□ No
53. How much progress are you making with Toyota's 14 principles of management?		
1. Base your management decisions on a long-term philosophy, even at the expense of short-term financial goals.	□ Yes	□ No
2. Create continuous process flow to bring problems to the surface.	□ Yes	□ No
3. Use "pull" systems to avoid overproduction.	□ Yes	□ No
4. Level out the workload (*heijunka*). (Work like the tortoise, not the hare.)	□ Yes	□ No
5. Build a culture of stopping to fix problems, to get quality right the first time.	□ Yes	□ No
6. Standardized tasks are the foundation for continuous improvement and employee empowerment.	□ Yes	□ No
7. Use visual control so no problems are hidden.	□ Yes	□ No
8. Use only reliable, thoroughly tested technology that serves your people and processes.	□ Yes	□ No
9. Grow leaders who thoroughly understand the work, live the philosophy, and teach it to others.	□ Yes	□ No

(Continued)

EXHIBIT 20.2 (Continued)

Culture Change (15-year horizon to make change)	Is it Covered?	
10. Develop exceptional people and teams who follow your company's philosophy.	□ Yes	□ No
11. Respect your extended network of partners and suppliers by challenging them and helping them improve.	□ Yes	□ No
12. Go and see for yourself to thoroughly understand the situation (*genchi genbutsu*).	□ Yes	□ No
13. Make decisions slowly by consensus, thoroughly considering all options; implement decisions rapidly.	□ Yes	□ No
14. Become a learning organization through relentless reflection (*hansei*) and continuous improvement (*kaizen*).	□ Yes	□ No

Management Practices at the Pier Nine Restaurant

As an international speaker, there have to be some perks—one of which is to eat seafood around the world. One venue in Brisbane is eagerly awaited by my stomach: the Pier Nine (PN) Restaurant. It all started during one lunchtime where I had only 45 minutes to eat. I had run overtime on the morning session. I walked into Pier Nine explaining the issue to the maître d'. "No problem, sir. I can recommend the wild barramundi."

The way the rushed order was handled, and the stunning meal, has had me coming back ever since. Each time I visit I receive the same excellent quality of service, food, and wine that blend into an experience that has me salivating even as I write. I started to talk to the management and staff, and practices emerged that we can learn from to turn our organization into a Pier Nine (PN).

Recruiting Staff

When PN management want staff they ask their staff to look around their friends and previous work colleagues. Every staff member knows the culture, so it is not strange to find that staff introduce friends whom they have worked with, who have a compatible work ethic, and are likely to fit in. Why rely on advertising when recommendations could be so much better for finding the right staff?

Bonus Scheme

The bonus scheme is interesting. The staff bonus depends on the "mystery diner" feedback (see the following discussion), whereas the management bonus is linked to staff satisfaction. If staff satisfaction is down, the management bonus is adversely affected. The CEO knows that happy staff leads to happy customers, which leads to happy shareholders.

Mystery Diner

Many organizations use a *mystery buyer* to keep up service levels. PN ensures that this role is treated importantly. They take the mystery diner feedback into the bonus scheme. Every day, staff members know that any customer could be that "mystery diner," so they make sure all customers have a positive experience.

Suppliers as Friends

As mentioned in an earlier chapter, the owner pointed out a serviceman delivering the linen tablecloths. He was a burly man dressed in a yellow T-shirt and shorts. The owner said that this person is critical to the business and a friend of the staff and provides a valuable service. He ensures the tablecloths are always accounted for and that those used each day are taken by him and cleaned. The supplier is part of the team to such an extent that the supplier is invited to the Christmas staff dinner, as are the cleaners. How's that for vertical integration of the supplier into the organization?

Staff Satisfaction Surveys That Mean Something

PN runs regular staff satisfaction surveys, at least three or four a year, and takes the feedback seriously. The feedback is discussed with management and staff promptly and actions implemented swiftly to rectify any issues.

Dealing with Complaints

The owner has an interesting policy here. While the customer is always right, the management back their staff 100%. If a customer is unhappy, a member of management immediately rectifies the situation by offering the customer a free meal at some later date. But he or she ensures that the wine is paid for separately, as wine quality is seldom an issue. Management treat each such occasion as a learning experience and at the same time believe the staff version of the facts. The key about this procedure is that it forces the disgruntled customer to come back there while at the same time not giving away too much. In both meals, the drinks will have been billed to and paid for by the customer as the owner will point out, "Your complaint is about xxx and not about the wine." Far too often we give too much away to a disgruntled customer.

Work with Passion

As you enter PN you see a hub of activity. Staff all know what they have to do, and it is a restaurant where I always get the wine waiter to match the wine with the food. All staff I have spoken to over the five or six occasions I have had the pleasure of dining there have been courteous, knowledgeable, and attentive. There is definitely an air about PN that causes staff to feel it is a pleasure to be of service.

Everyone to the Pump

There is a seamless division between management and staff. When times get busy all staff can act as frontline staff, and they do this without a second thought.

Handling the Downtimes

During January, when all the business customers are roasting on the beach or golf course, and diner numbers are lower, staff are encouraged to take their holidays. Part-time staff are retained even though they are not required. As the owner has said, "It is important to give your staff longevity of employment, and ride through the slow times."

Honoring Long-Serving Employees

All long-term employees get long service leave. This comprises a few extra weeks' holiday in that year. This perk is given to staff for every 10 to 15 years of service.

Dealing with Conflict

In a high-pressure service environment staff do on occasion step on each other's toes. The owner recounted an experience with two employees who, away from the customers' eyes, were involved in a bit of rough-and-tumble. The owner took the brawling staff members aside when they had cooled down and said, "Is this the sort of behavior that is expected from great staff in a great restaurant?" Both staff members, who were expecting to be fired, merely left at the end of the day with the shame of having been involved in the fight. They turned up at work the next day vowing to always stay in control.

Pay Above the Odds

It has been said so many times: "If you want monkeys, pay them peanuts." Paying slightly *above* the market rate does not actually cost much. But losing one good staff member for higher pay can cost you over $20,000 in recruitment fees and lost time. This money could and should have been invested in giving staff a premium wage for a premium effort.

Notes

1. Jeffery Liker, *The Toyota Way,* McGraw-Hill, 2003.
2. David Magee, *How Toyota Became #1: Leadership Lessons from the World's Greatest Car Company,* Portfolio, 2008.

CHAPTER 21

Making Your Day More Successful

If you have only a few minutes to skim over this chapter, this is what you should focus on:

- Revolutionizing the working day
- Bringing back the morning break

While leadership is examined in detail in Chapter 32, I wish here to discuss some missing links that are not appreciated enough.

Managing Your Scarcest Resource: Your Time

Every CEO calendar is different. Some enlightened CEOs go for road shows each year, touring their empire, meeting staff face to face, getting close to the action; others are known only through the periodic video footage as part of an employee-update session that employees attend only because the clever Human Resources department has guaranteed quality refreshments.

A number of things absolutely clutter the CEO's calendar: (1) the monthly accounts preparation; (2) the monthly board meeting, where up to a week can be written off each month; (3) up to three months in any year that are handicapped by an annual planning fiasco; and to top it off, (4) the month and a half of time that is impacted by the annual reporting process.

All four of these bottlenecks can be and are significantly curtailed in a 21st-century better-practice organization in the following ways:

- Month-end reporting can and should be finished inside three working days (see Chapter 26).
- Board papers can become totally electronic and rewrites made a thing of the past (see Chapter 22).

- The annual planning process can and should be replaced by quarterly rolling planning (see Chapter 24).
- The annual reporting process can be out within 15 working days after year-end and signed off by board and auditors.

Exhibits 21.1 and 21.2 show how the CEO's year can be very different if these issues are tackled.

The significant differences between these two calendars are that the CEO has more added value through:

- Limiting involvement to no more than a day in the monthly reporting process
- Revolutionizing the board reporting process by limiting board meetings to eight or fewer a year, reducing the wish to rewrite monthly reports, and introducing electronic board papers
- Replacing the annual planning process with four quarterly updates, rolling out six quarters each time
- Spending less time reporting year-end activities

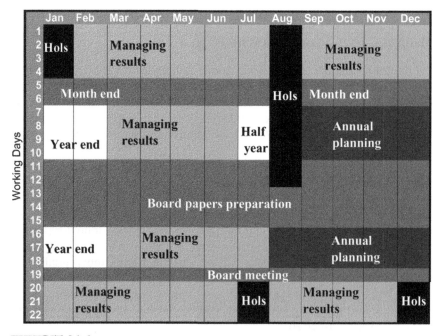

EXHIBIT 21.1 Typical CEO's Calendar Where Four Time Wasters Remain Unchallenged

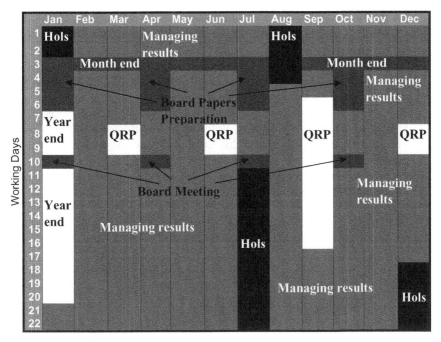

EXHIBIT 21.2 Twenty-First-Century CEO's Calendar

Revolutionizing the Working Day

As the CEO, you have a profound impact on how the organization functions. Within two years of your tenure as CEO, you can well and truly clog up productivity. Here are some ways you can undermine performance:

- By asking for too many reports without quantifying the time that should be invested. You always need to quantify the work required (e.g., say, "I need only a page on this and do not spend more than half a day on it").
- By encouraging a time-consuming meeting culture. You need to ban all morning progress/briefing meetings from your calendar so staff can always know that you are available in the morning.
- By rewriting reports in your own manner instead of promoting reports to be kept *au naturel* with reviewers signing, "I concur with the recommendations, but not written by me."
- By starting one project after another instead of actively promoting a finishing culture by coming down hard on all late projects, each and every week.

- By working excessive hours, getting to the top by working hard, not *smart*. Instead, you can promote a work/life balance and work on the key goals more.
- By encouraging a "cover-your-backside" culture by orchestrating witch hunts over decisions that have been wrong instead of promoting the culture that a mistake is a learning exercise.
- By trying to second-guess every eventuality before a decision is made instead of having a Sir Richard Branson "screw-it-let's-do-it" approach. This is where you ask "will this idea bring the company down if it goes wrong? Are there any reasons why we should not do this project?" If nothing major is raised you just implement the idea, for if it fails it will not be the end of the world.

In Exhibit 21.3 there is a suggested migration of your typical working day as you climb the management mountain.

As previously mentioned, the typical manager's day is filled with meetings with the productive project work being *squeezed in* where possible, leading to an inefficient and elongated day where reports are finished late in the evening, either at work or at home.

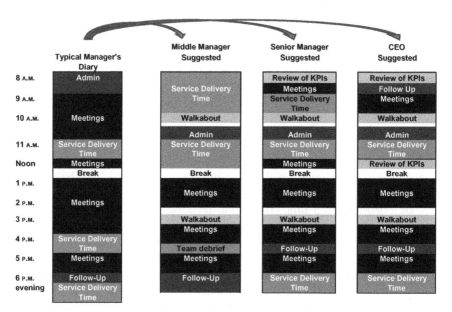

EXHIBIT 21.3 Transforming the Working Day

Better-practice changes to the day include:

* Moving all meetings (unless vital) into the afternoons
* Introduction of CEO's twice-daily office walkthroughs
* Moving of email and mail opening to midmorning
* Daily focus on the KPIs for the SMT and CEO
* More commitment to a lunchtime break into which you have introduced networking events

Planning a Sabbatical

Many great leaders understand the benefit of a sabbatical, an extended vacation often with an executive management program at a prestigious university. These sabbaticals are awarded to members of the senior management team, commonly on a five to seven year cycle, to keep them fresh and revitalized. Or as one knowledgeable person said to make the senior manager more marketable so they can move on! The CEO can get burned out quickly. One great legal practice I have come across has a six-week sabbatical every two years for all the partners. They are required to go abroad and broaden their knowledge. Not surprisingly, they come back refreshed, and wind up staying with the firm. As a CEO, you will argue there is no one to replace you. This is surely the first sign that you have not developed your senior management team enough.

I have a good friend who is a dentist, running his own practice. He is frustrated with his working life and cannot see any other option than to sell out and start an entirely new business. He has never had a sabbatical in nearly 30 years of dentistry. I am sure that if he managed a 10-week trip abroad he would be totally rejuvenated. He may even decide to stay in dentistry perhaps focusing in on the high-end, cosmetic work and selling the "drilling-and-filling" practice to another young and upcoming dentist.

Bring Back the Morning Tea Break

As an auditor I visited many companies and experienced firsthand the daily procession during the morning tea break. Looking back, I recall some interesting characteristics of this ritual, such as: Older staff had been around long enough to know just about everything and were treated as mentors; staff morale was high, with a real team spirit; Mondays were full of weekend stories; and everybody seemed to know what was going on.

I also remember later, as a management consultant, how pleased I was to see this "inefficient" process disappear in the late 1980s and early 1990s. Yet the practice of the morning break seems so sensible now, as it had a number of benefits, including:

- Reducing the emails and phone calls because you can catch up with Pat Carruthers over the morning or afternoon break.
- Reducing the number of meetings because issues can be tossed around over a few breaks.
- As an enforced break it provides a time for reflection: Am I working on my long-term goals?
- It is a chance to catch up on some fluid intake.

Look at the current situation: Everybody has breaks at different times; you never know if someone is free to cover that brief point you want clarification on; your email inbox is full to overflowing, much of which is of no consequence; there are many meetings covering points that the morning break would have dealt with; few people have a rounded knowledge of the business; and worst of all, where is our sense of perspective? How many of us actually work in life-and-death jobs, such as surgeons?

One organization I have come across converted a large meeting room to a "Meet & Eat Room" for social events, morning and afternoon breaks, lunches, and so on. The executive management team members were also encouraged to use these facilities and take the opportunity to get to know their staff and other members of the organization in a less formal situation, where they could discuss anything from current work issues to social issues and events. Not surprisingly, this change led to a reduction in both staff turnover and grievances, and to greater team spirit.

SMT Lunches and the Monthly Team Breakfast

It is interesting that during the 1980s another valuable communication tool disappeared—the SMT luncheons. While it was no doubt a perk, much communication was exchanged that has now been replaced by hour-long meetings. I know which I would prefer.

Are we so much more efficient now? Are we having more enjoyment at work? I don't think so. Just walk around tomorrow and look at the stress permanently etched into everyone's forehead.

If a morning break is not appealing, and the executive luncheons are a nonstarter, how about a monthly onsite breakfast for all staff? I know of a private-sector organization that holds monthly onsite breakfasts for over 100 of the staff (McDonalds delivers the breakfast) and each department presents on a topic. There are awards, banter, and departments are mixed among the tables. Everybody attends from the CEO down.

Focusing on One's Goals During the Day

Very successful people have the uncanny ability to engage in periods of reflection during the day in which they question whether the activities they are on or about to start are really on the road toward their long-term goals. Many tasks we undertake have no real purpose. We are doing them because we are familiar with them, or we are doing them because we have to, which means that events are shaping your future for you, rather than your shaping your own future.

Imagine if you could take a couple of minutes three or four times a day to reflect on whether you are heading in the right direction. A brief look at your treasure map or a look at your four-quadrant to-do list would help you immensely.

The *One Minute Manager*[1] talks about one-minute goal setting, where you are encouraged to regularly review progress against your major goals.

Note

1. Spencer Johnson and Kenneth H. Blanchard, *The One Minute Manager*, Harper Collins, 1982.

CHAPTER 22

Reporting to the Board

If you have only a few minutes to skim over this chapter, this is what you should focus on:

- Costing of the monthly board papers (Exhibit 22.1)
- Tabling board papers electronically
- Do not give the board "management information"
- Set timely board meetings less frequently
- A3 (U.S. standard fanfold)-page board dashboard with summary financials (Exhibit 22.6)

The board reporting process needs to occur more efficiently and effectively for both the board and management. In one of the classic "catch 22" situations, boards complain about getting too much information too late, and management complain that too much of their time is tied up in the board reporting process. Boards obviously need to ascertain whether the management team is steering the ship correctly as well as the state of the crew and customers before they can relax and strategize about future initiatives.

Board papers can reach mammoth proportions, tying up vast amounts of management time in preparation. I have seen organizations where one week a month is written off by the senior management team on this process. The result of these excesses is often late board meetings with the papers being sent to the directors only a day or two before the meeting. The board meetings themselves can then be side tracked by the detail with the strategic overview inadequately addressed.

Selling the Change to the Board

First, we need to examine why the carefully thought-out recommendations that we make in our reports seldom catch the imagination of the CEO or board. Many managers, in Myers-Briggs terms, are commonly categorized as "thinking and judgmental" people. We thus assume that as logic is our foundation stone, so it is for others; therefore, we use logic to sell change. Yet the majority of sales are closed by selling through the emotional drivers of the buyer and not by logic. Think of your last car purchase!

In order to sell the changes recommended, we need to work with one of the influential members of the board:

- Show him the costs involved.
- Show him the proposed format changes, seeking his input and support.
- Absorb his suggested changes.
- Prepare a presentation to sell a new board reporting regime that meets with their approval and support.
- Ask the member to be the first to support your presentation after you have delivered it to the board.

The presentation should be reviewed by a public relations (PR) expert before you discuss it with the chosen board member. PR experts know all about selling change by the emotional drivers.

Costing Board Papers

Directors themselves are often guilty of requesting changes to board report formats or additional analysis without first finding out what the exercise will involve or giving staff guidelines as to how much detail is required.

What amount of senior management time is absorbed by the board reporting process? It is important to cost this out and report this to the board—they will be horrified. I estimate that for a company with 500 full-time employees the annual cost for preparing monthly board papers is between $300,000 and $500,000 (see Exhibit 22.1).

Scoping Information Requests

A request for information from the board often can take on a life of its own. A simple request soon becomes the Charge of the Light Brigade as the request is passed down the management tree. Often, the director who asked the question had visualized a 30-minute job and now Pat Carruthers embarks on a massive exercise. Upon its arrival at the board, a lengthy report costing over $20,000 is briefly passed over after a cursory glance.

EXHIBIT 22.1 Costing the Monthly Board Papers

500 FTE Organisation with Monthly Board Reporting				
SMT Team Accounts	Accounting Team	BHs	Direct Reports	SMT
Board papers				
Preparing board financial report from management reports	2 to 3			
Review reports before they go to board				1 to 1.5
Preparing business unit progress reports to the board				4 to 6
Review by CEO				0.5 to 1
Preparing one-off board reports		10 to 20	5 to 10	6 to 10
Working days per month	2 to 3	10 to 20	5 to 10	11.5 to 18.5
Average salary cost	$60,000	$45,000	$45,000	$150,000
Average productive weeks	42*	42*	42*	32**

Costings	Low	High
Average personnel cost	$200,000	$300,000
Consultants' reports	$100,000	$200,000
Estimated annual cost	$300,000	$500,000

*Take out holiday, public hols, sick leave, and training and you are left with 42 weeks.
**Senior management have a further 10 weeks a year stuck in meetings.

There needs to be more direct communication between the directors and the staff who are going to research the request. The board should issue a set of instructions about size and examples of their ideal paper. In addition, each paper request should come with a half-page form stating:

- Suggested length (e.g., fewer than 5 pages, 5–10, 10–20, 20–30, up to 50)
- Indication of time to be spent
- Maximum level of investment on paper
- Board member to liaise with during with the project
- Whether a draft should be seen before further work is invested on the report

Failing that, all directors should be asked by the chairperson to scope their request in terms of time to be spent on it and costs to be incurred.

EXHIBIT 22.2 Last Page of All Reports

Concur with findings:......................... (CFO)
Concur with findings:......................... (CEO)

"I would like to know about *xxxxxxx*. I would suggest we invest no more that *x* days and $*x,xxx* on this."

Avoiding Rewrites of Board Reports

Some organizations have made a major cultural change to report writing, committing the board, CEO, and senior management team (SMT) to avoid rewrites at all costs. The board no longer considers the quality of the board papers as a reflection of the CEO's performance. Organizations have learned to delegate and empower their staff so that the SMT and board papers are seldom rewritten. The papers are being tabled with the originators name on the top of the paper. Provided that the SMT agrees with the recommendations the CFO and CEO sign a caveat at the bottom of each report (see Exhibit 22.2).

The board understands that the report is not written in SMT-speak. Board members are encouraged to comment directly to the writer about strengths and areas for improvement with report writing. The writers are also in the dual role of both presenter and writer, where necessary. Thus the SMT will have a much more relaxed week leading up to the board meeting having largely delegated the report writing and the associated stress. The rewards include motivated and more competent staff and general managers being free to spend more time contributing to the bottom-line.

Tabling Board Papers Electronically

Many of the procedures that support a board meeting have changed little since Charles Dickens's time. Board members would receive large board papers that they had difficulty finding the time or inclination to read. In the 21st century we should be using technology in this important area.

The financial report should be made available as soon as it has been finished via a secure area of the organization's intranet. Other board papers likewise can then be read, as and when they are ready, instead of the final paper determining when all of the papers are sent to the board.

There are organizations that specialize in electronic board paper systems. These have led to paperless board meetings. The board members have a screen in front of them and the chairperson simply says, "Let's turn to page 50 and discuss the purchase of XYZ." Immediately the first page of the paper is on the screen, and board members can access the notes they made when they read the paper. These systems offer many features, including:

- Access to papers from anywhere, any time, as soon as they are available
- Intuitive and simple to use
- Notes easily attached to pages
- Instantaneous edits, page numbering, and so on
- Absolute security of board papers

Do Not Give the Board "Management Information"

It is far too common for the finance team to give the financial report for management to the board and then wonder why the board is asking stupid questions, such as "Why was $10,000 spent on uniforms this month?"

We need to present a more summarized reporting pack. My suggestion is as follows:

- Page 1, a dashboard on the key result indicators reporting progress in the organization's critical success factors. (We should not give them the balanced scorecard.)
- Page 2, detail on problems with the organization's critical success factors.
- Page 3, consolidated profit-and-loss statement (P/L) (showing categories that are greater than 10% of total).
- Page 4, balance sheet rounded to nearest 1, 10, 50 million (whatever is appropriate).
- Page 5, forecast of P/L (given once every quarter).
- Page 6, forecast cash flow (including high/low range at any point in time during the next six months).
- Page 7, status of major capital projects.

Follow the rules of summary headings and materiality as discussed in Chapter 11.

Training Session for All Writers of Board Papers

A logical step to lock in efficiency of board writing is to hold a training workshop. Staff who are likely to be involved in writing board reports are requested to attend by the CEO. The outcome would be that writers in the organization would know what the board wants; they will have practiced what makes a good board paper, and will have heard from one of the directors, who would discuss what he wants in a board paper. This workshop would be no more than half a day, and facilitated by an external expert covering best practice.

Set Timely Board Meetings Less Frequently

Look to restructure the operations of the board, setting bimonthly meetings, with the time saved by board members being invested elsewhere, such as:

- Sitting on subcommittees that are looking at improvements in key areas of the business
- Assisting the organization with specialist knowhow by presenting topics appropriate to management and staff
- Helping the company by opening doors to new markets

Since board meetings are to be strategic, there is no need for monthly meetings; enlightened companies now have bimonthly meetings, or at most eight board meetings a year.

Exhibit 22.3 shows an efficiency scale for holding board meetings after the month-end in question. The more time you have to complete a paper to the board, the longer it will take. Save everybody's time by limiting the time they can spend on these papers.

In some cases management is meeting with the board six weeks after month-end. There is, of course, another month-end in between, so they have to be careful to talk about the correct month. This situation is ridiculous.

Exhibit 22.4 provides some tips for preparing a board report.

EXHIBIT 22.3 Board Reporting Timescales Ranking

Within 10 working days of month-end (M/E)	Within 11–15 working days of M/E	Within 16–20 working days of M/E	Over 20 working days of M/E
Exceptional performance	Better practice benchmark	Adequate performance	Inferior performance!

EXHIBIT 22.4 Checklist for Preparing a Board Paper

1. If a board request is a major exercise, do you seek clarification of terms of reference, objectives, and time budget directly from a director to avoid misunderstanding through communication? (Do not become part of a Charge of the Light Brigade.)	☐ Yes	☐ No
2. Do you ask to see an example of good board papers and copy the style? (This can be used to defend the board paper structure against changes.)	☐ Yes	☐ No
3. Do you plan your report with a top–down approach? Remember, the board may not get past the first page. Obtain a copy of the *Guide to Managerial Communication: Effective Business Writing and Speaking*, 8th Edition, by Mary Munter (Prentice Hall, 2008).	☐ Yes	☐ No
4. Do you support all facts and provide a source for all statistics?	☐ Yes	☐ No
5. Have you attended a business communication course?	☐ Yes	☐ No
6. Do you spend about 20% of the time on quality assurance? This will have a big impact on the acceptance of the report.	☐ Yes	☐ No
7. Do you prepare a PowerPoint presentation at the same time and insert some of the slides into the text to help emphasize summary points?	☐ Yes	☐ No
8. Do directors give staff guidelines as to how much detail is required?	☐ Yes	☐ No
9. Are reports sold to the thought leader prior to the meeting?	☐ Yes	☐ No
10. Is there direct communication between the directors and the staff who write reports?	☐ Yes	☐ No
11. Do board members request a copy of the slides plus notes rather than a full scripted version?	☐ Yes	☐ No
12. Do you set tight board meetings (within ten working days of month-end)?	☐ Yes	☐ No
13. Are your key measures monitored?	☐ Yes	☐ No

A previous business partner was a member of a board where papers of over 200 pages were issued to the board 24 hours before the meeting! The more complex the meeting, the bigger the papers, the less time given to read them. The preparation of the papers was no different from those prepared in the time of Charles Dickens. Papers had to be numbered at the last minute, the last paper determined when the board would see all the papers, and the senior management team was spending a week to a month in this process, which diverted them from making money for the organization.

Using a Dashboard to Report Key Result Indicators to the Board

In most organizations that have boards, there is a major conflict as to what information is appropriate for the board. Since the board's role is clearly one of governance and not of management, it is inappropriate to be providing the board with key performance indicators (KPIs) unless the company is in trouble and the board needs to take a more active role. To me, KPIs are the very heart of management; used properly, many of them are monitored 24/7 or at least weekly. These are certainly not measures to be reported monthly or bimonthly to the board.

We need indicators of overall performance that need be reviewed only on a monthly or bimonthly basis. These measures need to tell the story of whether the organization is being steered in the right direction, at the right speed, and whether the customers are happy and the staff are happy and acting in a responsible and environmentally friendly way.

In Chapter 16, I call these measures *key result indicators (KRIs)*. These KRIs help the board focus on strategic rather than management issues.

A good dashboard with the KRIs going in the right direction will give confidence to the board members that management know what they are doing and the ship is being steered in the right direction. They can then concentrate on what they do best—focusing on the horizon for icebergs or looking for new ports to call and coaching the CEO as required. This is instead of the board parking itself on the bridge of the ship and thus getting in the way of the captain, who is trying to perform important day-to-day duties.

A dashboard should be a one-page display, such as the two examples in Exhibits 22.5 and 22.6. The commentary should be included on this page.

Here are the key features of these two dashboards:

- These are each one-page documents with brief commentary covering the issue and what is being done about it.
- The trend analysis goes back at least 12 months (some businesses need to go back a rolling 15 to 18 months). Remember, business has no respect for your year-end; it is merely an arbitrary point in time.
- You can use the title of the graph to explain what is happening. "Return on capital employed" becomes "Return on capital employed is increasing."
- You may need to maintain somewhere between 8 and 12 graphs and report the most relevant ones to the board.
- These KRI measures need to cover the six perspectives of a balanced scorecard in order to show whether the organization is being steered

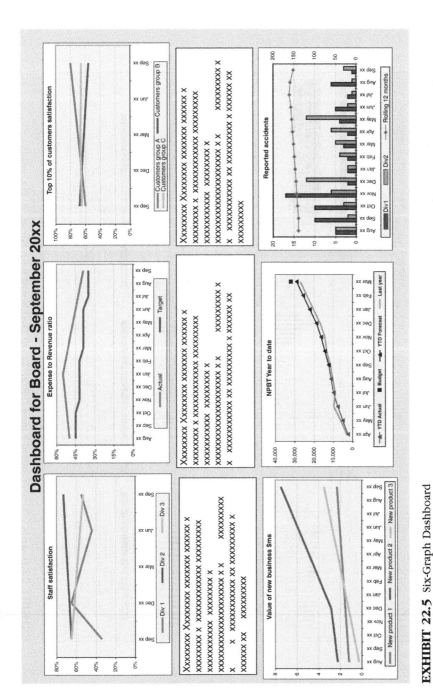

EXHIBIT 22.5 Six-Graph Dashboard

Source: David Parmenter, *Key Performance Indicators: Developing, Implementing, and Using Winning KPIs, 2nd Edition.* Copyright © 2010 by David Parmenter. Reprinted with the permission of John Wiley & Sons, Inc.

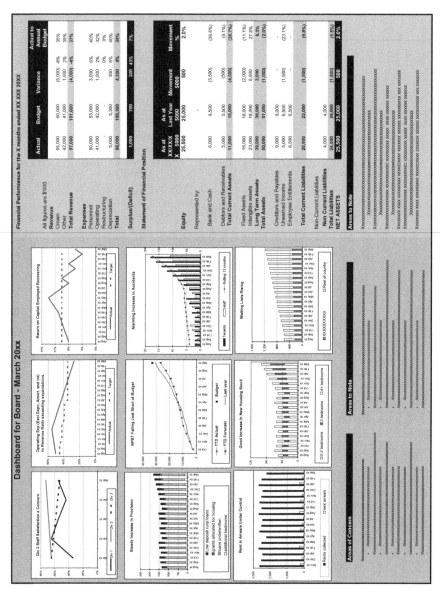

EXHIBIT 22.6 An A3 (U.S. Standard Fanfold)-Page Board Dashboard with Summary Financials

in the right direction at the right speed. (See www.davidparmenter.com/ webcasts and listen to presentations on KPIs and read the whitepapers/ articles.)

One accountant came to a workshop I was delivering where I demonstrated the dashboard. The organization where he worked had a board meeting the next day, and in the evening, based on previous board papers, he proceeded to prepare a dashboard showing trend information on the key result indicators. The board was very appreciative.

CHAPTER 23

Annual Planning Is Not Working

If you have only a few minutes to skim over this chapter, this is what you should focus on:

- Throw out your annual planning and associated monthly budget cycle
- If you keep an annual plan, do it in two weeks

This chapter is an extract from a white paper I deliver around the world that has revolutionized how many finance teams manage the annual planning process. Due to space constraints I have highlighted the main better practices that will also be carried over into quarterly rolling planning and forecasting. For further information it may be worth accessing this white paper.[1]

Throw Out Your Annual Planning and Associated Monthly Budget Cycle

The standard annual planning process takes too long, is not focused on performance drivers, is not linked to strategic outcomes or critical success factors, leads to dysfunctional behavior, builds silos, and is a major barrier to success. Organizations around the world are questioning the value of the traditional annual budgeting process.

Jeremy Hope has stated that not only is the budget process a time-consuming and costly exercise generating little value, it also and more importantly is a major limiting factor on how your organization can perform. He has many examples of how companies, following the philosophies he has expounded, have broken free and achieved success well beyond their expectations. Jeremy Hope has said:

"The same companies that vow to respond quickly to market shifts cling to budgeting—a process that slows the response to market developments until it's too late."[2]

Let us now look at why the budget process as it currently stands is counterintuitive. A survey performed a few years ago found that:

- The average time for a budget process was four months.
- Around 66% of CFOs stated their budget was influenced more by politics than strategy.
- Nearly 90% of CFOs were dissatisfied with their budget process.
- Around 60% of CFOs acknowledged that there was no link from the budgets to strategy.

I can assure you that this level of dissatisfaction is similarly found among boards, general managers, and budget holders. Another writer pointed out that "the incessant game playing extended the budget round and limited the need for us to stretch or seek breakthrough solutions." Does this sound familiar?

Here is the answer: Throw out the annual budgeting cycle—it takes too long and is not linked to strategy, strategic outcomes, or your organization's critical success factors.

By 2015, very few progressive organizations will do annual planning as we know it today.

I was presenting Beyond Budgeting and KPIs in Dunedin, New Zealand, and was introducing myself to the managing director of a large road contracting company. He politely informed me that he was mainly interested to hear the KPI part, as the beyond-budgeting session would be of little interest because they are already doing it. In fact the group has never had an annual planning process. He said if the group could predict when it was going to be sunny and when it was going to rain, annual planning would be useful.

The business encompasses concrete, transport (local and rural), fuel distribution, and road construction. The group has around 1,000 staff and a constant profit growth, the envy of many larger organizations.

The growth path has been either to grow from scratch, as in Wellington, or buy existing family companies. As the CEO says, expansion is often driven by opportunity. The group has 23 companies and in addition has a number of joint ventures.

The group monitors key ratios and has different divisions depending on size of operations so the companies can compare with each other. The ratios the group monitors include:

- Return per km (revenue and cost per km)
- Margin per liter
- Delivery cost per liter
- Concrete cost per cubic meter
- Cubic meter delivered by pay hour

Monthly reports are short and based on major cost categories (not at detail account code level). They do not waste time showing a consolidated result each month; this is done at year-end only.

There is much delegation to the branches, which manage staff levels with given limits, set staff salaries, and choose which suppliers to use (providing there is not a national contract in place).

All readers are encouraged to read *Beyond Budgeting* by Jeremy Hope and Robin Fraser.[2] It is also worthwhile to read Jeremy's articles and his other books. He has an uncanny ability to be always at least five years ahead of whatever better corporate accounting practices should be. His work also embraces remuneration and performance management.

The future for your organization is quarterly rolling planning, which has been covered. However, it will take upward of nine months to implement and your annual planning cycle may be just around the corner. This chapter will help develop better practices that will be carried over into quarterly rolling planning and forecasting.

If You Must Keep an Annual Plan, Do It in Two Weeks

There are many ways to improve the annual plan process, and if followed these can achieve a swift two-week process. These steps are covered in my whitepaper on the topic (see www.davidparementer.com).

Never Budget at Account Code Level

As accountants we have never needed to set budgets at account code level. We simply have done it because we did it last year, without thinking. Do you need a budget at account code level if you have good trend analysis

EXHIBIT 23.1 How a Planning Tool Consolidates Account Codes

Forecasting at Account Code Detail		Forecasting by Categories		Notes
Stationery	4,556			
Uniforms	3,325			
Cleaning	1,245			
Miscellaneous	7,654			No detail required
Consumables	2,367			
Tea & Coffee	2,134			
Kitchen Utensils	145			
	21,426	Consumables	21,400	
Salaries and Wages	25,567,678	Salaries and Wages	27,400,000	Budget Holder calculates S&W to the nearest $100 k
Taxes	2,488,888	Taxes	2,900,000	Taxes are automatically calculated by model
Temporary Staff	2,456,532	Other Employment Costs	4,200,000	This number is the balancing item
Contract Workers	2,342,345			
Students	234,567			
	33,090,010	Employment Costs	34,500,000	Budget holder estimates costs to the nearest $0.5 m

captured in the reporting tool? I think not. We therefore apply Pareto's 80/20 principle and establish a category heading that includes a number of general ledger codes.

Here are some rules I have developed:

- Limit the categories in a budget holder's budget to no more than 12—a budget line if the category is over 20% of total (e.g., show revenue line if revenue category is over 20% of total revenue). If category is between 15 and 20%, look at it and make an assessment.
- Map the general ledger account codes to the categories in the rule above—a planning tool can easily cope with this issue without the need for a revisit of the chart of accounts (see Exhibit 23.1).

- Accurate forecasting of personnel costs requires analysis of all current staff (their end date if known, their salary, the likely salary review and/ or bonus), all new staff (their starting salary, their likely start date).

Accurate Revenue Forecasting Will Involve Talking with the Right People at Your Main Customers

Many organizations liaise with customers to get demand forecasts only to find them as error prone as the ones done in-house. The reason is that you have asked the wrong people. You need to meet with the staff who are responsible for ordering your products/services.

> One participant told me that he decided to contact his major customers to help with demand forecasting. Naturally, he was holding discussions with the major customers' headquarter staff. On reflection he found it better but still error prone, so he went back to them: "How come these forecasts you supplied are so error prone?" "If you want accurate numbers, you need to speak to the procurement managers for our projects," was the reply. "Can we speak to them?" "Of course. Here are the contact details of the people you need to meet around the country."
>
> A series of meetings were then held around the country. He found that these managers could provide very accurate information and were even prepared to provide it in an electronic format. The sales forecast accuracy increased sevenfold due to focusing on getting the demand right for the main customers.

The lesson to learn is that when you want to forecast revenue more accurately by delving into your main customers' business, ask them, "Who should we speak to in order to get a better understanding of your likely demand for our products in the next three months?"

Bolt Down Your Strategy Beforehand

Leading organizations always have a strategic workshop out of town. The session is to look forward. Normally, board members will be involved because their strategic vision is a valuable asset. These retreats are run by an experienced external facilitator. The key strategic assumptions are thus set before the annual planning round starts; also the board members can set out what they are expecting to see.

Avoid Phasing the Annual Budget

The annual plan has never needed to be broken down into 12 monthly breaks before the year had started. We carry out this task because we did it last year. This predetermination of the monthly budgets has created a reporting yardstick that makes a mockery of reporting in your organization. Every month your managers write variance analysis that I could do just as well from my office in New Zealand. It is a timing difference.

Quarterly data for the next year is perfectly adequate. You want to have the ability to phase the monthly budgets closer to the event. This is explained in Chapter 24 on quarterly rolling planning.

Have Trend Graphs for Every Category Forecasted

Better quality forecasting can be achieved through analysis of the trends. There is no place to hide surplus funding when a budget holder is accountable for the past and future trends. This graph, shown in Exhibit 23.2, if made available for all the categories that budget holders are required to forecast, will increase forecast accuracy. Budget holders will want to ensure their forecasts make sense against the historic trend.

Budget Committee to Sit in a "Lock-up"

You need to persuade the budget committee that a three-day lockup is more efficient than the current scenario of months of discussion over an annual plan that will be wrong in any case. Sell the change to them: Do they want a long-drawn-out painful process or a short-and-sharp painful

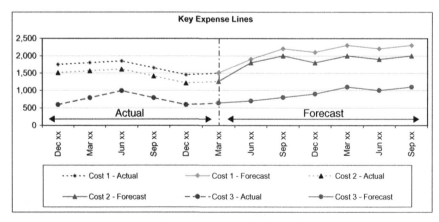

EXHIBIT 23.2 Forecast Expenditure Trend Graph

process? Explain that the lockup process will save the organization substantial sums. It will permit managers to focus on making money rather than talking about guessing the possibilities of next year, a process you will never get right.

During the lockup each budget holder has a set time to:

- Present a set number of slides (e.g., three standard ones and one of their own making).
- Discuss their financial and nonfinancial goals for the next year (e.g., including staff training and succession planning).
- Justify their annual plan forecast and explain any unusual trends evident from the trend graphs.
- Raise extra funding issues.
- Raise key dependency issues (e.g., the revenue forecast is contingent on the release to market and commissioning of products X and Y).

Notes

1. David Parmenter, *Timely Annual Planning Process in Two Weeks or Less*, 2010 www.davidparmenter.com.
2. Jeremy Hope and Robin Fraser, *Beyond Budgeting: How Managers Can Break Free from the Annual Performance Trap*, Harvard Business Review, April 2003.
3. Ibid.

CHAPTER 24

Quarterly Rolling Forecasting and Planning

If you have only a few minutes to skim over this chapter, this is what you should focus on:

- How the rolling forecast works for an organization (Exhibit 24.1)
- The nine-year-old's birthday cake analogy
- QRF is based on a planning application—not on Excel
- A fast, light touch
- Rolling forecasting is a quarterly and not a monthly process

This Chapter is an extract from a white paper[1] David Parmenter, *How to implement quarterly rolling forecasting (QRF) and quarterly rolling planning (QRP)—and get it right first time* 2010 www.davidparmenter.com, at some point it would be worth reading the other issues that I have had to omit due to space constraints.

The Quarterly Rolling Forecast

Quarterly rolling forecasting and planning is a process that will revolutionize any organization, whether public or private sector! It removes the four main barriers to success that an annual planning process erects: an annual funding regime where budget holders are encouraged to be dysfunctional, a reporting regime based around monthly targets that have no relevance, a three-month period where management is not particularly productive, and a remuneration system based on an annual target. The only thing certain about an annual target is that it is certainly wrong; it is either too soft or too hard for the operating conditions.

QRF normally go out six quarters, and this is a bottom-up process with the monthly forecasts for the next quarter being the reporting benchmarks.

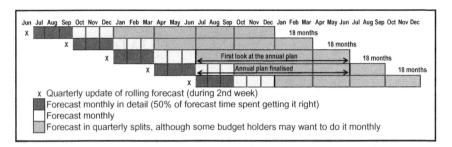

EXHIBIT 24.1 How the Rolling Forecast Works for an Organization with June Year-End

QRP takes QRF a step further—budget holders are now funded quarterly in advance from the approved forecast.

The quarterly forecasting process is where management sets out the required expenditure for the next 18 months. Each quarter, before approving these estimates, management sees the bigger picture six quarters out. All subsequent forecasts, while firming up the short-term numbers for the next three months, also update the annual forecast. Budget holders are encouraged to spend half the time on getting the details of the next three months right, as these will become targets, on agreement, and the rest of the time on the next five quarters. The quarterly forecast is never a cold start as they have reviewed the forthcoming quarter a number of times. Provided you have appropriate forecasting software, management can do their forecasts very quickly; one airline even does this in three days! The overall time spent on the four quarterly forecasts should be no more than five weeks.

Most organizations can use the cycle set out in Exhibit 24.1 if their year-end falls on a calendar quarter-end. Some organizations may wish to stagger the cycle, say May, August, November, and February. I will now explain how each forecast works using a June year-end organization.

December: We forecast out to the June year-end with monthly numbers and the remaining period in quarterly breaks. Budget holders obtain approval to spend January-to-March numbers subject to their forecast still going through the annual plan goalposts. The budget holders at the same time forecast next year's numbers for the first time. Budget holders are aware of the expected numbers and the first cut is reasonably close. This is a precursor to the annual plan. This forecast is stored in the forecasting and reporting tool. This update process should take only one elapsed week.

March: We reforecast to year-end and the first quarter of next year with monthly numbers, the remaining period in quarterly breaks. Budget holders obtain approval to spend April-to-June numbers. The budget holders at the same time revisit the December forecast (the last forecast)

of next year's numbers and fine-tune them for the annual plan. Budget holders know that they will not be getting an annual lump-sum funding for their annual plan. The number they supply for the annual plan is guidance only.

For the annual plan, budget holders will be forecasting their expense codes using an annual number and in quarterly lots, for the significant accounts such as personnel costs. Management review the annual plan for next year and ensure all numbers are broken down into quarterly lots and this is stored in a new field in the forecasting and reporting tool, called "March X4 forecast." This is the second look at 20X3/X4, so the managers have a better understanding. On an ongoing basis you would need only a two-week period to complete this process.

June: We can reforecast the end-of-June numbers and we should be able to eliminate the frantic activity that is normally associated with the *spend-it-or-lose it* mentality. Budget holders are now also required to forecast the first six months of next year monthly and then on to Dec 20X4 (six months into 20X4/X5) in quarterly numbers. Budget holders obtain approval to spend July-to-September numbers provided their forecast once again passes through the annual goalposts. This is stored in a new field in the forecasting and reporting tool, called "June X4 forecast." This update process should take only one elapsed week.

September: We reforecast the next six months in monthly numbers, and quarterly to March 20X5 the first nine months of 20X4/X5. Budget holders obtain approval to spend October-to-December numbers. This is stored in a new field in the forecasting and reporting tool, called "September X4 forecast." This update process should take only one elapsed week.

You will find that the four cycles take about five weeks, once management is fully conversant with the new forecasting system and processes.

The key points of a rolling forecast are:

- Budget holders provide an annual plan through the bottom-up quarterly rolling forecasting regime but are not assigned those funds. This is done on a quarter-by-quarter funding basis.
- Monthly reporting is more meaningful as it measures performance against the most recent forecast and not a monthly split of the original annual plan.
- Each subsequent forecast is still expected to put the ball through the posts at the end of the field (year-end annual plan), the difference being that the planning also looks at the next game at the same time as the budget holders are always looking forward 18 months).
- Forecasting is carried out on an appropriate planning tool that can handle a bottom-up forecast once a quarter. Excel is not, and never has been, an appropriate tool for a key company system.

QRF Quickly Creates the Annual Plan Goalposts

The QRF process will allow you to have a quick annual planning process. Budget holders will become more experienced at forecasting (they are doing it four times a year). They have already looked at the next year a number of times, and realize that there is no use demanding more than they need as the real funding is sorted out on a quarter-by-quarter basis where slush funds cannot be hidden.

Organizations that have truly adopted the beyond-budgeting principles will also throw out the annual plan target. Why should one view of year-end be any better than a subsequent, more current view? The March quarter forecast is no longer called the *annual plan*, but simply the *March quarter forecast*. The board will want to monitor the extent of forecast creep and this can be easily shown in a graph.

QRP Creates a Quarter-by-Quarter Funding Mechanism

The key is to fund budget holders on a rolling quarter-by-quarter basis. In this process the management team asks, "Yes, we know you need $1 million, and we can fund it, but how much do you need in the next three months?" At first, the budget holder will reply, "I need $250,000 this quarter." The management team replies, "Pat, how is this? Your last five quarterly expenditures have ranged between $180,000 and $225,000. Pat, you are two team members short and your recruiting is not yet underway— be realistic—you will only need $225,000, tops."

It will come as no surprise that when a budget holder is funded only three months ahead the funding estimates are much more precise and there is nowhere to hide those slush funds.

Some organizations are recognizing the folly of giving a budget holder the right to spend an annual sum and at the same time saying, "If you get it wrong, there will be no more money." By forcing budget holders to second-guess their needs in this inflexible regime you enforce a defensive behavior—a stockpiling mentality. In other words, you guarantee dysfunctional behavior from day one! The quarterly rolling planning process thus highlights "free funds" that can be reallocated for new projects earlier on in the financial year.

The released funds can provide for new initiatives that the budget holder could not have anticipated at the time of the budget round. This will get around the common budget holder's dilemma: "We cannot undertake that initiative, though we should, as I did not include it in my budget." In the new regime, the budget holder would say, "I will put it in my next update and if funds are available I am sure I will get the go-ahead."

This more flexible environment, as long as it is communicated clearly and frequently to budget holders, will have good buy-in. The logic of quarterly rolling funding can be shown in an analogy.

> The quarterly rolling funding process has a lot in common with the cutting of a nine-year-old's birthday cake. A clever parent says to Johnny, "Here is the first slice. If you finish that slice and want more, I will give you a second slice. Instead, what we do in the annual planning process is divide the cake up and apportion all of it to the budget holders. Like nine-year-olds, budget holders lick the edges of their cake so that even if *they* do not need all of it, *no one else* can have it. Why not, like the clever parent, give the managers what they need for the first three months, and then say, "What do you need for the next three months?," and so on. Each time, we can apportion the amount that is appropriate for the conditions at that time.

QRF Is Based on a Planning Application—Not on Excel

Forecasting requires a good, robust tool, not an error-prone spreadsheet built by some innovative accountant that no one can understand any more. The main hurdle is the finance team's reluctance to divorce itself from Excel. It has been a long and comfortable marriage albeit one that has limited the finance team's performance.

Acquiring a planning tool is the first main step forward, and one that needs to be pursued not only for the organization but also for the finance team members' future careers. It soon will be a prerequisite to have planning tool experience, and conversely, career limiting to be an Excel guru.

QRF Should Be Based on the Key Drivers

A forecasting tool needs to be based on the key drivers and thus able to quickly inform management should there be a major change in any of these drivers. In-depth interviews with the senior management team (SMT) coupled with some brainstorming will quickly identify the main drivers, which may include:

- What if we contract? (e.g., stop production of one line, sell a business)
- What if we grow through acquisition?
- What if we lose a major customer?
- What if there is a major change to key economic indicators? (e.g., interest rates, inflation)

7 day quarterly rolling forecasting/planning process

Process =>	Prior work: Forecast pre-work	Present forecast workshop	1	2	3	4	5	Week end	6	7
(header)			Budget holders prepare and load their forecast		First look at numbers	Submissions by BHs to management board (for more funding or to justify unrealistic forecast)			Re-run of forecast and give presentation to CEO	Final alterations and finishing off documentation
Activities by team =>										
Strategic Planning	Attend					Review to ensure linkage to strategic plan–advise if any discrepancies			Attend	
SMT	Set assumptions				First look at numbers	Review submissions etc, full time			Hear presentation and give instructions for final changes	
Finance Team	Prepare system, the presentation, calculate known costs overheads, personnel costs etc	Give presentation to BHs	Help BHs with forecast (extended team)		Quality checks	Further QC and prepare presentation			Present forecast presentation	Finish off documentation
BHs		Attend	Prepare forecast			Present forecast and business plan where there is a major change			Present to SMT if required	Document and file all calculations

EXHIBIT 24.2 Timeline for the First Three Quarterly Forecasts within a Financial Year

Source: David Parmenter, *Pareto's 80/20 Rule for Corporate Accountants.* Copyright ©2007 by John Wiley & Sons. Reprinted with permission of John Wiley & Sons.

10 day Annual Planning Process (4th quarter QRP)

	Prior work		1	2	3	4	5	W/E 6	7	8	9	10
Process =>	Budget prework	Present budget workshop	Budget: revisit of previous quarters forecast (first look at year end)			First look at numbers	rework some budgets	Submissions by BHs to management board			Compilation of final draft budget for Management Board approval	Final alterations and finishing off documentation
Activities =>												
Strategic Planning		Attend					Reviewing to ensure linkage to Plan, and advising of any discrepancies				Attend	
SMT	Set assumptions					First look at numbers		Review submissions etc, full time			Hear presentation and give instructions for final changes	
Finance team	Prepare system, the presentation, overheads, personnel costs, travel standard costs etc	Give presentation to BHs	Help BHs with budget plans (extended team)			QA	Help BHs	Further QA			Complete preparation and present AP presentation	
BHs		Attend	Prepare budget				Attend	Present to SMT when called			Document and file all calculations	

EXHIBIT 24.3 Timeline for the Fourth-Quarter Forecast (which Generates the Annual Plan)

Source: David Parmenter, *Pareto's 80/20 Rule for Corporate Accountants*. Copyright ©2007 by John Wiley & Sons. Reprinted with permission of John Wiley & Sons.

- What if a major overseas competitor sets up in our region?
- What are the plant capacity ramifications from gaining a large increase in business? (e.g., shut down a major local competitor)

If you have second-guessed the likely SMT requests and have designed the model around them, you will have a planning tool that can quickly model the implications of such changes robustly.

QRF Has a Fast, Light Touch (Completed in One Week)

QRFs should be performed within five working days (see Exhibit 24.2). The one exception will be that the fourth quarter forecast, which creates the annual plan (see Exhibit 24.3), will have one extra week for additional negotiations and quality assurance. QRFs can be quick because:

- Consolidation is instantaneous with a planning tool.
- Since you have run a workshop on budget preparation with budget holders, they know what to do.
- The model is based on Pareto's 80/20 principle.
- Training has been given to budget holders so they can enter directly into the planning tool.
- The quarterly repetition aids efficiency.
- Forecasting is at a high level, at category, not account code level (e.g., only 12 to 15 categories per budget holder).
- Repeat costs can all be standardized for the whole year (e.g., New York-to-London return flight: US$2,500, overnight in London: US$250).

Exhibits 24.2 and 24.3 show that this process will take only seven working days for three of the four quarters and up to ten working days for the quarter where you are setting the annual plan goalposts.

It is important for the CEO to support a quick timeframe and make it clear to all budget holders that late forecasting submissions, from now on, will be a career limiting activity.

Notes

1. David Parmenter, *How to implement quarterly rolling forecasting and quarterly rolling planning—and get it right first time*, 2010 www.davidparmenter.com.

CHAPTER 25

CEO Feedback

If you have only a few minutes to skim over this chapter, this is what you should focus on:

- Appendix H for a template of a CEO 360-degree feedback survey
- Lessons on running a CEO 360-degree feedback

Managing One's Ego

Having a big ego is the downfall of many CEOs. To get to the top one has to have an unfailing belief in oneself. This, however, is so often a double-edged sword. I strongly recommend the following:

- Regular mentorship sessions.
- 360-degree feedback, where you keep the report in your desk. (See Appendix H for a template survey.)
- Regular staff opinion surveys. This is covered in Chapter 27 where the importance of running a staff survey three or four times a year is pointed out. A valid survey can be achieved through a small statistical sample and its findings, when communicated to all staff, will be endorsed by them.

Measuring Your Performance as a CEO

Why is it that as CEO you are getting little or no balanced performance feedback? It is a situation you need to manage rather than leave to the board, which can mismanage this process easily. As a modern CEO you should get a 360-degree feedback done annually as set out in Exhibit 25.1. See Appendix H for a template for a CEO 360-degree feedback survey.

EXHIBIT 25.1 CEO 360-Degree Feedback Process

Benefits of Balanced Feedback on Your Performance

There are a number of benefits you can receive when getting feedback on your performance. They include:

- The board can see a more rounded picture of performance. The board has limited opportunity to observe, usually seeing the CEO only at board or committee meetings. Some members may not realize the scope of the CEO's job or may be tempted to judge performance on the basis of popularity instead of on actual performance.
- It improves communication between board and CEO on performance feedback. The lack of balanced performance feedback can result in serious miscommunication.

Performance reviews may be routine at lower levels of corporations, but they are still a rarity at the top. Most CEOs are far more willing to submit to an annual physical examination than a rigorous performance appraisal. And when boards do conduct reviews, they often focus on executive pay rather than issues like leadership and effectiveness.

Wall Street Journal, April 4, 1998

One CEO commenting on his dismissal said: "It came as a total surprise. Not a single board member felt comfortable enough to tell me I was in trouble." He went on to say "CEOs really want the feedback about how we're doing and what we can be doing to improve what's going on."[1]

- It minimizes opportunity for conflict. Personality clashes between individual board members and the CEO can also be a cause of concern. Working together on a comprehensive performance review process with the CEO and backing it up with a clear policy is the best way to avoid such problems.
- It provides the company with better legal protection. With the growing emphasis on employee rights legislation and the vulnerability of boards of directors to lawsuits, a formal appraisal on file protects both the board and the CEO in the event of disputes. The formal appraisal provides a consistent work record over time and helps to avoid contentious situations.

Some of the Subjective Areas You May Wish to Cover in the 360-Degree Process

Each 360-degree feedback process is tailored to fit the organization. Questions need to be designed to assess the performance in the subjective areas to be reviewed. Some of the subjective areas you may wish to cover in the CEO's 360-degree process are:

- Internal leadership
- Leadership of external parties (e.g., active participation in trade association, etc.)
- Vision and the ability to sell it to the staff
- Performance measurement within the organization
- Team building and the ability to inspire
- Human resources management
- Customer satisfaction
- Innovation
- Policy development
- Strategic management—giving adequate attention to planning and mapping out the future of the organization
- Financial management
- Professional development of CEO
- Effectiveness of the CEO to delegate
- Communication within the company
- Board relations (including communication with the board—formal and informal)
- Union relations

Lessons on Running a CEO 360-Degree Feedback

Lesson 1: Make It Clear Who Owns the 360-Degree Report   This is a question of ownership. Who owns the 360-degree report, the CEO or the board? If the results are for the CEO only, then the selection of respondents is likely to be more balanced. However, if the results are to be used for appraisal or salary reviews, then the selection of respondents may be biased toward receiving positive feedback. Worst of all, if the board selects the respondents, it is likely to create conflict between the CEO and the board.

> I came across a CEO where the chairman of the board had undertaken a disorganized 360-degree feedback process. The CEO was incensed with the feedback, feeling it did not fully recognize his contribution, and it impaired the working relationship for months. It is important to be proactive and insist on a process that gives you balanced feedback.

Lesson 2: Divorce the 360-Degree Feedback from the Remuneration Review   The 360-degree feedback is best left as a performance development tool and hence the report should be owned by the CEO. This does not preclude using the 360 in the salary review, as the CEO can table the report if she wishes.

Lesson 3: Annual Performance Feedback Is Insufficient   It is common practice for managers and staff to get two or three formal performance feedback reports a year. This helps provide timely information and helps assess whether the person is making progress in the right direction. We suggest that the CEO have a 360-degree feedback process performed twice a year. Thus it is important that the process be efficient, cost effective, and focused around Pareto's 80/20.

Lesson 4: Two Vital Questions in Your 360-Degree Feedback   The following two questions should be asked: (1) What are three things that the CEO is doing well? and (2) What are three things that the CEO can improve upon?

Note

1. *Wall Street Journal,* April 27, 1998.

CHAPTER 26

Implement Reporting That Works

If you have only a few minutes to skim over this chapter, this is what you should focus on:

- Yesterday's sales report (Exhibit 26.1)
- Weekly sales to key customers (Exhibit 26.2)
- Weekly overdue-projects report (Exhibit 26.3)
- Reporting a business unit's performance (Exhibit 26.7)
- Current projects-in-progress report (Exhibit 26.8)
- Monthly progress-against-strategy report (Exhibit 26.10)
- The A3 (U.S. standard fanfold) investment proposal (Exhibit 26.12)

Daily/Weekly Reporting

For leading organizations decision information is based on daily/weekly information on progress within the critical success factors (CSFs). In these organizations the month-end has become less important and consequently the management papers are reduced to 15 pages or less.

In one company the senior management team (SMT) has a "Nine O'clock News Report" every morning, followed by further weekly information. At the monthly management meeting even the human resources manager is able to enter the sweepstakes guessing the month-end result. Talking about the monthly numbers is a small part of the meeting, which happens in the first week of the following month.

Leading corporate accountants are now providing the CEO and management with timely information so the management team intuitively knows whether the month is a good or bad one during that month, enabling them to do something about it.

As CEO you will need your corporate accountants to provide the following daily and weekly reporting:

- Yesterday's sales reported by 9:00 A.M. the following day.
- Transactions with key customers reported on a weekly basis.
- Weekly reporting on late projects and late reports.
- Weekly information of key direct costs.
- Key performance indicators (KPIs) reported daily/weekly (see Chapter 16).

Yesterday's Sales Report

If the CEO and SMT receive a report on the daily sales, they will better understand how the organization is performing. Exhibit 26.1 shows the sort of detail they will be interested in.

Weekly Key Customer's Sales

In a similar vein, it is important for the SMT to monitor how products are being purchased by the key customers. This is especially important after a launch of a new product, or after your competitors launch a new competing product. Exhibit 26.2 shows the sort of detail that will hold most interest.

Weekly Reporting on Late Projects and Late Reports

Many managers are innovative people who love to get on with a project but often fail to tie up the loose ends or finish it. I am always encountering projects that are stuck in limbo and so will be of value to the organization only when someone refocuses and completes them. Set out in Exhibits 26.3 and 26.4 are two report formats that I believe should be tabled weekly to the senior and middle management to enable them to focus on completion. Exhibit 26.3 has a dual focus, on the project manager and the project. Exhibit 26.4 is a shame-and-name list. It focuses management on those reports that are well past their deadline. The version number helps management realize the cost of revisions. The manager's in-tray column focuses on the guilty manager and helps encourage action.

Month-End Reporting

To complement the reporting during the month, a CEO needs swift month-end reporting, to confirm the numbers and limit the time wasted preparing them. A 21st-century month-end reporting regime would include:

- A flash report of the month's result within ±10% of final result by 5:00 P.M. first working day

- Monthly report pack available by at least the third working day
- Interesting monthly information

Issue a "Flash Report" at the End of Day One

Issue a flash report on the profit-and-loss bottom-line to the CEO stating a level of accuracy of say ±10%. Immediately inform the CEO of any real

Daily Sales Report

	Yesterday's Sales	Daily Average Last 90 Days	Variance	>$100k & 10%
Sales by Key Product				
Product 1	450	400	50	
Product 2	440	560	(120)	✗
Product 3	375	425	(50)	
Other products	185	175	10	
Total Sales	1,450	1,560		✗
Sale by Branch				
Branch 1	580	700	(120)	✗
Branch 2	440	420	20	
Branch 3	220	210	10	
Branch 4	180	160	20	
Other branches	30	70	(40)	
Total Sales	1,450	1,560		✗
Sale by Customer Type				
Platinium customers	710	600	110	✓
Gold customers	480	440	40	
Silver customers	380	410	(30)	
Bronze customers	280	510	(230)	✗
Total Sales	1,450	1,560	(110)	✗

($000s)

 EXHIBIT 26.1 Yesterday's Sales Report

Weekly Sales with Key Customers

	$000s		
	Last Week's Sales	Weekly Ave Last 180 days	Variance
Customer #1			
Product 1	450	400	50
Product 2	400	460	(60)
Product 3	340	310	30
Product 4	375	425	(50)
Other products	185	105	80 ✓
Total Revenue	1,750	1,700	50
			0
Customer #2			0
Product 1	340	480	(140) ✗
Product 2	380	450	(70)
Product 3	120	190	(70)
Product 4	180	190	(10)
Other products	180	220	(40)
Total Revenue	1,200	1,500	(300) ✗
			0
Customer #3			0
Product 1	220	160	60
Product 2	190	140	50
Product 3	160	120	40
Product 4	190	150	40
Other products	1,140	1,130	10
Total Revenue	1,500	1,300	200 ✓

Graph of Customer #2 - Product 1

Wk - 12 Wk - 11 Wk - 10 Wk - 9 Wk - 8 Wk - 7 Wk - 6 Wk - 5 Wk - 4 Wk - 3 Wk - 2 Wk - 1 Current Week

▨ Customer #2 purchases of product 1

- - - Weekly average (based on last 6 months weekly average)

Areas to note:
1. Xxxxxxxxxxxxxxxxxxxxxxxxxxxxxxxxxxxxxxxxxxxxxx
xxxxxxxxxxxxxxxxxxxxxxxxxxxxxxxxxxxxxxxxxxxxxxxxxxxxxxxxxxxxxxxxxxxxxxxxxxx xxxxxxxxxxxxxxxx xxxxxxxxx
xxxxxxx xxxxxxxxxxxxx xxxxxxxxxxxxxxxxxxxxxxxxxxxxxxxxxxx
2. Xxxxxxxxxxxxxxxxxxxxxxxxxxxxxxxxxxxxxxxxxxxxxx
xxxxxxxxxxxxxxxxxxxxxxxxxxxxxxxxxxxxxxxxxxxxxxxxxxxxxxxxxxxxxxxxxxxxxxxxxxx xxxxxxxxxxxxxxxx xxxxxxxxx
xxxxxxx xxxxxxxxxxxxx xxxxxxxxxxxxxxxxxxxxxxxxxxxxxxxxxxx
3. Xxxxxxxxxxxxxxxxxxxxxxxxxxxxxxxxxxxxxxxxxxxxxx
xxxxxxxxxxxxxxxxxxxxxxxxxxxxxxxxxxxxxxxxxxxxxxxxxxxxxxxxxxxxxxxxxxxxxxxxxxx xxxxxxxxxxxxxxxx xxxxxxxxx
xxxxxxx xxxxxxxxxxxxx xxxxxxxxxxxxxxxxxxxxxxxxxxxxxxxxxxx
4. Xxxxxxxxxxxxxxxxxxxxxxxxxxxxxxxxxxxxxxxxxxxxxx
xxxxxxxxxxxxxxxxxxxxxxxxxxxxxxxxxxxxxxxxxxxxxxxxxxxxxxxxxxxxxxxxxxxxxxxxxxx xxxxxxxxxxxxxxxx xxxxxxxxx
xxxxxxx xxxxxxxxxxxxx xxxxxxxxxxxxxxxxxxxxxxxxxxxxxxxxxxx

 EXHIBIT 26.2 Weekly Sales to Key Customers

EXHIBIT 26.3 Weekly Overdue-Projects Report

Manager	Number of Projects Currently Outstanding	Number of Outstanding Projects Last Month	Total Projects Currently Being Managed
Kim Bush	7	0	8
Pat Carruthers	5	3	10
Robin Smith	3	3	12
XXXXXXX	3	2	5

List of Major Projects That Are Past Their Deadline	Original Deadline	Project Manager (Sponsor)	Risk of Noncompletion
xxxxxxxxxxxx	1/06/0X	AB (YZ)	(neutral face)
Annual report	1/07/0X	DE (RS)	(happy face)
Strategic plan publication	1/08/0X	AB (RS)	(sad face)
Balanced scorecard report	1/09/0X	DE (YZ)	(happy face)
Outcomes 2010	1/12/0X	AB (YZ)	(sad face)

Will be completed within five working days	Will be completed this month	Will be completed this quarter	Risk of noncompletion at year-end
(happy face)	(neutral face)	(neutral face)	(sad face)

problems with the flash report numbers within the next couple of days. You may find that a flash report is not required if you can report within three working days. See Exhibit 26.5 for an example of a flash report.

It is important not to provide too many lines as you may find yourself with another variance report on your hands if you are unlucky enough to have a CEO who fails to look at the big picture. It is important not to give too many numbers as you will set up another round of variance reporting. Remember to state your degree of accuracy (e.g., ±5%, ±10%). Never attempt a flash report until the accounts payable, accounts receivable, and accruals cutoffs have been successfully moved back to the last working

EXHIBIT 26.4 Weekly List of Overdue Reports

Past Deadline Reports Week Beginning 20/xx/xx				
Report Title	Date: First Draft	Manager's In = Tray	Version Number	Original Deadline
Annual Report	1/2/xx	DP	>10	15/9/xx
20xx/20x1 annual budget	15/9/xx	DP	>20	15/3/xx
xxxxxxxxxxxxxxxxxx	1/9/xx	DP	>10	30/7/xx
xxxxxxxxxxxxxxxxxx	30/8/xx	DP	5	15/4/xx
xxxxxxxxxxxxxxxxxxxxxxxxx	15/2/xx	DP	4	30/1/xx
xxxxxxxxxxxxxxxxxx	30/3/xx	PC	>10	1/2/xx
xxxxxxxxxxxxxxxxxxxxxxxx	1/8/xx	PC	1	15/5/xx
xxxxxxxxxxxxxxxxxxxxx	15/2/xx	PC	1	30/1/xx
xxxxxxxxxxxxxxxx	1/9/xx	PC	3	1/2/xx
xxxxxxxxxxxxxxxx	15/3/xx	PC	7	1/3/xx
xxxxxxxxxxxxxxxxxxxx	1/9/xx	MM	7	30/7/xx
xxxxxxxxxxxxxxxxxx	15/3/xx	MM	1	15/1/xx

Actions to Be Taken:

Xxxxxxxxxxxxxxxxxxxx xxxxxxxxxxxxxxxxxxxx xxxxxxxxxxxxxxxxxxxx xxxxxxxxxxxxxxxx

Xxxxxxxxxx xxxxxxxxx xxxxxxxx xxxxxxxxx xxxxxxxxxxx xxxxxxxx xxxxxxxxx xxxxxx

Xxxxxxxxxxxxxxxxxxxx xxxxxxxxxxxxxxxxxxxx xxxxxxxxxxxxxxxxxxxx xxxxxxxxxxxxxxxx

Xxxxxxxxxx xxxxxxxxx xxxxxxxx xxxxxxxxx xxxxxxxxxxx xxxxxxxx xxxxxxxxx xxxxxx

Xxxxxxxxxxxxxxxxxxxx xxxxxxxxxxxxxxxxxxxx xxxxxxxxxxxxxxxxxxxx xxxxxxxxxxxxxxxx

Xxxxxxxxxx xxxxxxxxx xxxxxxxx xxxxxxxxx xxxxxxxxxxx xxxxxxxx xxxxxxxxx xxxxxx

xxxxxxxxx xxxxxxxxxx xxxxxxxxxxx xxxxxxx xxxxxxxxx xxxxxxx

EXHIBIT 26.5 Flash Report Given to CEO During First Working Day

Flash Report for the Month Ending 31 December 20xx				
	This Month $000s			
	Actual	Target	Variance	
Revenue				
Revenue 1	5,550	5,650	(100)	⇔
Revenue 2	3,550	3,450	100	⇔
Revenue 3	2,450	2,200	250	√
Other revenue	2,250	2,350	(100)	⇔
Total Revenue	13,800	13,650	(100)	⇔

EXHIBIT 26.5 (Continued)

Flash Report for the Month Ending 31 December 20xx				
	This Month $000s			
	Actual	Target	Variance	
Less: Cost of sales	(11,500)	(11,280)	(220)	⇔
Gross Profit	2,300	2,370	(320)	×
Expenses				
Expense 1	1,280	1,260	(20)	
Expense 2	340	320	(20)	
Expense 3	220	200	(20)	
Expense 4	180	160	(20)	
Other expenses	170	110	(60)	
Total Expenses	1,790	1,950	160	⇔
Surplus/(Deficit)	510	420	90	

Areas to Note
1. xxxxxxxxx xxxxxxx xxx Xxxxxxxxx xxxxx xxxxx xxxxxxxxx xxxxxxxxxxxx xxxxxxx xxxxxxxxxxxxxxxxxxxxxxxxxxxxxxxxxxxxxxxxxxxxxxxxxxxx xxxxxxxxxxxxxx xxxxxxxxx xxxxxxx xxxxxxxxxxxx xxxxxxxxxxxxxxxxxxxxxxxxxxxxxxxxxxx
2. Xxxxxxxxxxxxxxxxxxxxxxxxxxxxxxxxxxxxxxxxxxx xxxxxxxxxxxxxxxxxxxxxxxxxxxxxxxxxxxx xxxxxxxxxxxxxxxxxxxxxxxxxxxxxxxxxxxxx xxxxxxxxxxxxx xxxxxxxx xxxxxxx xxxxxxxxxxx xxxxxxxxxxxxxxxxxxxxxxxxxxxxxxxx
3. Xxxxxxxxxxxxxxxxxxxxxxxxxxxxxxxxxxxxxxxxxxx xxxxxxxxxxxxxxxxxxxxxxxxxxxxxxxxxxxx xxxxxxxxxxxxxxxxxxxxxxxxxxxxxxxxxxxxx xxxxxxxxxxxxx xxxxxxxx xxxxxxx xxxxxxxxxxx xxxxxxxxxxxxxxxxxxxxxxxxxxxxxxxx
4. Xxxxxxxxxxxxxxxxxxxxxxxxxxxxxxxxxxxxxxxxxxx xxxxxxxxxxxxxxxxxxxxxxxxxxxxxxxxxxxx xxxxxxxxxxxxxxxxxxxxxxxxxxxxxxxxxxxxx xxxxxxxxxxxxx xxxxxxxx xxxxxxx xxxxxxxxxxx xxxxxxxxxxxxxxxxxxxxxxxxxxxxxxxx

day of the month. Otherwise, you will be using the accruals to change final numbers so they closely match your flash numbers! That is a practice I would not recommend.

Monthly Report Pack Available by at Least the Third Working Day

I go around the world helping accounting teams report to the senior management team within three working days from month-end. This is the beginning of a journey to virtual reporting whereby CFOs can tell their CEOs how much profit has been made at any time during the month. The methodology for this is outlined in a whitepaper[1] and through webcasts

EXHIBIT 26.6 Speed of Reporting

	Day One reporting	2 to 3 days	4 to 5 days	Over 5 days
Rating	Exceptional performance	Better practice benchmark	Adequate performance	Inferior performance and career limiting!!

that can be accessed via www.davidparmenter.com. A ranking guide for where your organization fits is shown in Exhibit 26.6.

Here are some facts about month-end reporting:

- The costs involved in preparing are huge, far outweighing the benefits.
- Month-end locks the accounting team into being a processing center.
- It does not create much value, telling management that the horse has bolted after the event.
- Month-end reporting is part of the trifecta of lost opportunities (the other two are budgeting and annual reporting).
- Late month-end reporting can be career limiting as it is being achieved more and more quickly and some organizations are even doing it in one day (day one reporting).
- It diverts the finance team away from what you and the CEO want—more advisory time from the finance team.

Monthly Reports That Are Worth Reading

I also go around the world helping accounting teams prepare decision-based reports for the senior management team. These reports are set out in a whitepaper[2] and some are covered in webcasts that can be accessed via www.davidparmenter.com. I have included some examples in this chapter.

What is good monthly reporting? Good reporting should:

- Not be delayed for detail—three working days is better practice, five working days is a minimum requirement.
- Be consistent—between months, judgment calls, maintain format.
- Be a true and fair view and error free.
- Be concise—fewer than nine pages.
- Have a separate reporting line only if category is over 10% of total revenue or expenditure, whichever is relevant. Thus the report will have only 10 to 15 lines.
- Have an icon system to highlight major variances.
- Be a merging of numbers, graphs, and comments on the one page, thus doing away with the essay in front of the financial statements!

- Have graphs that say something—a title that describes the main issue, a trend going back at least 15 months (neither your operations nor your graphs should start at the beginning of the year!).

When finished, make them available to the entire finance team!

Reporting a Business Unit's Performance

Exhibit 26.7 is an example of business unit's report. The profit and loss (P&L) is summarized in 10 to 15 lines. Two graphs are shown under the

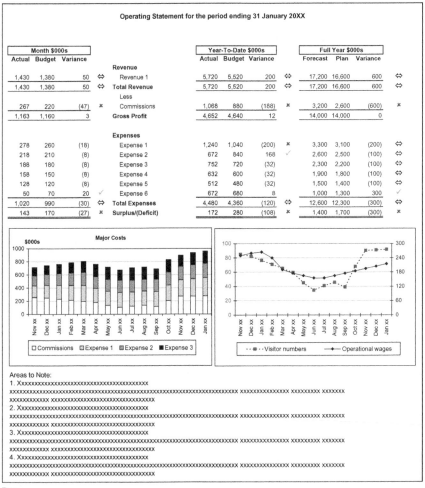

Operating Statement for the period ending 31 January 20XX

Month $000s					Year-To-Date $000s				Full Year $000s			
Actual	Budget	Variance			Actual	Budget	Variance		Forecast	Plan	Variance	
				Revenue								
1,430	1,380	50	⇔	Revenue 1	5,720	5,520	200	⇔	17,200	16,600	600	⇔
1,430	1,380	50	⇔	Total Revenue	5,720	5,520	200	⇔	17,200	16,600	600	⇔
				Less								
267	220	(47)	✗	Commissions	1,068	880	(188)	✗	3,200	2,600	(600)	✗
1,163	1,160	3		Gross Profit	4,652	4,640	12		14,000	14,000	0	
				Expenses								
278	260	(18)		Expense 1	1,240	1,040	(200)	✗	3,300	3,100	(200)	⇔
218	210	(8)		Expense 2	672	840	168	✓	2,600	2,500	(100)	⇔
188	180	(8)		Expense 3	752	720	(32)		2,300	2,200	(100)	⇔
158	150	(8)		Expense 4	632	600	(32)		1,900	1,800	(100)	⇔
128	120	(8)		Expense 5	512	480	(32)		1,500	1,400	(100)	⇔
50	70	20	✓	Expense 6	672	680	8		1,000	1,300	300	✓
1,020	990	(30)	⇔	Total Expenses	4,480	4,360	(120)	⇔	12,600	12,300	(300)	⇔
143	170	(27)	✗	Surplus/(Deficit)	172	280	(108)	✗	1,400	1,700	(300)	✗

Areas to Note:
1. Xxxxxxxxxxxxxxxxxxxxxxxxxxxxxxxxxxxxxxxxxxx
xxxxxxxxxxxxxxxxxxxxxxxxxxxxxxxxxxxxxxxxxxxxxxxxxxxxxxxxxxxxxxxxxxxx xxxxxxxxxxxxxxx xxxxxxxx xxxxxxx
xxxxxxxxxxxxx xxxxxxxxxxxxxxxxxxxxxxxxxxxxxxx
2. Xxxxxxxxxxxxxxxxxxxxxxxxxxxxxxxxxxxxxxxxxxx
xxxxxxxxxxxxxxxxxxxxxxxxxxxxxxxxxxxxxxxxxxxxxxxxxxxxxxxxxxxxxxxxxxxx xxxxxxxxxxxxxxx xxxxxxxx xxxxxxx
xxxxxxxxxxxxx xxxxxxxxxxxxxxxxxxxxxxxxxxxxxxx
3. Xxxxxxxxxxxxxxxxxxxxxxxxxxxxxxxxxxxxxxxxxxx
xxxxxxxxxxxxxxxxxxxxxxxxxxxxxxxxxxxxxxxxxxxxxxxxxxxxxxxxxxxxxxxxxxxx xxxxxxxxxxxxxxx xxxxxxxx xxxxxxx
xxxxxxxxxxxxx xxxxxxxxxxxxxxxxxxxxxxxxxxxxxxx
4. Xxxxxxxxxxxxxxxxxxxxxxxxxxxxxxxxxxxxxxxxxxx
xxxxxxxxxxxxxxxxxxxxxxxxxxxxxxxxxxxxxxxxxxxxxxxxxxxxxxxxxxxxxxxxxxxx xxxxxxxxxxxxxxx xxxxxxxx xxxxxxx
xxxxxxxxxxxxx xxxxxxxxxxxxxxxxxxxxxxxxxxxxxxx

 EXHIBIT 26.7 Reporting a Business Unit's Performance

table, one graph looks at the trend of the major expenditure items and the other at revenue if the business unit is a profit center. A good idea is to have a graph that contrasts financial and nonfinancial numbers (in this case tourist numbers against personnel costs). The notes are the main highlights and action steps to take. No other commentary is provided on the business unit's P&L. The business unit manager can discuss other issues in person with the CEO.

Each business unit may have up to five different graphs and the two that show the most pertinent information are shown in that month's report. Each business unit report will look slightly different. The titles of the key lines and graphs may be different.

Snapshot of All Projects Currently Started

Project reporting can be a huge burden on a project team. It consumes significant amounts of time, creating documents that are too long, poorly structured, and often lacking quick-reference action points.

Project management software was first designed for very complex projects such as "putting a man on the moon." Project managers charging in excess of $200 per hour for their time can spend it completing endless progress schedules. As a rule of thumb, if more than 5% of the project time is spent on reporting, balance has been lost. Project reporting is best managed by progressively updating a PowerPoint presentation. This means that at any time the project team can give an interesting and informative progress update.

I believe it is only worthwhile measuring metrically, that is, measuring accurately without estimate, those performance measures that are so fundamental to the organization that they affect nearly every aspect of its operation (e.g., the KPIs, which are explained in Chapter 16).

Project progress certainly does not fit into this category and hence I promote two simple types of project reporting, as shown in Exhibits 26.8 and 26.9. One gives a snapshot of all projects currently started and the other focuses on the progress of the top-ten projects.

Using this report enables management and the SMT to see the overall picture and answer these questions: Have we got too many projects on the go? What projects are running late? What projects are at risk of noncompletion?

Reporting Progress of the Top-Ten Projects

To minimize the time spent reporting progress I promote a five-band and four-color project progress status (see Exhibit 26.9). Using this method, a

Project office status report – June xx

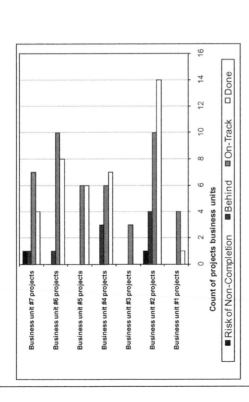

Count of projects business units

■ Risk of Non-Completion ■ Behind ■ On-Track □ Done

Projects at Risk of Non-Completion at year-end.

Xxxxxxx xxxxxxx xxxxxxx xxxx xxxxx
Xxxxxxxxx xxxxxx xxxxxxxx xxxxx
Xxxxxxxxxx xxxxxxxx xxxxxxxxxxxx xxxxxxxxxxx xxxxxxxxx xxxxxxx xxxxxxxx xxx
xxxxxx xx.

Previous project at Risk of Non-Completion

Xxxxxxxxxx xxxxxxx xxxxxxx xxxxxxxxx xxxxxxxxx xxxxxxxx xxxxxxxx xxxxxx xxx
xxxxxx xxxxxxxxxx.

Highlights:

1. Xxxxxxxxx xxxxxxxxxx xxxxxxxxx xxxxxxxx xxxxxxxxx xxx xxxxxx
xxx xxxxxx xxxxxxx xxxxxxx xxxxxxx xxxxxx.

2. Xxxxxxxxx xxxxxxxxx xxxxxxxx xxxxxxxx xxxxxxx xxxxxx.

3. Xxxxxxxxxx xxxxxxxxx xxxxxxxx xxxxxxxx xxxxxxxx xxx xxxxxx xxx
xxxxxx xxxxxxx xxxxxxx xxxxxx.

4. Xxxxxxxxxx xxxxxxxxx xxxxxxxx xxxxxxxx xxxxxxxx xxx xxxxxx
xxx xxxxxx xxxxxxx xxxxxxx xxxxxx xxx

5. Xxxxxxxxx xxxxxxxxx xxxxxxxx xxxxxxxx xxxxxxxx xxx xxxxxx
xxx xxxxxx xxxxxxx xxxxxxx xxxxxx xxx xxxx xxxxxx xxxxxxxxx.

6. Xxxxxxxxxx xxxxxxxxx xxxxxxxx xxxxxxxx xxxxxxxx xxxxx xxxxxx xxx
xxxxxxx xxxxxxx xxxxxxxx xxxxxxxx xxxxxxxx xxx xxxxxxx xxxxxxxxx
xxxxxxx xxxxxxx xxx. Xxxxxxxxxx xxxxxxxx xxx xxxxxxxx xxxxxxxxxx
xxxxxxx xxx xxxxxx xxx xxxxxx xxxxxxx xxxxxxxx xxxxxxx xxx.

 EXHIBIT 26.8 Current Projects-in-Progress Report

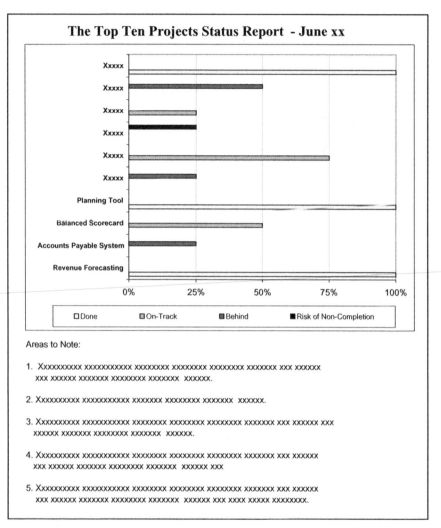

EXHIBIT 26.9 Top-Ten-Projects Report

project is either 0%, 25%, 50%, 75%, or 100% complete, and it is either at risk of noncompletion, behind schedule, on-track, or finished.

A project that is 15% complete would be shown as 25% complete, and next month, when it might be 30% complete, it would still stay at the 25% bands. Project managers are simply asked which quadrant and what color best reflects progress to date.

Managers at first may try to hide lack of progress. This soon becomes apparent when a project has been at the 25% band for three months and supposedly is still on-track. This method applies Pareto's 80/20 principle and also acknowledges that progress reports by their very nature are arbitrary and no two project managers would come up with the same progress evaluation.

The key message in the last quadrant is to *finish the project* no matter what the sunk cost is. It is thus not particularly helpful for the accounting team to constantly focus on the overrun. It would be far better to focus on the remaining costs and compare these against the benefits of finishing. Post-project is the place for postmortems. This will help reduce the tendency for staff to remove themselves from an overrunning project to a project with a new budget.

Reporting the Strategic Objectives/Risks/Costs Pressures

Finance teams are realizing that the finance report needs to also focus on strategic issues. If the finance team does not do this, another team will do it. I have come across the following reporting that I recommend to you:

- *Monthly reporting on the progress of the strategic objectives/themes and the initiatives within them.* Exhibit 26.10 is an example that uses a simple traffic-light display.
- *Monthly/quarterly report about major risks over a certain figure.* Note that you are talking about uncertainty, so avoid using "$3.75 million" when "$3 to 4 million" would be better. See Exhibit 26.11.

The One-Page Investment Proposal

One of the important principles that make Toyota so successful is the need for transparency. This view is carried through to its investment proposals. All proposals have to fit on an A3 page (U.S. standard fanfold). This is a very difficult task (see Exhibit 26.12). It ensures clarity of thought and reduces the possibility that the proposal will be 50 pages long because it represents a $500 million investment. Toyota has recognized that a large investment document will not be read or fully understood by all the decision makers. In fact, the larger the document, the less clarity there is for

Progress Against Strategy
Status as 30 June xx

Warning: little progress made
Some progress but behind schedule
On track or finished

Comments (required action if amber or red)

Strategy one xxxxxxxxxxxxxxxxxxxxxxx

A1 Initiative xxxx xxxx xxxxxxx xxx xxx
Completed in third week of May

A2 Initiative xxxx xxxx xxxxxxx xxx xxx
xxxxxxxxx xxxxxxx xxxx xxx xxxx xxxxx xxxxx xxxx xxxxxx xxxxxxxx xxxx xxxx x xxxxxx x xxxxxx
xxxxxxx xxxx xxxx

A3 Initiative xxxx xxxx xxxxxxx xxx xxx

Strategy two xxxxxxxxxxxxxxxxxxxx

B1 Initiative xxxx xxxx xxxxxxx xxx xxx
xxxxxxxxx xxxxxxx xxxx xxx xxxx xxxxx xxxx xxxxx xxx xxxxxx xxxxxxxx xxxx xxxx x xxxxxx x xxxxxx
xxxxxxx xxxx xxxx

B2 Initiative xxxx xxxx xxxxxxx xxx xxx
Completed in March

B3 Initiative xxxx xxxx xxxxxxx xxx xxx
On track, completion date mid Sept

Strategy three xxxxxxxxxxxxxxxxxxxx

C1 Initiative xxxx xxxx xxxxxxx xxx xxx
Completed in third week of May

C2 Initiative xxxx xxxx xxxxxxx xxx xxx
Completed in third week of May

C3 Initiative xxxx xxxx xxxxxxx xxx xxx
On track, completion date end Dec

Strategy four xxxxxxxxxxxxxxxxxxxxxxx

D1 Initiative xxxx xxxx xxxxxxx xxx xxx
xxxxxxxxx xxxxxxx xxxx xxx xxxx xxxxx xxxx xxxxx xxx xxxxxx xxxxxxxx xxxx xxxx x xxxxxx x xxxxxx
xxxxxxx xxxx xxxx

D2 Initiative xxxx xxxx xxxxxxx xxx xxx
xxxxxxxxx xxxxxxx xxxx xxx xxxx xxxxx xxxx xxxxx xxx xxxxxx xxxxxxxx xxxx xxxx x xxxxxx x xxxxxx
xxxxxxx xxxx xxxx

D3 Initiative xxxx xxxx xxxxxxx xxx xxx
Completed in third week of May

EXHIBIT 26.10 Monthly Progress-against-Strategy Report

Major Risks

Status as 30 June xx of all risks with a potential cost of over $xm

■ Major risk
▨ Some risk
□ Little or no risk

	$m	2011	2013	2014	Risk Level	Mitigation action
Risks to xxxxxxxxxxxxxxxxxxxxxxxx						
xxxx xxxx xxxxxxx xxx xxxx	2	1	1			xxxxxxxxxx xxxxxxx xxx xxxx xxxxx xxxx xxxxxx xxxxxxxx xxxx xxxx x xxxxxxx x xxxxxx
xxxx xxxx xxxxxxx xxx xxxx	3	2	1			xxxxxxxxx xxxxxxx xxxx xxxx
xxxx xxxx xxxxxxx xxx xxxx	6	2	2	2		xxxxxxxxxx xxxxxxx xxxx xxxx xxxx xxxxx xxxx xxxxxx xxxxxxxx xxxx xxxx x xxxxxx x xxxxxx
xxxx xxxx xxxxxxx xxx xxxx	1	1				xxxxxxxxxx xxxxxxx xxxxxx xxxxxxxx xxxx xxxx x xxxxxx x xxxxxx
						xxxxxxxxx xxxx xxxx
Risks to xxxxxxxxxxxxxxxxxxxxxxxxxx						
xxxx xxxx xxxxxxx xxx xxxx	2	2				xxxxxxxx xxxx xxxx
xxxx xxxx xxxxxxx xxx xxxx	2	2				xxxxxxxxx xxxxxxx xxxxxxx xxxx xxxxx xxxx xxxxxx xxxx xxxx x xxxxxx x xxxxxx
						xxxxxxxx xxxx xxxx
Risks to xxxxxxxxxxxxxxxxxxxxxxxxxx						
xxxx xxxx xxxxxxx xxx xxxx	5	2	2	1		xxxxxxxxx xxxxxxx xxxxxx xxx xxxx xxxxx xxxx xxxxxx xxxx xxxx x xxxxxx x xxxxxx
xxxx xxxx xxxxxxx xxx xxxx	2	1	1			xxxxxxxx xxxx xxxx
xxxx xxxx xxxxxxx xxx xxxx	3	3				xxxxxxxxx xxxxxxx xxxxxx xxxxxxxx xxxx xxxxx xxxx xxxxxx xxxx xxxx x xxxxxx x xxxxxx
						xxxxxxxx xxxx xxxx
	26	**16**	**7**	**3**		

EXHIBIT 26.11 Quarterly Major-Risks Report

Investment Proposal for xxxxxxxxxxxxxxxxxxxxxxxxxxxxxxxxxxxxx xx/xx/xxxx

Current Situation

Xxxxxxxxxxxxxxxxxxxxxxxxxxxxxxxxxxxxxx
xxxxxxxxxxxx

Xxxxxxxxxxxxxxxxxxxxxxxxxxxxxxxxxxxxxx
xxxxxxxxxxxx

□ % of total orders under $5,000
■ % of total value of orders under $5,000

2008 2009 2010

Proposal

Xxxxxxxxxxxxxxxxxxxxxxxxxxxxxxxxxxxxxx
xxxxxxxxxxxx

Significant Variances:

- Xxxxxxxxxxxxxxxxxxxxxxxxxxxxxxxx
- Xxxxxxxxxxxxxxxxxxxxxxxxxxxxxxxx
- Xxxxxxxxxxxxxxxxxxxxxxxxxxxxxxxx
- Xxxxxxxxxxxxxxxxxxxxxxxxxxxxxxxx

Xxxxxxxxxxxxxxxxxxxxxxxxxxxxxxxxxxxxxx
xxxxxxxxxxxxxxxxxxxxxxx

Plan

- Xxxxxxxxxxxxxxxxxxxxxxxxxxxxxxxx
  xxxxxxxxxxxxxxxxxxxx

- Xxxxxxxxxxxxxxxxxxxxxxxxxxxxxxxx
  xxxxxxxxxxxxxxxxxxxx

Acceptable business related purchases using the Purchase card

Small tools	
Auto spares	

Unacceptable business related purchases using the Purchase card

Cash advance	
Computer Hardware	

Implementation

1. Xxxxxxxxxxxxxxxxxxxxxxxxxxx
2. Xxxxxxxxxxxxxxxxxxxxxxxxxxx
3. Xxxxxxxxxxxxxxxxxxxxxxxxxxx
4. Xxxxxxxxxxxxxxxxxxxxxxxxxxx
5. Xxxxxxxxxxxxxxxxxxxxxxxxxxx
6. Xxxxxxxxxxxxxxxxxxxxxxxxxxx
7. Xxxxxxxxxxxxxxxxxxxxxxxxxxx
8. Xxxxxxxxxxxxxxxxxxxxxxxxxxx
9. Xxxxxxxxxxxxxxxxxxxxxxxxxxx

Controls

- Xxxxxxxxxxxxxxxxxxxxxxxxxxx
  xxxxxxxxxxxxxxxx

- Xxxxxxxxxxxxxxxxxxxxxxxxxxx
  xxxxxxxxxxxxxxxx

Labour Costs and Time Analysis

Labour and Materials Savings

Time Savings

Estimated Costs of Set Up

Return on Investment

Timeline

9/3/20XX	9/4/XX to 30/4/20XX	Etc	Etc	Xx/xx/xx	Xx/xx/xx	Xx/xx/xx	Xx/xx/xx	Xx/xx/xx
Present at ccc	Policy guidelines issuer selection	Training for pilot programme	Xxxxxx xxxxxxx	Xxxxxx xxxxxxx	Xxxxxx xxxxxxx	Xxxxxx xxxxxxx	Xxxxxx xxxxxxx	Xxxxxx xxxxxxx

EXHIBIT 26.12 The A3 (U.S. Standard Fanfold) Investment Proposal

decision making. Please reread the section on Toyota for more clever ideas (Chapter 20).

Notes

1. David Parmenter, *Quick Monthly Reporting—by Day Three or Less!*, Waymark 2010.
2. David Parmenter, *Decision-Based Reporting*, Waymark 2010.

CHAPTER 27

Seeking Staff Opinion
on a Regular Basis

If you have only a few minutes to skim over this chapter, this is what you should focus on:

- Appendix G for an easy-to-perform staff-satisfaction survey
- Designing a staff survey

A Staff Survey Run Three or Four Times a Year

As a manager, you can be either an advocator for better practices or a blocker. One important process that needs your support is the regular gathering of staff opinions. There have been changes since the monster surveys of old that were carried out once every two or three years.

It goes without saying that the people in an organization *are* the organization. Since Kaplan and Norton introduced the concept of a balanced scorecard (BSC),[1] it has become increasingly more important for companies to track staff satisfaction and act upon those major areas of concern. (See Appendix G for an example of an easy-to-perform staff-satisfaction survey.) Kaplan and Norton dedicated a section of the BSC to "learning and growth." Some organizations that have introduced the BSC have gone one step further by adding another section called "employee perspective."

It is necessary to find a way to cost-effectively and efficiently gain feedback on a quarterly or four-month basis if you have a BSC or are serious about measuring employee satisfaction.

A quick review of the benefits of a staff opinion survey includes:

- Providing a channel for receiving suggestions, ideas, and other forms of feedback from staff
- Probing for sources of discontent within an organization, thus having the opportunity to address them

- Canvassing opinions on new policies and procedures
- Highlighting those areas of the culture that are working well

Increasingly today staff opinion surveys are being delayed or deferred. Some of the problems that influence the senior management team (SMT) to delay staff opinion surveys lie in:

- An overstretched human resources (HR) function
- A lack of in-house survey experience
- Poor implementation of the last staff opinion, so why bother?
- Lack of funding
- Limited buy-in from the SMT

With the downsizing and disenfranchising of HR, the HR functions are overstretched. Initiatives such as a staff opinion survey are put on the back burner.

Many organizations have experienced problems with their staff opinion surveys. They have become albatrosses around the neck of HR because of the huge cost, the time spent trying to design the perfect questionnaire by committee, and the inability to handle the huge volume of information.

Poor implementation of the previous staff opinion survey is a common problem—the staff opinion report becomes the end product, rather than a building block, for HR initiatives. The HR function, having expended all available energy, has little left to carry out the new initiatives required.

Organizations of around 300 to 400 staff can be quoted $30,000 for a staff opinion survey covering all staff. This often is not within the budget of an underfunded HR function. Carrying out a *rolling sample survey* is considerably cheaper, with costs ranging from $9,000 for the first run to $6,000 for subsequent runs.

Lack of buy-in from the SMT is a common problem as few have experienced a successful staff opinion survey and many clearly do not understand what value HR can offer. Some of the SMT may even wish to delay any such initiative as they fear it may be a vehicle for negativity.

Designing a Staff Survey

All the above issues can be resolved if one is prepared to accept the following points:

- A *quick* staff opinion survey is a good one.
- Get management buy-in by having the CEO launch recommendations with a tour of the offices by the SMT (they might get to like it).

- Qualitative feedback creates at least half the value of an opinion survey.
- Keep the questionnaire focused on issues that you can do something about.
- A *keep-it-simple (KIS)* questionnaire is a good questionnaire.
- Use a rolling sample approach.

A quick staff opinion survey is a good one. From planning to feedback to staff, a six-week (or, at the most, eight-week) timeframe is possible. One client said to me:

> *I believe these surveys often fail because the executive do not wish to hear or tackle the negative/critical comments and prefer to bury their heads in the sand. I believe the responsibility for developing change initiatives, as a result of such a survey, lies with the executive, as should ownership of the information that is provided by the survey. I would argue that HR's role as owner of the process is to make it all happen in an efficient and easy manner.*

I would add that if the SMT is not prepared to present the findings in an open environment, then do not bother doing a staff opinion survey.

Qualitative feedback creates at least half the value of an opinion survey and ensures that you get balance. You should ask for comments on three things the organization excels at and three main areas in which the organization should improve; this will be a substantial information source. See Exhibit 27.1 for a checklist.

Keep the questionnaire focused on issues that you can do something about. Why build up expectations?

A KIS questionnaire is a good questionnaire. It should be able to be completed in ten minutes; anything over 30 questions will not allow enough time for commentary.

Use a *rolling* sample. All you need to do is analyze the total staff into three samples. Each sample has coverage of staff/managers/SMT, departments, demographics, and so forth. You now have samples ready not only for the first survey, but the subsequent two. Thus everybody will have the opportunity to give feedback, over say an 18-month period. New staff will be allocated an appropriate survey time when their details are entered into the database.

One service sector organization, with over 2,000 staff on one site, has now developed a rolling staff survey. Every three months, up to 200 staff are picked at random and asked to complete a survey. To ensure

(Continued)

it is done, they organize a set time when the selected staff go to a room to complete the questionnaires. The survey company personnel are present so that they can answer any questions and seek clarification on the comments staff make right there and then. This approach gives valuable quarterly trend analysis and avoids the time-consuming delays of waiting for returns to come in.

EXHIBIT 27.1 Staff-Satisfaction Checklist

1. Have you selected a sample of staff covering each division/   ☐ Yes   ☐ No
   branch/team, ensuring good vertical and horizontal slices?
2. Have you used a web-based survey package such as   ☐ Yes   ☐ No
   SurveyMonkey?
3. Have you made the questionnaire simple and able to be   ☐ Yes   ☐ No
   completed within ten minutes?
4. Have you avoided asking questions you will not act upon?   ☐ Yes   ☐ No
   (Remember there is limited time to implement change)
5. Do you give a short timeframe (eight working days to   ☐ Yes   ☐ No
   complete) and follow up, by phone, on all those who have
   not responded by day 5, three days before the deadline?
6. Do you categorize all comments so that themes emerge?   ☐ Yes   ☐ No
   (We use an access database and then transfer to word for
   final tailoring.)
7. Have you prepared an informative report with practical   ☐ Yes   ☐ No
   suggestions, ensuring that feedback comments are handled
   carefully to maintain confidentiality?
8. Have you delivered enough PowerPoint presentations so all ☐ Yes   ☐ No
   staff and managers can attend? All staff should have the
   opportunity to attend a feedback session as many who
   have not commented will still want to ensure their big
   issues have been covered.
9. Have you implemented at least one recommendation within   ☐ Yes   ☐ No
   one month after issuing the survey?

Note

1. Robert S. Kaplan and David P. Norton, *Translating Strategy into Action: The Balanced Scorecard*, Harvard Business School Press, 1996.

CHAPTER 28

Importance of the Human Resources Team

I f you have only a few minutes to skim over this chapter, this is what
you should focus on:

- Savings created by the Human Resources team
- Why managers do not have the time and expertise to be a surrogate HR Department
- Warning signs your Human Resources function is being marginalized

Increasingly, the Human Resources (HR) function is being cut back and marginalized by CEOs who are dinosaurs, solely focusing on measuring short-term financial performance. These organizations are not interested in the measures in other perspectives (balanced scorecard), such as learning and growth, customer satisfaction, staff satisfaction, environment and community, and internal business processes. These perspectives were discussed in Chapter 17.

This marginalization is often carried out by CEOs who are more focused on their next move than on the future of the organization. These CEOs move on quickly before the dubious practices they have implemented to maximise their bonuses start reaping havoc within the organization.

I wish to explore some of the ways the Human Resources (HR) Department can add value and the consequences of depleting the size of the HR team.

Selecting the Right People for the Business

Most readers can reflect back on a recruitment that they approved that did not work out. In most cases this would have been based on interviews and references. HR practitioners have found there are far more effective

ways to recruit, starting by making an in-depth focus on the job requirements, followed by behavioral event interviews, simulated exercises, and
assessment centers. All of this takes experienced in-house resources to
manage and deliver. As we all know, the cost of hiring the wrong person
can be much greater than just the individual's salary costs.

Reducing the Need to Recruit

I was fortunate enough to work for Arthur Andersen & Co. in the Manchester
office in the United Kingdom. They showed me a picture of people climbing up a mountain, roped together. The picture was symbolic not only of
teamwork but also of the philosophy of actively encouraging staff beneath
you to come up into your job. As you can imagine, recruiting costs at the
middle and senior management levels were next to nothing. An HR team
can help the organization migrate to a culture like this.

Reducing Recruitment Costs

If some of the skilled recruiters are generating somewhere between $350,000
and $600,000 in fees, you can safely assume their pay packet is somewhere
between $120,000 and $200,000. It does not take a rocket scientist to point
out that contracting out is certainly not a cheap option.

With fees around 12.5 to 15% of gross remuneration, ten management
positions can cost you $125,000 to $150,000 in recruiting fees.

While the HR function may not wish to take all of recruiting in-house,
it can, through initiatives, substantially reduce costs. One organization I
have come across has been very proactive, giving staff a $5,000 bonus if
they suggest a person who ends up being recruited for a sales-related
position (with certain provisos regarding length of stay, and so forth).

Developing Managers and Staff

Building organizational capacity is often left to on-the-job-training. Some
enlightened organizations are investing in building in-house development
centers. Such initiatives require experienced people (your HR team) supple-
mented with some external experts.

One finance sector organization has put around 180 managers through
development centers to improve their management competency. Following
the center, some managers realized that they would like to redirect their
career within or outside the organization.

Enhancing the Organization's Performance through Changing the Culture

A new culture can improve the bottom line in many ways: less absenteeism, lower turnover, more initiative, higher productivity, and possibly greater business opportunities created by staff.

Any culture change requires a high level of buy-in. Organizations that have been successful have had an experienced HR team to support change processes.

One organization in the service sector has successfully tied the culture of the recent re-launch of the company into the company's employment contracts. The re-launch of the company was based around staff empowerment and trust. Call center staff are allowed to approve company expenditures even where the company may not be liable. Decisions are reviewed post the event for performance management purposes.

One organization in the private sector successfully developed its own in-house "culture change" course. Internal teams were set up to identify a company with outstanding customer service. An airline was identified and liaised with. Consultants then assisted the internal teams to develop a customized course to guide the organization's staff through the culture change.

Savings through Reducing Sick-Pay Payments

Organizations that have programs to get sick staff back to work quickly, report great success with significant reductions in sick pay and other related levies.

An estimate of how much HR can add to the bottom line is shown in Exhibit 28.1. In this exhibit, I have developed some broad estimates based on discussions I have held with organizations, for a hypothetical company in the service sector with approximately 500 staff.

Managers Do Not Have the Time and Expertise to Be HR Experts

Thinking back to your most recent management position, how much time did you allow for performance feedback to your staff? If I were a betting man, I would say you found the six monthly assessments difficult to fit in. Organizations are now giving feedback three to four times a year to ensure performance is on track. If managers are spending time managing performance, how can they develop and maintain expertise in recruitment techniques, accident prevention, or management development?

EXHIBIT 28.1 Savings Created by the HR Team

	High	Low
	000's	000's
Health-care insurance savings through accident prevention and a good back-to-work program	400	150
Reducing cost of absenteeism (less use of temporary staff)	60	15
Reduction in recruiting costs through retention of staff and more in-house involvement	150	125
Reducing cost of redundancies through managed contraction	150	50
Reduction in cost (including legal costs) of unfair dismissals	90	30
Savings	850	370
Direct costs of HR function	[450]	[180]
Contribution to the bottom line	400	190

EXHIBIT 28.2 Checklist of Warning Signs Your HR Department Is Being Marginalized

1. HR does not report directly to the CEO.	☐ Yes	☐ No
2. Absence of an HR report in the board papers.	☐ Yes	☐ No
3. HR staff are not replaced when they leave.	☐ Yes	☐ No
4. No data capture or monitoring of the money spent on training.	☐ Yes	☐ No
5. Percentage spent on training is down over the last five years.	☐ Yes	☐ No
6. No clear documentation of the organization's core competencies.	☐ Yes	☐ No
7. No succession planning for management roles.	☐ Yes	☐ No
8. HR position is not headed by a trained HR professional.	☐ Yes	☐ No
9. No regular staff opinion survey.	☐ Yes	☐ No
10. SMT positions are recruited by the CEO (often previous work associates).	☐ Yes	☐ No
11. The CEO and SMT have not had 360-degree feedback.	☐ Yes	☐ No
12. Coaching and mentoring that has not been established (vital in my progressive organization)	☐ Yes	☐ No
13. Lack of HR trend analysis in absenteeism, health and safety, headcount, demographics, and so on.	☐ Yes	☐ No

See Exhibit 28.2 for signs that your HR function is being marginalized. I have come across a multinational company that proclaims it has successfully delegated this responsibility to managers. This, however, requires a different company culture, where managers are extensively trained; in this case all managers attend an intensive management course where "you are not the same person coming out of the course as you were going in."

Possible consequences of removing an internal HR function can comprise the following:

- Overreliance on external advisers, which may cost more in the long run, defeats the objective of cost saving.
- A trend to purchase rather than grow trained staff makes the organization over-reliant on the training provided by other employers.
- Remuneration is out of kilter, especially at the senior levels.
- The organization's culture is talked about, but nothing is really done about it.
- New recruits are not performing as anticipated.
- Staff turnover and absenteeism are rising.
- Young talented staff never learn good management skills.

Steps You Can Take Right Now

If you are in position to make or recommend structural changes to your organization, this is what I recommend you do:

Step 1. Start marketing the value the HR team are creating.

Step 2. Relocate the HR function so that it is close to the CEO's office.

Step 3. Ensure the HR function is led by a broadly educated and skilled HR professional.

Step 4. Investigate your recruiting costs, as the HR team should be able to make savings.

Step 5. Ask for an informative two-to-three-page HR report to be included in the monthly board papers.

Step 6. Ensure that your HR advisers are involved in the business planning. They have much to give, and it represents the ideal forum to enhance their perceived value.

CHAPTER 29

Performance Bonus Schemes

If you have only a few minutes to skim over this chapter, this is what you should focus on:

- Super profits should be retained
- Bonus scheme free of profit-enhancing adjustments
- Trialing the performance bonus scheme before you go live (Exhibit 29.5)

The Billion-Dollar Giveaway

Performance bonuses give away billions of dollars each year based on methodologies where little thought has been applied. Who are the performance bonus experts? What qualifications do they possess to work in this important area other than prior experience in creating the mayhem we currently have?

When one looks at their skill base, one wonders how they got listened to in the first place. Which bright spark advised the hedge funds to pay a $1 billion bonus to one fund manager who created a paper gain that never eventuated into cash? These schemes were flawed from the start; *super profits* were being paid out, there was no allowance made for the cost of capital, and the bonus scheme was only *high-side focused*.

The Foundation Stones

There are a number of foundation stones that need to be laid down and never undermined when building a *performance bonus scheme (PBS)* that makes sense and will move the organization in the right direction.

Base the PBS on a Relative Measure

You should base the PBS on a relative measure rather than a fixed annual performance contract. Most bonuses fail at this first hurdle. Jeremy Hope and Robin Fraser[1] have pointed out the trap of an annual fixed performance contract. If you set a target in the future, you will never know if it was appropriate, given the particular conditions of that time. You often end up paying incentives to management when in fact you have lost market share. In other words, your rising sales did not keep up with the growth rate in the marketplace.

Relative performance target measures are where we compare performance to the marketplace. Thus the financial institutions that are making super profits out of this artificially lower interest rate environment would have a higher benchmark set retrospectively, when the actual impact is known. As Jeremy Hope says,[2] "Not setting a target beforehand is not a problem as long as staff are given regular updates as to how they are progressing against the market." He argues that if you do not know how hard you have to work to get a maximum bonus, you will work as hard as you can.

Super Profits Should Be Retained

Super profits should be excluded from a performance bonus scheme and retained to cover the possible losses in the future. In boom times, annual performance targets give away too much. These *super-profit years* come around infrequently and are needed to finance the dark times of a recession. Yet, what do our "remuneration experts" advise? A package that includes a substantial slice of these super profits, yet no sharing in any downside. This downside, of course, is borne solely by the shareholder.

There needs to be recognition that the boom times have little or no correlation with the impact of the teams. The organization was always going to achieve this, no matter who was working for the firm. As Exhibit 29.1 shows, if an organization is to survive, super profits need to be retained. If you look at Toyota's great years, the percentage paid to the executives was a fraction of that paid to the Detroit-based CEOs, whose performance was not as successful.

This removal of super profits has a number of benefits:

- It avoids the need to have a deferral scheme for all unrealized gains.
- It is defensible and understandable by employees.
- It can be calculated by reference to the market conditions relevant in the year. Where the market has got ten substantially larger, with all the main players reporting a great year, we can attribute a certain amount of period-end performance as super profits.

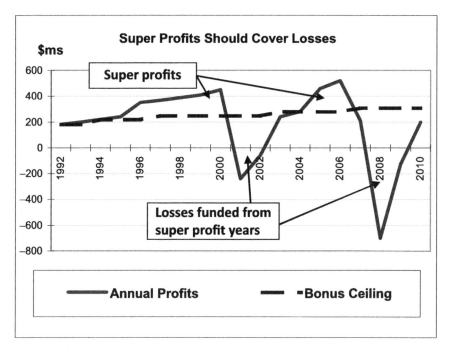

EXHIBIT 29.1 Retention of Super Profits

When designing a bonus scheme the super-profits component should be a deduction from the profits rather than creating a ceiling for the bonus scheme. If a bonus pool has maxed out, then staff will rather play golf than go hard to win further business. The ceiling in Exhibit 29.1 is shown for illustration purposes only.

Free of Profit-Enhancing Adjustments

All profits included in a performance bonus scheme calculation should be free of all major "profit-enhancing" accounting adjustments. Many banks will be making super profits in 2010–2012 as the massive writedowns are written back when loans are recovered to some extent. This will happen as sure as night follows day.

I remember a classic case in New Zealand where a merciless CEO was rewarded solely on a successful sale of a publically owned bank. The loan book was written down to such an extent that the purchasing
(Continued)

bank merely had to realize these writedowns to report a profit in the first year that equated to nearly the full purchase price. This activity is no different from many other white-collar crimes that occur under the eyes of poorly performing directors.

One simple step you can take is to eliminate all short-term accounting adjustments from the bonus scheme profit pool of senior management and the CEO. These eliminations should include:

- Recovery of written-off debt
- Profit on sale of assets

The aim is to avoid the situation where management in a bad year will take a massive hit to their loan book so they can feather their nest on the recovery. This type of activity will be alive and well around the globe.

These adjustments do not have to be made for the loan team's bonus calculations. We still want them motivated to turn around nonperforming loans.

Taking into Account the Full Cost of Capital

The full cost of capital should be taken into account when calculating any bonus pool. Traders can trade in the vast sums involved only because they have a bank's balance sheet behind them. If this were not so, then the traders could operate at home and be among the many solo traders who also play in the market. These individuals cannot hope to make as much profit due to the much smaller positions their personal cash resources facilitate.

Each department in a bank should have a cost of capital, which takes into account the full risks involved. In today's unusual environment, the cost of capital should be based on a five-year average cost of debt and a risk-weighting associated with the risks involved. With the losses that bank shareholders have had to stomach, the cost of capital should be set in some higher-risk departments as high as 25%.

With the current artificially low base rate, a fool could run a bank and make a huge bottom line. All banks should thus be adjusting their cost of capital based on a five-year average in their PBSs.

"At-Risk Portion of Salary"

Any "at-risk portion of salary" should be separate from the performance bonus scheme. In the finance sector it is traditional for employees to have

EXHIBIT 29.2 At-Risk Component of Salary

	Remuneration		
	Mgr 1	Mgr 2	Mgr 3
Base salary, paid monthly	48,000	64,000	80,000
At-risk salary (bonus is paid separately)	12,000	16,000	20,000
Salary package	60,000	80,000	100,000
Relative measure, set retrospectively	not met	met	exceeded
Percentage of at-risk salary paid	40%	100%	100%
At-risk salary paid	4,800	16,000	20,000
Share of bonus pool	nil	5,000	10,000
Total period-end payout	4,800	21,000	30,000

a substantial share of their salary at risk. The bonus calculation has been a very primitive calculation.

I propose that the at-risk portion of the salary should be paid when the expected profits figure has been met. (See Exhibit 29.2.) Note that as already mentioned this target will be set as a relative measure—set retrospectively when actual information is known.

Where the relative target has been met or exceeded, the at-risk portion of the salary will be paid. The surplus over the relative measure will then create a bonus pool for a further payment, which will be calculated taking into account the adjustments already discussed.

Avoid Linkage to Share Price

Performance bonus schemes should avoid any linkage to share price movements. No bonus should be pegged to the stock market price as the stock market price does not reflect the contribution that staff, management, and the CEO have made.

Only a fool believes that the current share price reflects the long-term value of an organization. Just because a buyer, often ill informed, wants to pay a certain sum for a packet of shares does not mean the total shareholding is worth that amount.

Providing share options is also giving away too much of shareholder's wealth in an often-disguised way.

Linked to a Balanced Performance

Performance bonus schemes should be linked to a balanced performance. The balanced scorecard has offered another avenue to pay performance. PBSs using a balanced scorecard are often flawed on a number of counts:

EXHIBIT 29.3 Performance-Related Pay System That Will Never Work

Category	Perspective Weighting	Measure	Measure Weighting
Financial	60%	EVA	25%
		Unit profit	20%
		Market growth	15%
Customer	20%	Customer satisfaction survey	10%
		Dealer satisfaction survey	10%
Internal	10%	Above-average rank on process industry quality survey	5%
		Decrease in dealer delivery cycle time	5%
Innovation and learning	10%	Suggestions/employee	5%
		Satisfaction survey	5%

Source: International Institute of Management.

- The balanced scorecard is often based on only four perspectives, ignoring the important "environment and community" and "staff satisfaction" perspectives.
- The measures chosen are open to debate and manipulation.
- There is seldom a linkage to progress in the organization's critical success factors.
- Weighting of measures leads to crazy performance agreements such as in Exhibit 29.3.

An alternative would be to link the PBS to the organization's critical success factors. See an example of an airline PBS in Exhibit 29.4.

In this exhibit all teams have the same weighting for the financial results. Some readers will feel this is too low. However, when you research more on the balanced scorecard philosophy you will understand that the greatest impact to the bottom line, over the medium and long term, will be in the organization's critical success factors.

The operational team, at one of the airports, has a major focus on timely arrival and departure of planes. You could argue that this should have a higher weighting, such as 30%. However, this team does impact many other CSFs. This team clearly impacts the timely maintenance of planes by making them available on time, and impacts the satisfaction of our first-class, business-class, and gold-card-holders passengers. The public's perception of the airline is reflected in the interaction between staff and the public along with press releases and the timeliness of planes.

Ensuring that staff are listened to, are engaged successfully, are constantly striving to do things better (Toyota's *kaizen*) is reflected in the

EXHIBIT 29.4 How a Performance-Related Bonus Could Be Linked to the Critical Success Factors (Airline)

	Operational Team	Public Relations Team	Maintenance Team	Accountants
Financial performance	30%	30%	30%	30%
In the critical success factors (CSFs)				
Timely departure and arrival of planes	20%	0%	20%	0%
Timely maintenance of planes	10%	0%	30%	0%
Retention of key customers	10%	0%	0%	0%
Positive public perception of organization—being a preferred airline	10%	30%	0%	0%
"Stay, say, strive engagement with staff"	10%	20%	10%	20%
Encouraging innovation that matters	10%	20%	10%	20%
Accurate, timely information that helps decisions	0%	0%	0%	30%

weighting of "stay/say/strive" and "encouraging innovation that matters." There is no weighting for "accurate timely information that helps decisions" because other teams such as IT and accounting are more responsible for this and I want to avoid using precise percentages such as 7% or 8%, which tends to give the impression that a performance pay scheme can be a scientifically based instrument.

The public relations team has a major focus on creating positive spin to the public and to the staff. All great leaders focus in this area. You need not look past Richard Branson in this respect. The weights for the public relations team will focus on the team in the key areas that it can contribute. By having innovation success stories and recognition celebrations, staff will want to focus on this important area of constant improvement.

The maintenance and accounting teams' focus is more narrowed. The accounting team has a higher weighting on "stay/say/strive" and "encouraging innovation that matters" to help focus its attention in these important areas. This will improve performance and benefit all the other teams the accounting team impacts through its work.

Avoid Having "Deferral Provisions"

Performance bonus schemes should avoid having "deferral provisions," which attempt to avoid paying out unrealized gains. All unrealized gains are just that. In many cases they are a *mirage*. While we need to reward those who got in on the ground floor of a climbing stock, we need to recognize that the extent of the gain is largely due to a bounceback.

Already some banks have adopted a deferral mechanism on unrealized gains. While this is understandable, we need to consider the likely impacts:

- We do not want all stocks sold and bought back the next day as a window-dressing exercise that dealers/brokers could easily arrange with each other.
- The financial sector is driven by individuals who worship the monetary unit, rather than any other more benevolent force. This is a fact of life. A deferral system will be very difficult for them to accept.
- Staff will worry about their share of the pool when they leave; the last thing you want is a team leaving so its members can cash out their deferral pool while it is doing well.
- Deadwood may wish to hang around for future paydays out of their deferred bonus scheme.

It is my belief that while some sectors may be able to successfully establish a deferral PBS, the financial sector is fraught with difficulties. I believe it would be better to focus on the other foundation stones, especially the removal of super profits.

Tested to Minimize "Gaming Risk"

All performance bonus schemes should be tested to minimize risk of being "gamed" by participants in the scheme. All schemes where money is at stake will be gamed. Staff will find out ways to maximize the payment by undertaking actions that will often not be in the general interest of the organization.

The testing of the new scheme should include:

- Reworking bonuses paid to about five individuals over the last five years to see what would have been paid under the new scheme and compare against actual payments made.
- Consulting with some clever staff and ask them, "What actions would you undertake if this scheme were running?"
- Discussing with your peers in other companies better practices that work. This will help move the industry standard, at the same time avoiding implementing a scheme that failed elsewhere.

Not Linked to KPIs

Performance bonus schemes should *not* be linked to key performance indicators (KPIs). KPIs are a special performance tool; it is imperative that these are not included in any performance-related pay discussions. KPIs are too important to be gamed by individuals and teams to maximize bonuses. While KPIs will show, 24/7, daily, or weekly, how teams are performing, it is essential to leave the KPIs uncorrupted by performance-related pay.

Certainly most teams will have some useful monthly summary measures, which I call *result indicators*, that will help teams track performance and be the basis of any performance bonus scheme. See Chapter 16 for more information.

Schemes Need to Be Communicated

All PBSs should be communicated to staff using public relations experts. All changes to such a fundamental issue as performance-related pay need to be sold through the emotional drivers of the audience. With a PBS, this will require different presentations when selling the change to the board, CEO, senior management team (SMT), and the management and staff. They all have different emotional drivers. We need to note that nothing is ever sold by logic (e.g., remember your last car purchase).

Thus, we need to radically alter the way we pitch the sale of the new performance-related pay rules to the CEO, the SMT, the board, and the affected staff. We have to focus on the emotional drivers that matter to all these parties. The emotional drivers will all be different.

Many change initiatives fail at this hurdle because we attempt to change the culture through selling logic, writing reports, and issuing commands via email. It does not work. The new performance-related pay scheme needs a public relations machine behind it. No presentation, email, memo, or paper should go out unless it has been vetted by your PR expert. In addition, I would also road-test the delivery of all your presentations in front of the PR expert before going live.

Road Tested

Performance bonus schemes should be road-tested on the last complete business cycle. When you think you have a good scheme, test it on the results of the last full business cycle, the period between the last two recessions. View the extent of the bonus on the net profit.

You need to appraise the PBS as you would a major investment in a fixed asset where you have committed a future stream of income to pay for an asset. See Exhibit 29.5 for an example of this road-test, and Exhibit 29.6 for a checklist.

EXHIBIT 29.5 Trialing the Performance Bonus Scheme Before You Go Live

	1991	1992	1993	1994	1995	1996	1997	1998	1999	2000
Annual profits (excluding all cost of capital charges)	180	180	200	220	240	350	370	390	410	450
Removal of accounting entries			(30)							
Super profits clawback	(30)	(30)	(30)	(32)	(35)	(10)	(20)	(30)	(30)	(40)
Full cost of capital						(60)	(62)	(62)	(75)	(75)
Adjusted profit	150	150	140	188	205	280	288	298	305	335
Expected profit based on market share	140	140	140	160	180	260	260	265	280	290
Profits subject to bonus pool	10	10	0	28	25	20	28	33	25	45
Percentage of pool (33% in this example)	3	3	0	9	8	7	9	11	8	15

	2001	2002	2003	2004	2005	2006	2007	2008	2009	Last Year
Annual profits (excluding all cost of capital charges)	(240)	(60)	290	310	460	520	210	(700)	(125)	200
Removal of accounting entries			(20)		(40)	(40)				
Super profits clawback					(20)	(30)				
Full cost of capital	(25)	(28)	(40)	(42)	(65)	(70)	(30)	(30)	(35)	(30)
Adjusted profit	(265)	(88)	230	268	335	380	180	(730)	(160)	170
Expected profit based on market share			190	220	300	350	170			160
Profits subject to bonus pool	0	0	40	48	35	30	10	0	0	10
Percentage of pool (33% in this example)	0	0	13	16	12	10	3	0	0	3

EXHIBIT 29.6 Checklist to Ensure Foundations Are Laid Carefully

Be based on a relative measure rather than a fixed annual performance contract

All fixed in advance, annual targets for bonuses are removed	☐ Yes	☐ No
Relative measures are introduced to take account of:		
▪ Comparison against market share	☐ Yes	☐ No
▪ Comparison against other peers	☐ Yes	☐ No
▪ Changes in input costs (e.g., where base rate is zero banks)	☐ Yes	☐ No
Progress against the relative measures are reported three or four times a year	☐ Yes	☐ No

Super profits should be retained for the loss-making years lying ahead

▪ Super-profit scenarios have been analyzed	☐ Yes	☐ No
▪ Historic trends analyzed to estimate when super profits are being made	☐ Yes	☐ No
▪ Drivers of super profits identified (e.g., the interest margin banks had in 2009 meant that even a fool would have made super profits)	☐ Yes	☐ No
▪ Super profits removed from net profit as a percentage of each $m made rather than have a ceiling	☐ Yes	☐ No
▪ Model tested against last 10 or 20 years retained profit/losses to ensure formula is right	☐ Yes	☐ No

The profits in a bonus calculation should be free of all major "profit-enhancing" accounting adjustments

Eliminate all short-term accounting adjustments including:		
▪ Recovery of written-off debt	☐ Yes	☐ No
▪ Profit on sale of assets	☐ Yes	☐ No
▪ Recovery of goodwill	☐ Yes	☐ No

Taking into account the full cost of capital

All departments having a specific profit-sharing scheme should have a "cost of capital", that takes into account the full risks involved	☐ Yes	☐ No

Separate out "at-risk portion of salary" from bonus element

Test the new system on previous years	☐ Yes	☐ No
Human Resources to discuss the change on a one-to-one basis with all managers affected	☐ Yes	☐ No
Prepare an example of the new scheme and publish in a secure area of the HR team's intranet section	☐ Yes	☐ No

Avoiding linkage to share price movements

Removed all bonuses that are linked to share prices	☐ Yes	☐ No
Removed all share options from remuneration	☐ Yes	☐ No

(Continued)

EXHIBIT 29.6 (Continued)

Linked to a balanced performance		
Remove all KPIs from bonus schemes	☐ Yes	☐ No
Evaluate progress against the success in the critical success factors	☐ Yes	☐ No
Avoid having a deferral scheme for all unrealized gains	☐ Yes	☐ No
All bonus schemes must be "game" tested		
Rework bonuses paid to about five individuals over the last five years to see what would have been paid under the new scheme and compare against actual payments made	☐ Yes	☐ No
Consult with some clever staff and ask them "What actions would you undertake if this scheme were running?"	☐ Yes	☐ No
Discuss with your peers in other companies better practices that work—this will help move the industry standard at the same time as avoiding implementing a scheme that failed elsewhere	☐ Yes	☐ No
Do not link KPIs with performance-related pay		
Removed all KPIs from performance-related pay	☐ Yes	☐ No
Removed all KPIs from job descriptions	☐ Yes	☐ No
Removed all KPIs from annual performance agreements	☐ Yes	☐ No
Communicating with staff using public relations experts		
Sold changes via the emotional drivers	☐ Yes	☐ No
Have prepared presentations that are targeted specifically at the:		
▪ Board	☐ Yes	☐ No
▪ CEO	☐ Yes	☐ No
▪ Senior management team	☐ Yes	☐ No
▪ Staff on performance-related pay schemes	☐ Yes	☐ No
Road-test the bonus scheme on last complete business cycle (e.g., between 10 to 20 years)	☐ Yes	☐ No

Notes

1. Jeremy Hope and Robin Fraser, *Beyond Budgeting: How Managers Can Break Free from the Annual Performance Trap*, Harvard Business Press, 2003.
2. Jeremy Hope, "How to Identify, Measure, and Eliminate Hidden Costs" and "Why Annual Targets Distort, Mislead and De-motivate and How to Manage Without Them," *BBRT*, 2004.

CHAPTER 30

Avoiding a Rotten Takeover or Merger

If you have only a few minutes to skim over this chapter, this is what you should focus on:

- How mergers go wrong
- Takeover or merger scorecard
- The investment banker's story

It is often quoted, and even great leaders seem to forget, that history has a habit of repeating itself. Company executives, and the major institutional investors (whose support is often a prerequisite), need to learn the lessons, both from overseas and at home, and think more carefully before they commit to a takeover.

How Mergers Go Wrong

There are many other reasons why you should beware of a TOM.

The Synergy Calculations Are Totally Flawed

The Economist[1] ran a very interesting series on six major takeovers or mergers (TOMs). In the articles they commented that over half of the TOMs had destroyed shareholder value, and a further third had made no discernible difference. In other words, there is a one-in-six chance of increasing shareholder value (per KPMG report as stated in *The Economist*, July 22, 2000).

TOM advisers and hungry executives are as accurate with potential cost savings estimates as they are with assessing the cost of their own home renovations (in other words, pretty hopeless).

Press clippings are easily gathered with CEOs stating the anticipated savings have taken longer to eventuate. The reason is as follows: It can take up to four years to merge the IT platforms together, and even when this is achieved, many of the future efficiency and effectiveness initiatives have been put on the back burner.

They never allow enough for the termination and recruitment costs involved in merging entities.

Loss of Focus on Customers

There is no better way to lose sight of the ball than a merger. Merging the operations will distract management and staff from the basic task of making money. While meeting after meeting occurs at the office and sales staff focus on their future (either applying for positions elsewhere or joining in the ugly scramble for the new positions), the customers are up for grabs. Researchers, sales staff, marketers are all back at their desks busily trying to perform damage-limitation exercises as they either jockey for the life-boats or stay on board to try to keep the ship afloat. It would be an interesting Ph.D. to assess the loss of customers due to merger activity.

Culture Clash

TOMs are like herding cats. Where have cultures merged successfully? In reality, one culture takes over another. This is okay where one culture is fundamentally flawed. However, in many mergers both entities have cultures that work. Now you have a problem. Many competent staff may choose to leave rather than work in a culture that does not suit their working style.

There Is No Heart in a Merged Organization

How long does it take for a company to develop a heart? This is more than just the culture—this includes the living and pumping lifeblood of the organization. I think it takes years and some *consistency* among the management and staff. The *merged* organization cannot have a heart. The organization can be kept on life support, but just like an acute patient it is effectively bedridden and will be in intensive care for some time.

The Loss of Years of Intangibles (Passion, History, Research, Projects)

An organization is a collection of "thousands of years" of experience, knowledge, networking, research, projects, and methodologies. If a major blue-chip company said that it was going to de-establish all its staff and management, shareholder analysts would think management had simply lost their marbles. The stock values would fall. This is exactly what a merger does. Research and development is another victim. How do you keep on projects and maintain the level of momentum with unhappy research staff? At worst, you will be moving one team to a new location, making redundant those whom you believe are making the least contribution, and hemorrhaging talent. Research basically gets decimated. It would be interesting to look at the impact on research post the Wellcome/Glaxo merger.

The Wrong Management Rises to the Top

I have this theory that the main beneficiaries of a merger are the piranhas, those managers who relish the fight to the top. For them, burying a dagger in someone's back needs to be a daily occurrence—it is the equivalent of a caffeine fix—they are addicted to it. The result is quite interesting: The merged company very soon becomes dysfunctional as more and more of these caustic managers rise to the top. The senior management meetings make the feeding frenzy over a carcass, on the plains of Africa, look like an orderly thing. These managers do not live and breathe the organization; the ones who did have long since left as there is no heart in the new organization.

Financial Time Bombs Start Going Off

There are many financial time bombs that impact shareholder value.

Severance packages can create further waste as staff, especially the talented staff, leave before generous severance terms disappear. Thus to retain such staff further salary incentives need to be made that create further pressure on the bottom line.

The TOM is often the time when the shareholders realize that the dilution they have been a silent party too comes into full swing, with the conversion of options. The surge of the share price as speculators play with the stock means that options can be exercised profitably by the executives who then leave the shareholders holding the rotten TOM.

Avoiding a Lemon

Some companies are still making paper money like Enron did. They are a sham and we need to be able to avoid purchasing a lemon. The "Enron documentary" should be compulsory watching for all investors and employees with pensions invested in their companies. The lessons from Enron and other collapses I believe have led to the opinion that all company collapses are predictable.

EXHIBIT 30.1 Warning Signs of a Lemon

Checklist	Is it covered?	
Stock market loves the share for over a 2–3 year period	□ Yes	□ No
CEO has become a media loved person	□ Yes	□ No
The company has adopted some bizarre HR practices	□ Yes	□ No
There is an over hyped culture within the company	□ Yes	□ No
The key positions in the top are head hunted visionaries	□ Yes	□ No
The investment bankers are earning large transactions fees	□ Yes	□ No
There are no questioning articles in the press	□ Yes	□ No
Excessive company executive remuneration	□ Yes	□ No
Senior management team consists of many rags to riches stories	□ Yes	□ No
Outside superstars are recruited in with media fan fare	□ Yes	□ No
A high proportion of the income comes from "invisibles"	□ Yes	□ No
The organisation has created a new market, service that the market does not yet understand	□ Yes	□ No
Take-overs are becoming a regular occurrence in the company	□ Yes	□ No
There are signs that business ethics are questionable	□ Yes	□ No
Very innovative company	□ Yes	□ No
Taxi drivers are talking about the share	□ Yes	□ No
The company has changed its executive jet twice in the last three years!	□ Yes	□ No
Excessive media interest borne from media spin	□ Yes	□ No
Executives are charismatic in front of analysts and the press	□ Yes	□ No

Exhibit 30.1 is a checklist. Score more than five, and you had better *disinvest* before your funds are de-invested from you, by others.

Human Beings Find It Hard to Conceptualize the Intangibles

For many of us, conceptualizing the abstract is very difficult. A company is most definitely an abstract quantity. It is not a balance sheet—it is much more and much less. Executives in major corporations can write off the annual gross national product of a small country on a failed merger and still not lose sleep at night. The numbers are so large that they appear unbelievable and senior management seem to be able to pass them off as just a poor management decision. Yet they are a catastrophe for the investor whose savings are now reduced and the pensioner who was relying on the dividends to cover their yearly living expenses.

It is impossible for the average board and SMT to completely appreciate the full implications of a merger.

Mergers Are Seldom Done from a Position of Strength

Most mergers are defensive, management on the back foot trying to make something happen. Defensive TOMs are not a great idea as the companies escaping from a threat often import their problems into the marriage.

Alternatively, they occur because management consider themselves invincible. They talk to the general public through the press, reveling in their moment in the limelight. Their brief track record of stellar growth is now extrapolated out of all proportions.

There Is Never Enough Time to Fully Evaluate the Target

A merger is like an auction. The buyer rarely has more than a cursory look at the goods before bidding. Management often do not want to find the dirty laundry as it would mean going back to square one again.

During the starry days of courtship it is important not to limit due diligence in the haste to close the deal as you tend to know less about each other than you think. The dirty laundry often takes years to discover and clean.

Takeover or Merger Scorecard

Exhibit 30.2 is a scorecard based on the lessons executives need to complete before boldly going where others have mistakenly gone before (five out of six TOMs fail to achieve the synergies planned). If the merger must go ahead, then please look at the list in Exhibit 30.2 and get to it. I will not wish you good luck as that would not be adequate!

EXHIBIT 30.2 Takeover or Merger Scorecard

1. Can your company turn away from a deal if it does not stack up?	□ Yes	□ No
2. Have you done an evaluation of the potential downside?	□ Yes	□ No
3. Are all the following team players experienced in accurately assessing the full costs of the TOM and accurately estimating synergistic savings?		
■ Advising brokers	□ Yes	□ No
■ TOM advisers	□ Yes	□ No
■ Board	□ Yes	□ No
■ Executive	□ Yes	□ No
4. Have all other alternatives to the TOM been fully explored?	□ Yes	□ No

(Continued)

EXHIBIT 30.2 (Continued)

5. Have safeguards been put in place to ensure that the benefits from this TOM accrue to shareholders, staff, local community, as well as the executive "share option holders"?   ☐ Yes   ☐ No

6. Does your company have experience in doing a proper due-diligence process?   ☐ Yes   ☐ No

7. Has your company enough time to do a proper due-diligence process?   ☐ Yes   ☐ No

8. Has an impact assessment been undertaken on the organization if the TOM fails?   ☐ Yes   ☐ No

9. Has the company got enough cash reserves to "weather any eventual storm" arising from the TOM?   ☐ Yes   ☐ No

10. Have you performed a culture audit? A TOM is like merging two families and many problems are overlooked in the frenzied courtship.   ☐ Yes   ☐ No

11. Have you locked-in a portion of your advisers' fees to a successful realization of the proposed TOM benefits? (remember, many of your advisers have never worked in an organization that has had a successful TOM.)   ☐ Yes   ☐ No

12. Have you performed an assessment of asset fit—quality, condition, and usage?   ☐ Yes   ☐ No

13. Is your target company a "CAMEL"—an organization that can withstand difficult times? It should be a company with adequate Capital, good Asset quality, good Management, record of sound Earnings growth, and good Liquidity.   ☐ Yes   ☐ No

14. Has an assessment been done on the locked-in employment terms and conditions? This is especially relevant in certain countries, e.g., Australian.   ☐ Yes   ☐ No

15. Has an evaluation been performed of the current pressure on the environment in which the organization is trading? At the time you are the weakest, post-merger, the industry is likely to have a major crisis.   ☐ Yes   ☐ No

16. Has an assessment been performed on the technology systems integration? (few understand the implications of a TOM and the time frames involved. The IT team may not have the skills to cope with the now-larger environment.)   ☐ Yes   ☐ No

17. Has the TOM been initiated through sound reasoning? Many mergers based on a defensive or cost-cutting strategy fail.   ☐ Yes   ☐ No

18. Have you carefully selected the target? Or if you have been approached, have you really ascertained why they want to sell?   ☐ Yes   ☐ No

19. Have you checked the adequacy of provisioning for potential bad debts and underperforming loans?   ☐ Yes   ☐ No

EXHIBIT 30.2 (Continued)

20. Is the business tied to contractual conditions that enable customers to pull out of profitable contracts? (A lesson that an Australian bank has learned)	□ Yes	□ No
21. Have you established an integration plan that would include the setting up of a council that would oversee the key integration projects?	□ Yes	□ No
22. Current relationship between the companies is favorable (in other words they have not been fierce rivals in the past).	□ Yes	□ No
23. Do you have the resources to select the new management structure ASAP?	□ Yes	□ No
24. Have you got a contingency plan for the potential loss of key staff? (Uncertainty and very generous severance clauses may force executives you want to keep to activate the severance clause for fear of losing the generous terms.)	□ Yes	□ No
25. Are you prepared to go through the potential pain of lower revenue as management and staff are diverted by the merger?	□ Yes	□ No
26. Are you prepared to be made surplus to requirements when the dust has settled and the bloodletting is finished?	□ Yes	□ No
27. Have you set up a clear strategy for *after* the merger, including who is getting what job, thus avoiding the cancer of uncertainty?	□ Yes	□ No
28. Have you set up an in-house think-tank whose task is to speed up integration and to extract knowledge from the different parts of the joint company and use it in the new organization?	□ Yes	□ No
29. Have you ensured that the joint CEOs are able to work together until the designated CEO leaves? (Remember appearances count.)	□ Yes	□ No

Alternatives to a TOM

Why is it that senior management and boards rush like lemmings toward self-annihilation? It is understandable why the investment community and shareholders make the mistake—they are simply naive. Try and find an analyst who has been a successful manager in business. Their skill is in adding up numbers and the ability to write seemingly sensible evaluations based on little or no knowledge of why mergers cannot work. Shareholders usually have little time for research or are just plain greedy, looking for supernormal returns and believing all the promotional material, which does lift stock evaluations over the short term.

There are alternatives to a TOM. You can:

- Remain being a boutique operator with strategic alliances. This may be better than risking the fate of many failed TOMs.
- Pay back shareholders the surplus fat and let them reinvest elsewhere.
- Improve performance by focusing on underperforming assets (that is often the reason why the other company is interested in yours in the first place).
- Look to grow the old-fashioned way—by expanding from within.
- Invest as a silent partner (Warren Buffet style) in small but fast-growing companies with complementary services and extract value by internationalizing their innovations.

I met an interesting investment banker on the plane from Melbourne to Sydney who told me about the takeover-and-merger game that is being played by large investment bankers around the world. (It has never made any sense to me when everybody knows that only one in six mergers breaks even and many have lost billions off the balance sheet!) The game is called *transactional fees* and involves the study, by the investment bankers, in minute detail of the motivational factors of the key players. They end up knowing more about the private lives of the CFO, CEO, board members, and fund managers than they would like their own partner to know! Investment bankers first go to the CEO and CFO with a proposed merger-and-acquisition deal and they often fail. The CFOs and CEOs know that these deals seldom work.

The investment bankers then go to the influential board members, and the CFO and CEO have to fight it out in the boardroom, which they typically will win. The investment bankers, who have by now spent hundreds of thousands of dollars in research, are not finished. They go to the fund managers, who are the major shareholders, and say, "The board have lost their way; they do not recognize the value in this deal!" The fund managers put the hard word on the board, who in turn say to the CEO and CFO, "If we do not do this deal, the fund managers will change the board structure—but before that we will see that you go first." The CEO then says, "What the hell; we'll do it." Here is the interesting part: The CEO is offered a big sum to go quietly, and this, with the investment bankers' fees, is now amortized, through poorly thought-out accounting principles, slowly killing the combined company for years to come.

Note

1. *The Economist*, "How Mergers Go Wrong," July 22–August 26, 2000.

CHAPTER **31**

The Perils of Restructuring

If you have only a few minutes to skim over this chapter, this is what you should focus on:

- Reorganization scorecard
- Alternatives to a major reorganization
- Before you look at a reorganization

Why Do We Appear to Have an Addiction to Reorganization?

A major reorganization is as complex as putting in a new runway at Heathrow Airport while keeping the planes still landing and taking off. The steps, the consultation, the dynamics, and so forth are just as difficult. How is it that we are unable to fully understand the ramifications and costs of reorganizations, and why do organizations appear to have an addiction to them?

This is what I believe happens: The cost estimates, included here, are based on a notional organization with 5,000 employees:

- There is a period of chaos, where staff are disillusioned and many key staff in the third- and fourth-tier management ranks plan to leave (normally within the first six months).
- The bedding-in process of the new structure starts to kick in somewhere between 7 and 12 months. The completion of all the redundancies takes longer than expected and, yes, more than a few will come back as contractors at a higher cost.
- Costs go through the roof, especially consultancy fees. You will need help with this.
- Designing a new logo (if re-branding), cost can be anywhere between $30,000 and $70,000.

307

- New letterhead, new signage and stationery (if re-branding) will cost between $200,000 and $300,000.
- Culture-change advice will cost $50,000 to $100,000.
- Alignment of procedures will cost $50,000 to $100,000.
- Recruiting for new positions—assistance costs from $100,000 to $200,000 (yes, we need to allow everybody to apply).
- Bedding-in an IT system that can cope with the new structure, having discarded much equipment that was perfectly all right in the two smaller units, will be $750,000 to $2,000,000.
- Unwinding the property leases that both businesses had can take up to 24 to 36 months.

About 24 months after the reorganization was announced, productivity is back to normal; thus for the duration you have been effectively going backward. The 24-to-36-month period advantages may kick in provided that the reorganization has been successful. It is useful to remember that only one out of six takeovers or mergers actually work. I suspect that while reorganizations may have a greater success rate than this, it may well be less than 50%.

Around the world CEOs seem to think restructuring government departments is good for efficiency, improving service, and of course good for their political aspirations.

As Frances Urquhart[1] would say, "Some of you may think that restructuring a department frees the newly formed teams to deliver; others may think that the confusion and miscommunication that often go with a reorganization undermine people's confidence in what they do and in their team, giving rise to a period of stagnation. *You* may think that, but I cannot possibly comment."

Typical Reasons for a Reorganization

We Are Reorganizing to Improve Efficiency

Merging two units/teams together or splitting up teams and reforming them into new teams certainly does create a climate change. The question is whether it leads to efficiency. In order to become more efficient there needs to be a behavioral and procedural change. Staff need to change work habits so that logical efficiencies can be introduced.

One energy-sector company has made much progress with continuous-improvement programs. Senior managers are heavily involved in the change management and now this is part of the culture. They have workshops to identify areas where change needs to occur and people at the meetings agree to take on the process of change. They have had a number of successful projects.

One finance company has had a number of successes with business reengineering. They have made significant inroads by using preferred suppliers and eliminating paperwork or passing over the paperwork to them. Continuous improvement is now part of their culture. There is an ongoing requirement for staff to keep up in their field and bonuses are paid if they pass a tertiary exam, and so on.

The interesting point about these two examples is that they arose from business *reengineering* as opposed to business reorganization. Any efficiencies reorganizations achieve are simply those that are associated with reengineering the processes. Thus, one can surmise it would have been better to have performed a reengineering exercise in the first place.

One area that the uninitiated often make a mistake with is assuming large savings are available when merging corporate service functions, such as merging two accounting functions together. In many cases the costs of changing systems far outweigh the saving from any duplication of labor.

We Are Reorganizing to Improve Service

As stated earlier, a reorganization or merger is like putting in a new runway at Heathrow Airport. Simply laying down foundations, concrete, and a bit of infrastructure is not that hard (try telling that to the management at Heathrow Airport).

Likewise, the reorganized entity is a lot more complex than your planning will have indicated. Day-to-day routines are disrupted with meetings to discuss the new organization, staff applying for new positions, staff searching the papers and agencies for possible backstops—need I go on? Service does not improve, not in the first two years, anyway.

For service to improve you need a behavioral change. Staff need to buy into becoming more customer oriented, measuring their performance in a balanced way. You have only to see the quotes on the wall in any Tony's Tyre Service customer waiting room (a tire company in New Zealand) to understand that staff live and breathe service:

> "Every job is a self-portrait of those who did it—autograph your work
>   with quality."
> "Quality only happens when you care enough to do your best."

A positive behavioral change does not often occur with a reorganization—in fact, quite the reverse occurs in the first two years. So if you are looking for better service, maybe a service program is what is needed rather than a reorganization.

Reorganizing Will Show There Is a New CEO

Many CEOs like to stamp their authority by throwing out systems they do not understand and reorganizing the business to fit a model they are more familiar with. They like to show there is a new "broom" in the organization. This is typical of a CEO with an ego problem. Many reorganizations occur within the first 6 to 12 months of a new CEO arriving and they are making decisions often without full knowledge of the business. The cost to the enterprise is huge. In fact I suggest, as part of the recruitment process, that someone evaluate the reorganizations the CEO has done.

Exhibit 31.1 is a checklist that should be evaluated before a reorganization occurs.

 EXHIBIT 31.1 Reorganization Scorecard Checklist

1. Have you done an evaluation of the potential downside?	☐ Yes	☐ No
2. Have the senior managers got a convincing story to tell that will capture the minds and hearts of staff—without the staff becoming disillusioned very quickly and turning away from the organization?	☐ Yes	☐ No
3. Are all the following team players experienced in accurately assessing the full costs of the reorganization?		
▪ The board	☐ Yes	☐ No
▪ Senior management	☐ Yes	☐ No
▪ Advisers you have used	☐ Yes	☐ No
4. Have all other alternatives to the reorganization been fully explored?	☐ Yes	☐ No
5. Have you got a reorganization web page on the intranet site explaining the current status?	☐ Yes	☐ No
6. For all those staff who now appear to be surplus to requirements, has a reality check been done to ascertain how many of them may be your company oracles? (those people who have much company history, knowledge, and wisdom)	☐ Yes	☐ No
7. Have reasonable estimates been made for consultancy fees?		
▪ New organization logo, if necessary	☐ Yes	☐ No
▪ New letterhead and signage and stationery, if necessary	☐ Yes	☐ No
▪ Culture-change advice	☐ Yes	☐ No
▪ Alignment of procedures	☐ Yes	☐ No
▪ Recruiting costs for new positions	☐ Yes	☐ No
8. Have reasonable estimates been made for temporary staff, redundancy pay, and contractors?	☐ Yes	☐ No
9. Have reasonable estimates been made for legal costs, which can be significant if the change process isn't done well?	☐ Yes	☐ No
10. Have reasonable estimates been made for alignment of procedures?	☐ Yes	☐ No

EXHIBIT 31.1 (Continued)

11. Are you prepared to have key projects grind to a halt as staff lose interest, leave, or are diverted on reorganization exercises?	☐ Yes	☐ No
12. Have you allowed for lower productivity in the next 18 months as the dust settles? (Think of the lost time due to most managers reapplying for their own positions, endless reorganization meetings, etc.)	☐ Yes	☐ No
13. Have you got a contingency plan for the potential loss of key staff?	☐ Yes	☐ No
14. Have you scheduled in-house team-building exercises, as the reorganization will have created some disharmony among managers as they jockey for position?	☐ Yes	☐ No
15. Have all property-related costs been fully accounted for? (Subletting surplus office accommodation takes much longer than the leasing agent would lead you to believe.)	☐ Yes	☐ No
16. Have you discussed reorganization with two or more of your peers from other organizations?	☐ Yes	☐ No
17. Have you created a checklist on all changed IT requirements?	☐ Yes	☐ No
18. Have you organized any enticements for staff to help make them stay on? (They are going to be suffering in this reorganization.)	☐ Yes	☐ No
19. Have you organized training?	☐ Yes	☐ No
20. Have you updated the website for the new structure?	☐ Yes	☐ No
21. Have you created press releases for publications and letters to stakeholders, contractors, suppliers, and customers?	☐ Yes	☐ No
22. Have you developed a training program to help managers during the recruitment process?	☐ Yes	☐ No
23. Have you estimated the time and cost of unfair dismissal cases?	☐ Yes	☐ No
24. Are you prepared to create havoc in the lives of some of your staff? (A reorganization is going to be deleterious to family life of staff.)	☐ Yes	☐ No
25. Have you planned to have events that will put some fun back in the workplace? (reorganizations are unpleasant.)	☐ Yes	☐ No

Less than 15 affirmatives	Stop now—take a break, and think of another strategy for service improvement/enhancement.
15–20	High-risk reorganization—you may be able to increase your score through further preparation.
20–25	Well done—look out for the areas where you do not feel inclined to cover; they could be your Achilles heel.
Over 25 affirmatives	Congratulations, you are in a unique position—worth having your assessment checked by a third party.

There Are Alternatives to a Major Reorganization

Appoint a CEO Who Is a Successful Change Agent. I believe an inspirational CEO will create more value than any reorganization ever will. In fact it would be worthwhile looking to see if inspirational leaders ever fall back on reorganization to solve a problem I can recall the early days of George Hickton, a great leader (see Chapter 4 for more about his leadership). Very soon, with a combination of new blood and inspirational leadership, in a government department that dealt with supporting the unemployed and those on sickness benefit, income support was revolutionized. I believe it was one of the most impressive government departments I have had the pleasure of working for. I recall the time when Hickton was presenting at the Institute of Chartered Accountants conference where the front row was taken up by his direct reports, who were both interested and passionate about what the CEO was talking about. This was a rare sight, and I kept expecting David Attenborough, safari shorts and all, to come through the curtains at any moment, saying, "You are witnessing an event that is rarely caught on camera."

Move Buildings

BP plc was a large, clumsy multinational when Robert Horton, the new CEO, realized that the best way to change was to sell Britannic House, a large and spacious head office, and acquire a head office a third of the size. He called the business heads in and said, "Fit into that building and the staff that cannot make it will be made redundant." It turned out that there was a whole level of management whose working day was based on attending meetings. Surprisingly enough, when these meetings ceased to exist, BP found that it still was operating just as well, and some would say possibly even better.

Rotate Offices

Arthur Andersen's Manchester office had another solution to reorganizations. Each year the senior management team members (i.e., the partners) were instructed to move offices. This had the desired effect of energizing and giving the partners a chance to get on top of the paper war. The partners agreed that the hassle was a positive experience (albeit you needed to ask them a couple of weeks after the move!).

Improve the Leadership from Within

A reorganization may be an attempt to get around the problem that is created by inadequate or ineffective leadership from the senior management team and the management tier that reports just below that. One way of improving the issue is to undertake a *leadership survey*, which is a more in-depth look at leadership than 360-degree feedback can achieve.

You then support these leaders with mentors and follow an up-skilling leadership program. You need to seek mentors who have the *X* factor. Many would welcome the chance to pass on their knowledge and experience. I guess that if half the people who masterminded reorganizations had talked it through with their mentor, if they had one, many reorganizations would have stayed on the drawing board.

Before You Look at a Reorganization

Before you look at a reorganization, reflect on these points:

- Talk to your peers who have done a reorganization to reassess the likelihood of success and the cost involved.
- The next 18 months may be a period of lower productivity—is the organization prepared for this?
- Focus on your key employees first to ensure that the reorganization will not disenfranchise them.
- Evaluate the alternatives; there may be a better option.
- Two reorganizations in a three-to-four-year period indicates another problem (i.e., an addiction).

Note

1. *House of Cards*, BBC production (1991).

CHAPTER 32

Becoming a Serving Leader:
A Viking with a Mother's Heart

If you have only a few minutes to skim over this chapter, this is what you should focus on:

Five foundation stones of a serving leader
Locking in good leadership habits (Exhibit 32.1)
Ten areas of focus for a serving leader

"What makes a good leader?" I was asked across a dinner table. To answer this you need to understand what makes a *serving leader*. Servant leadership has been talked about for some time now. Robert Greenleaf and Larry Spears wrote their groundbreaking book, *Servant Leadership: A Journey into the Nature of Legitimate Power and Greatness*, over 30 years ago.[1]

How do you obtain the qualities and character that make people want to follow you over the top of the trenches? In this book I have featured a number of leaders who have demonstrated the importance of effective leadership. As a manager, you can bully, order, or coerce staff to undertake tasks in a prescribed manner. However, you are unlikely to succeed unless you have learned the lessons and put into practice the traits of the leaders featured in this book.

I have become interested in the leadership exploits of Sir Ernest Shackleton, Sir Edmund Hillary, Sir Winston Churchill, and some modern-day leaders. Shackleton, however, is arguably one of the greatest servant leaders ever and provides the backbone of this simple leadership model.

Shackleton looked after the comforts of the team. He was a mother hen. He genuinely cared for his team members as if they were his own flesh and blood. He saw a leader as one who served rather than one who was served. He dutifully took his turn performing the most menial of chores and expected his leadership team to do the same. He was "a Viking with a mother's heart."

There are many books on leadership and you can spend your entire life reading them. But they will make you more confused than enlightened. This chapter presents a simple model for servant leadership that can be easily understood and hopefully is straightforward to implement.

Five Foundation Stones of a Serving Leader

In order to succeed as a leader, you need five foundation stones in place. These have been derived from my observations of some famous leaders, some of which have already been featured in this book.

Foundation Stone #1: Minimize Personal Baggage

From the time we enter this world, we develop traits and habits that will be limiting factors in our management and leadership of people. We will always be running with a few cylinders misfiring unless we fully understand our behavior patterns and those around us. We inherit baggage from our ancestry, along with many great things. This baggage is added to by our parents, with too much smothering, too little attention, too much criticism, too little quality time—need I go on? I believe one important task in life is to lighten the load so that it is not crippling us when we decide to start "management summiting."

It is important to understand that to be a leader today you do not have to have handled all of your personal baggage; the key is the awareness of your weaknesses. There are plenty of "crippled" CEOs causing havoc in every organization that they work for. Yet there are those iconic CEOs who are a pleasure to work with. My point is that you owe it to your colleagues, your staff, your suppliers, contractors, family, partner, and offspring to do something about your own personal baggage.

We have a choice: to grow and challenge those behavior traits that will create havoc in the workplace, or to ignore them and seek new jobs like we do new partners, hooked on the romance period and leaving when the going gets tough. To make a major contribution, you will need to achieve through the contribution of others. This means acquiring a new set of behavioral skills more suited to working with and leading others.

I have addressed minimizing personal baggage in Chapter 5 of this book. I urge you to go back to that chapter and make inroads in this important area.

Ernest Shackleton developed his character and qualities immensely, from being the favorite brother of doting sisters to becoming the Antarctic explorer that men would follow regardless of risk and reward. Edmund Hillary changed remarkably from the shy and reclusive beekeeper to the media-savvy Nepalese school builder. Hillary changed from a person who hardly spoke in class to a person who, post the conquest of Everest, was giving lecture tours around the world.

Churchill emerged from a dysfunctional family, with a father who, through illness, destroyed his own brilliant political career, and a torrid time at Eton where failure was the norm as he refused to learn the "Eton way," to become a person whom people would follow to their last step and breath. Churchill constantly had an internal fight to keep his abrasive personality traits in check.

Foundation Stone #2: "Love Thy Neighbor as Thyself"

This foundation stone requires us to have some greater driving force than simply worshiping the dollar. Many great CEOs exhibit some spiritual element that has assisted them on their journey. Love for the "common man," hostmanship, humility, and integrity all form the building materials for this foundation stone.

Love for the "Common Man" Many of us pray to our God during the weekend and yet, on Monday, we seldom practice "Love thy neighbor as thyself" with our workplace relationships (suppliers, direct reports, colleagues, etc.). I recall two images. One is of an elderly couple having left my church forcing an oncoming car to give way in the one-way street, outside the church, with the other driver shouting the memorable words, "I suppose you have just been to church!" Another is of a dysfunctional professional firm where the language between the partners was not fit for *The Simpsons*, yet the partners would be "devout" sometime during the weekend.

While atheists can be great leaders, they must have a love for the "common man." Worshipping the dollar will always limit the leader's potential.

Many in the corporate world do not abide by "love thy neighbor as thyself," and that is why we quite happily create conflict in our working environment. Corporate life is littered with examples of unnecessary litigation, which has led to poor health in those individuals who are caught up in this self-inflicted process.

It might be appropriate for the CEO or the senior management team to start bringing some spiritual elements into the business world that would reinforce good and sound business ethics. For example:

- Respecting your colleagues' and your team members' time (i.e., allowing them quality time to process initiatives rather than interrupting them with another meaningless task).
- Investing time to actively listen (even when you are on the verge of exploding with frustration).

- Conducting your working relationships effectively with all colleagues (even those whom you would never invite to your weekend barbecue!).
- Not setting demanding goals when they are unnecessary (e.g., avoiding asking for a report by 9 A.M. tomorrow when you will only get around to reading it three days later).
- Appropriate assistance to poor performers.
- Better handling of stress, of yourself, your staff, and your colleagues.
- Taking control of your stimulant intake. (Do not underestimate the impact it has on your work colleagues.)
- Better treatment of your suppliers.

Levels of caring for the "common man" are contrasted in these examples:

- During World War II, Field Marshall Montgomery, unlike many of his peers in earlier wars, would never let his troops face the enemy in the desert unless they had better equipment, more firepower, and a larger force. He knew that these would ensure minimum casualties on his forces.
- It is worth noting that Churchill, Napoleon, and Alexander the Great did not care for the lives of their troops; they frequently put troops in hopeless positions at great cost to life. To this degree we can say that their foundation stones were not as sound as, say, Shackleton's foundation stones were.
- Edmund Hillary is legendary for his small acts of kindness. On hearing that a two-year-old boy was seriously ill in the hospital, he immediately wrote an inspirational note to him. Naturally it was also inspirational to the parents and to their now-healthy teenage son.

A leader should never forget the small details. It is those small acts of kindness and consideration that will build your legend.

Hostmanship   Jan Gunnarsson[2] says that *hostmanship* is the way we make people feel welcome. In his book and accompanying website, Jan provides inspiration and direction to anyone who wants to make a difference, as an individual, as part of a team, or within an organization. His hostmanship approach has had the approval of Tom Peters, and has had a profound impact on organizations applying it, on both the organization's culture and its interfaces with the outside world.

It is interesting to note that one's ability to be a *host* is influenced by one's past, both in experiences at home and with one's role models. It is no wonder so many of us have issues here.

Jan sees hostmanship as having six areas: serving, maintaining the big picture, taking responsibility, caring, knowledge, and dialogue. I have quoted from his work so you have a better understanding of his views.

Serving *is using your talents and experiences, first and foremost, because you have a genuine interest in someone else's well-being: "What can I do to make you feel better at this particular moment in time?" A desire to help someone achieve their goals and thereby be successful in life.*

Maintaining the big picture *in the world of Hostmanship is about seeing and understanding wholeness. The person who meets the guest is always the company's outward face, right there, right then. Even if we can't be responsible for everything that happens in this entirety, it is important that we understand that it is the guest's opinion of the entirety that affects their meeting with us.*

Taking responsibility *is about being courageous. We must take responsibility for how we choose to react to what happens. Taking responsibility is about standing on the other person's side and helping them improve the world we are both living in: a position which isn't always appreciated in "your own ranks," but at the end of the day it creates stronger and more personal meetings.*

Caring *is the heart of Hostmanship. Allowing caring to prevail in a business is about seeing the human in the people that seek us out. Adapting our systems and our culture with the notion that the people we work with and the people we meet are human.*

Knowledge *is about opening up to all cultures and people, regardless of origin or background. Knowledge is far more than just knowing. It is the ability to use your knowledge in the context of another person's needs.*

Dialogue *is being able to first listen, which is usually the toughest obstacle when a problem needs resolving. We need to listen and try to understand the context by entering into a dialogue. By opening yourself up for a dialogue at every meeting, you are taking all parties at the meeting seriously.*

These quotes come from a well-written brochure from Jan's website, which can be accessed on www.hostmanship.com.

How often when under pressure have you frowned when a staff member came to your office to ask for help? The great leaders know the visitor in front of them is their most important task and are able to welcome the interruption!

Humility   Humility does not mean that you do not use public relations, nor does it mean you do not lay claim to what is rightly your achievements. It simply means that when dealing with individuals you treat them as equals.

While Shackleton loved the limelight and enjoyed the public adoration, he was very humble when communicating with his team, whether in a recruitment confirmation letter or in day-to-day leadership issues. Time and again he gave up comforts for his men. During the Antarctic trip, he gave up his fur-lined sleeping bag, his bed, for a sick member, and his gloves at a point when he risked severe frostbite. He always shared the provisions with all no matter what their contribution. In other words, through humility greatness can be achieved.

Integrity—Set Values and Live by Them   In organizations where "money is god," you will constantly see a lack of values, and behavior among executives and staff that is fit only for the wilds of the Serengeti. When you look at the great collapses of major companies, you will always find a lack of values. Great organizations with high-meaning values can become compromised if these values are not maintained. The CEO must always be looking for breaches and ensuring that these are pointed out to all staff immediately.

Shackleton set high values and lived by them 24/7. When these values were compromised by members of the team, he was unforgiving. The four staff members who had jeopardized the safety of his men were later severely punished on return to the UK by the withholding of the Polar medal.

Foundation Stone #3: Master of Communication and Public Relations

You cannot lead unless others understand your vision and are sold the "flight tickets" for the journey. Mastering communication means under-standing the importance of one-to-one communications, being seen by your staff, working the public relations machine, and mastering the written and spoken word.

Avoid Public Fights   All great leaders realize that the world is a small place and "what goes around comes around." They take care to avoid alienating themselves from individuals whom they do not like. One of the best pieces of advice I have been given is to always approach those who are your adversaries, your roadblocks, and take them out for coffee or lunch. It is the hardest thing to do and yet the most effective.

Shackleton had little time for Scott but had only positive words for him when expressing an opinion in public. He knew it is a small world and he might need Scott's support one day.

Work the Public Relations Machine

"The Boss" loved the press and they loved him back. This is true of many great CEOs. One that comes to mind is Richard Branson. There is no one better at working the public relations machine than Branson. Please revisit the story in Chapter 18 about how Richard Branson holds a celebratory function for his staff.

Oral and Written Word

Leaders need to realize that being a good orator is a vital part of leadership. Time and effort needs to be devoted to delivering a meaningful message. Special coaching and endless practice should be seen as an important investment rather than a chore.

Both Shackleton and Churchill understood the importance of being a good presenter and writer. Churchill went on to be awarded the Nobel Prize for Literature in 1953 and his speeches are still considered some of the best of the 20th century.

Perhaps it is time you started sharing your views, thoughts, and experiences with a wider public.

Informal One-to-One Communication

Managers today have meeting after meeting. They believe it is more efficient than holding one-to-one meetings. Yes, in one hour ten people are listening to the manager, but at the end those ten people will walk out and carry on as if the last hour did not happen. The key to effective management is to hold fewer meetings and use more one-to-one sessions. They do not have to be long if you are doing plenty of walking around among the staff.

Shackleton always personalized communication. If a major change was about to be made, he would mention it in passing individually so that when he publically announced the change it came as no surprise. The bad news was never unexpected. He always canvassed the men when the likely options were unpleasant. In other words, when he said, "We will need to risk the trip to Elephant Island," the men knew that this was the only likely option.

Churchill's personal correspondence kept him close to key people and enabled him to forge very strong personal alliances.

Walkabout: Walking Among the Staff

Leaders can never be too visible to their staff. Great leaders take a walk at least twice a day when they are in the office. Not only does it give them some much-needed exercise but it ensures that they can catch up with staff they might not normally see during meetings. Unfortunately, today, more often than not, it is only the older, more experienced managers who walk around the office—the younger managers believe that an email will do!

Every night, no matter how many degrees below freezing it was, Shackleton would visit each tent for a pep-talk. He would wake in the early hours of the morning to keep the man on watch company (his need for a basic four hours' sleep would no doubt have been a considerable advantage). He always found time to cheer up team members who were feeling depressed about their prospects.

Churchill flew incredible journeys during World War II, at great risk to his health, to visit the different theaters of war. He was always inspecting what the scientists had to offer. He also regularly visited areas of London that had been riddled with bombs.

One week a year, George Hickton, a successful New Zealand CEO and leader, likes to take his executive team to run a part of the business with the existing staff by their side showing them the ropes. His executive teams in the past have run an employment center, a betting agency, and a tourist information center.

Richard Branson is very skilled in this area. He is forever seen with his staff, many of whom have pictures at their office or their home of when they met him. I would suggest that not many CEOs would have their photo taken as many times with their staff as he does.

On one occasion, when Virgin was opening yet another route, they organized a party for staff, asking them to bring their partner and their best friend … Branson stood by the door all night, kissing the women and shaking the hands of all the men. A professional photographer and support crew were on hand to ensure every person had a photo with Branson. Where do you think these photographs went?—center mantelpiece (wedding photo moved to the right). What do you think the staff member's best friend thought every time they looked at the photo?

We cannot all be like Branson, but we should be able to be recognized and spoken to by any staff members who see us. You know you have got it right when all staff feel confident at any time to come up and wish you "Good morning, Pat" when you arrive at work.

A better practice is to spend 20 minutes walking among your team members each day, posing a question or two to show you are up with the play and to keep them on their toes.

Eon Black, a CFO of BP New Zealand, was a past-master of walkabout. Every day he would do the rounds and have a great question to ask you. If you were having a bad day, you would often duck beneath the

> partition and commando-crawl to cover as soon as you heard his voice. His daily presence meant that if you had a question for him, you held it and waited for the visit: "Eon, did you want me to ...?"; "Eon, is this what you were after?" He was also kept abreast of whatever the team was achieving.

Foundation Stone #4: Have a Mentor and a Safe Haven

Finding and Using a Mentor

Shackleton realized the importance of mentorship and this is what he said in his book, *South: The Endurance Expedition:*[3]

> *Leonard Tripp, who has been my mentor, counselor, and friend for many years, and who, when the Expedition was in precarious and difficult circumstances, devoted his energy, thought, and gave his whole time and advice to the best interests of our cause.*

Edmund Hillary sought the help and advice of Admiral George Dufek, who was in charge of the American Antarctic fleet. Admiral Dufek helped Hillary choose the site of Scott Base, which has been used continuously now for over 40 years. Admiral Dufek also helped Hillary at other critical stages of the expedition.

In business many costly failures could have been averted if advice had been sought from a trusted and wise mentor. The key is the selection (and use) of your mentor/adviser and realizing that just because you have asked once, this does not preclude a second or third request for help.

Find a mentor and seek advice on those major decisions—you will notice the difference in *your* expeditions. Read Chapter 3.

Having a Safe Haven

All leaders will have many soul-searching moments during their journey. The magnitude of these can be quite severe if the leader is taking their team/organization on a significant conquest. In order to cope with these "downs" you need to have built a safe haven for yourself, a place where you can retreat and recover. Leaders need to nurture close family relationships and hobbies that offer relaxation and enjoyment. Without a safe haven, leaders will succumb to the sense of failure that can permeate them when all they have in their life is their chosen conquest that has now gone off the rails.

It is important to cultivate a passion that absorbs your time—the "safe harbor" when times are tough. Do you enjoy your home so much that every day away is a wasted day? If not, maybe you should pursue with more vigor your dream home. It could well be the haven you need. The importance of Chartwell House to Sir Winston Churchill is well documented and I recommend that you read about Churchill in Chapter 14.

Foundation Stone #5: Be Clear on Your Legacy

I firmly believe that the meaning of life for the human race can be summed up in one word—*legacy*. We all have a driving force to leave something behind to say we were here. It can be through our family, through industry, or through our devotion to others. This legacy says, "I was here; I added up to something; I had something to say; I changed peoples' lives for the better." Understanding one's legacy is important; it is a directional beacon that will guide you through life in a more purposeful way.

Andy Warhol famously said that everybody has 15 minutes of fame in them. We each have a unique mix of attributes, skills, and experiences that can be put to use in leaving a lasting legacy. The trick is to find them. It is not always obvious.

Shackleton knew from an early age that he would be an explorer. He wanted to be first to the Pole, first to cross the Antarctic and bring his men back safely.

Churchill also knew he was destined to leave a legacy. As Chapter 14 explains, he left a profound legacy: galvanizing the British and Americans to fight tyranny. His writing and recorded speeches are still the benchmark many aspire to.

Sir Edmund Hillary's legacy is in both mountaineering and the impact his Nepalese schools have had on the livelihood of generations of Nepalese. His story can be read in Chapter 7.

As a leader, you need to dream of your eventual goal—to see, feel, and hear what it would be like to succeed—using the neuro-linguistic programming techniques discussed in Chapter 1.

If you were to make a one-paragraph statement as to what your legacy is to be, what would it say? Forming this legacy in your mind gives meaning to life and puts up a guiding star in the sky that will shine brightly no matter what dark clouds are over you.

As shown in Exhibit 32.1, the foundation stones are the basis on which your leadership is built. It is important where possible to ensure that each one is developed and maintained. Once you have the foundation stones in place, you can use them as a platform from which to "juggle your time" between the twelve areas of focus that characterize the serving leader. Some foundation stones and focus areas impact on the organization's culture, and this influence is marked by a C in a box.

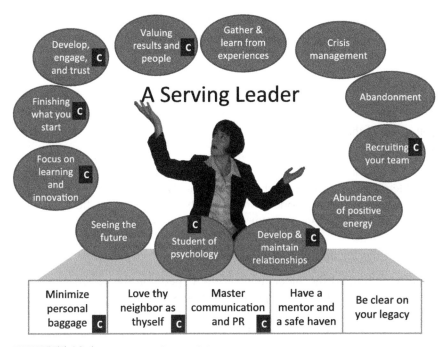

EXHIBIT 32.1 Serving-Leader Model

Areas of Focus for a Serving Leader

I have based the twelve areas of focus (Exhibit 32.1) on the lessons derived from Shackleton, Hillary, Churchill, and many other great leaders. To explain these 12 areas of focus I will frequently refer to Shackleton's leadership. His feat of saving the whole *Endurance* party in Antarctica is accepted by many, as one of the greatest demonstrations of leadership.

The Endurance party lived for two years in the harshest environment in the world, with early 20th-century equipment and no support from outside agencies. He managed to make a home on a floating ice-shelf and sail all his men to the uninhabited Elephant Island. He then sailed a small team across 800 miles of the roughest water in the world in little more than a lifeboat, after which they crossed unclimbed mountains and glaciers in an epic 30-hour traverse. This chapter attempts to pull together much that has been written about Shackleton in a way that it can be digested and embedded in our daily routines. (The full leadership story is told in *Shackleton's Way.*[4])

The concept of the serving leader will be explained as you read on. Shackleton managed to juggle the 12 serving-leadership balls (areas) with great aplomb.

Crisis Management

Letting Go of the Past

With the amount of carnage that many CEOs and senior management preside over, it is quite clear they have no qualms about moving on. When Shackleton witnessed the final sinking of the *Endurance* he knew it meant bankruptcy. Yet not for one moment did he let this event affect his optimistic plans for getting his team off the ice-floe and back to safety.

The Old Dogs for the Hard Road, Every Time

Shackleton valued the older men on the expedition, he referred to them as the "old dogs." On all his perilous journeys, where life and death were in the balance he always had the old dogs in the advance party. He made an interesting observation one day. The old dogs ate less, complained less, slept less, and were injured less!

In today's business world, where recruitment is often run by young human resources officers and equally young managers, the old dogs find it hard to change jobs when they are over 50. This is stupid.

Much of one's best work is done beyond the age of 50 (well, this is what I choose to believe, with of course a vested interest!). One is wiser, has seen it all before, knows where to conserve energy, and knows when to put the hard yards in.

Be Flexible in Tactics

Shackleton was always thinking ahead. However, some decisions would have to be reversed on a daily basis as conditions changed. The change in circumstances constantly meant a change in what could be taken along on the next leg of the return journey.

When they knew it was time to leave the breaking ice-floe, he had to assess what was the safest option, bearing in mind the various attributes of three potential destinations. The condition of the men and of the sea, and the fact that one lifeboat was only marginally seaworthy, had to be weighed. In a sequence over the course of just three days, the destination for their escape kept changing: Clarence Island or Elephant Island; King George Island; Hope Bay (on the Antarctic mainland); and finally, Elephant Island, where they landed safely.

The vagaries of business and those of an expedition are the same. You will never be able to predict accurately the future. We need to provision for worst-case scenarios and carefully assess what are the best options to take in the given circumstances.

Maintaining a Sense of Humor When All Looks Lost

Shackleton's sense of humor was always to the fore. He was in fact the life and soul of the group. He was constantly looking for ways to maintain morale. Sir Edmund Hillary was known for his sense of humor and always looked for it in others when recruiting team members.

As Tom Peters says about bad times, "I can say with conviction and confidence that this is when it gets fun for talented and imaginative leaders."[5]

Abandonment

Management guru Peter Drucker frequently used the word *abandonment.* He said that "the first step in a growth policy is not to decide where and how to grow. It is to decide what to abandon. In order to grow, a business must have a systematic policy to get rid of the outgrown, the obsolete, the unproductive." He also put it another way: "Don't tell me what you're doing, tell me what you've stopped doing."

Great leaders know when to cut the losses, admit they made an error of judgment, sell off old parts of their business, and move on. The act of abandonment gives a tremendous sense of relief to the leader for it stops the past from haunting the future. It takes courage and conviction— abandonment is a skill that one needs to cultivate.

Knowing when to abandon and having the courage to do so are the two attributes leaders need. To help you figure out what to abandon, seek advice from sages and, of course, your mentor. These people have been there before you and can recognize the difference between projects that should be persevered in and those that should be given up.

Peter Drucker observed in one organization that the first Monday of every month is set aside for "abandonment meetings at every management level." Each session targets a different area so that in the course of a year everything is given the once-over.

Recruiting Your Team

Pick Your Second-in-Command with Care

Shackleton's second-in-command was Frank Wild—an old dog, as Shackleton would say. He was totally dedicated to acting on behalf of the Boss in his absence. Wild followed the Boss on all his adventures. Like Shackleton he started off as a seaman and became a great explorer.

The Boss and Wild were the perfect fit. Wild left the planning to the Boss and focused on maintaining a happy and friendly morale no matter what transpired.

Recruit Carefully

Shackleton chose his people carefully; he was always looking for character, competence, and multiple skills. The Boss's interview questions penetrated the individual to see if he had a positive attitude and a light-hearted, even whimsical nature. His recruitment strategy was as follows:

- "Loyalty comes easier to a cheerful person than one with a heavy countenance" (the Boss's words).
- His inner-core members had to be loyal and strong leaders. The Boss knew the importance, not of just leading by oneself, but of ensuring leadership by others within the team.
- He set difficult tasks for the interviewees to see how keen they were to join.
- He used trials to test whether applicants were able to undertake the menial chores that such an expedition entailed, cleaning decks, sorting out tack, assisting at meal time etc,.

Abundance of Positive Energy

Jack Welch, former CEO of General Electric, says that it is important that a leader have "positive energy, the capacity to go-go-go with healthy vigor and an upbeat attitude through good times and bad."[6] Shackleton had an abundance of positive energy. He worked the hardest, slept the least, and led from the front. He was fitter than all the others on the team, with the possible exception of Frank Wild.

How many potbellied CEOs can say that? Many would not last five minutes on a treadmill.

Never Give Up

The Boss never gave up: He believed that "there's always another move, you just have to find it." Having arrived at the whaling town on South Georgia, the Boss made four attempts to rescue the men from Elephant Island and spent a further seven months rescuing his men who were stuck on the other side of Antarctic.

Shackleton was always a purveyor of hope and optimism. When setbacks occurred, he had to remain outwardly optimistic, despite his own feelings, to prevent a growing despair among his men. He knew that such despair could, in the face of adversity, lead to dissension, mutiny, or simply giving up.

- He kept the men so busy that they had little opportunity to brood over their predicament.
- When he sensed that the mood of the men was darkening, he would use a holiday observance or some other pretence to justify extra rations of food to boost morale.
- Hurley, a member of the *Endurance* expedition, said, "I always found him, rising to his best and inspiring confidence when things were at their blackest."

Many Minor Celebrations

The Boss loved a party. Every Saturday night they would celebrate and toast their loved ones. Birthdays were always honored. He even went to the trouble of taking a Christmas pudding along on the arduous walk to the then—"furthest south" with Scott. On Christmas Day, out came the small pudding with a piece of holly. Through near-starvation he had kept this to share with Scott and his other companion.

Successful senior managers have the knack of making work fun—a quality that often can be seen in how teams perform and enjoy their work. However, for many organizations the "fun" is restricted to obliterating the week with a number of stiff vodkas or half a dozen beers on Friday night.

Some suggestions to *make work more fun* in the office are:

- Be brave and create a workspace that has color and energy to foster a successful attitude.
- Celebrate success—one company has a newsletter called the *Success Express*.
- Create "CEO bouquets" gifts of either flowers, theatre tickets, or restaurant vouchers that are given out weekly for outstanding achievements.

- Put guidelines on the percentage of time that should be invested in management meetings, board papers, and so on, and monitor these time periods.

> I came across a team that had a half-day out-of-office session every month. They would hold this session after they had finished the month-end. The session would include training and planning activities for the remaining month. When asked how team morale was, the reply was "outstanding."

Young at Heart

"The Boss was so young at heart that he appeared to be younger than any of us," McIlroy, a member of his expedition, was quoted as saying. Shackleton was always looking for ways to amuse his team—plays, sing-a-longs, cards, moonlight football matches.

Yet this trait is seldom seen in the modern CEO.

Develop and Maintain Relationships

Key Decision Makers

Shackleton knew that his dream of being the first to the South Pole could be achieved only through the support of the Royal Geographical Society and wealthy sponsors who needed to be inspired by the epic proportions of the enterprise. Shackleton not only was close friends with these decision makers, he was a favorite with many of their wives—his charm, good looks, and attentiveness assured a constant stream of support.

Churchill said he would "make friends with the devil" if it would help Britain's cause in the war. He maintained close contact with many key decision makers across the world.

Be Aware of the Politics

Churchill knew the importance of the United States presence in the war. Many of his famous speeches were aimed not only at the British listening public but also at the Americans, who would surely suffer if the Nazis controlled the Atlantic.

Sir Edmund Hillary knew that he would never be in the leading party to conquer Everest if he remained with his fellow New Zealander, George Lowe.

Student of Psychology

Let Psychology Be Your Friend

Shackleton was ahead of his time. He read widely in psychology and wanted on his return to England to write his thoughts on the psychology of leadership. Generations have lost much by his failure to complete this task.

His understanding of psychology played a big part in saving the lives of his team. He appreciated the importance of understanding the team's physical as well as psychological needs.

- On the hike over the mountains of South Georgia, his two team members wanted to rest. Shackleton knew that this would be the end of them and his crew stuck on Elephant Island. He let them sleep for five minutes and then woke them up, saying they had slept for 30 minutes.
- On the famous boat trip, he took two members who would be of no use but could not be left behind. These two were the negative soothsayers who would have poisoned the minds of those left on Elephant Island.
- His selection of crews on the escape from the sinking ice-floe took account of the dynamics of the friendships, the seamanship, and finally the state of the boats. One team had to handle a constantly sinking boat.
- He noted that the moodiness of the expedition's photographer was improved by flattery and by including him in consultations about the expedition's course.
- He would sow a seed if he thought a change might be inevitable.
- During all the trials and tribulations, he never shared any doubts he might have had about their predicament.

Minimizing Emotional Damage

Shackleton was the master of conflict resolution: He avoided emotional outbursts. He would gently point out the reason why it should be done a different way. He would only tell staff off in private and when this was done it was normally in a careful manner.

He did not like all of his team members. One team member stole personal possessions left in the ice. During the difficult 18 months, he worked with everyone. Only on returning to England did he truly punish those who had crossed the line of acceptable behavior. He did not permit them to be holders of the Polar medal.

Shackleton's philosophy was: When staff members fail you, do not blame them. There were a number of instances where team members failed him. There was one near-mutiny and one captain sailed off early, leaving Shackleton and a small South Pole party to die (*Nimrod* expedition). I am sure Shackleton gave the captain a cool reception, on boarding the boat, but it is said he did not have a cross word with him. Shackleton's view was: "If they fail, it is because I have not trained them well enough or should not have recruited them." In other words, he took the blame.

Managing Anger

Shackleton was able to manage his anger and frustration. Many times, he had seen leaders letting go at the subordinates and had promised himself never to be like that.

He was very advanced for his time. He had the capability of choosing not to get angry. When you possess this mechanism, you realize that anger does not help; the emotional damage caused by the outburst cannot be healed quickly and in some cases the damage done can never be repaired. I am sure readers can recall, as if it was yesterday, emotional outbursts directed at them over ten years ago. The apology cannot wipe away the memory.

If you have an anger-management problem, the behavioral change takes around 12 weeks of constant modification. I know, as I went through a behavior-change program myself.

Keeping Trouble Close to You

Shackleton engaged the dissidents and avoided needless power struggles. At critical times, he ensured that the dissidents traveled with him rather than letting them pollute the minds of the younger expedition members.

Shackleton feared that the anxiety of the expedition's artist would spread like an infection to the other men, so he made sure that the artist always resided in his or Wild's tent.

Seeing the Future

The Future Must Be Owned by the Leader

Shackleton could visualize things ahead and plan accordingly. Extensive planning needs to be performed. The extent of his detail in planning included:

- Different gear to avoid the problems he had experienced in past expeditions
- Provisioning food and equipment that saved their lives many times
- The standardization of packing cases made of a new material (plywood) that could be reconstituted into building material for a hut

Bold in Planning but Careful in Execution

Shackleton and other great leaders, such as Edmund Hillary, were meticulous with their planning. This of course was very relevant to them as there was no courier to deliver missed items.

While the vision must be bold, every conceivable risk was minimized to ensure a safe outcome. Shackleton, like Hillary, *over-provisioned.* Hillary planned so that he could, if the "gods were smiling," surprise Fuchs by getting first to the South Pole in "motorized transport."

Shackleton's original plan was to be away for just over a year, but he had wisely provisioned for two years based on 4,000 calories a day.

Provision for the Team

Only the best was good enough for the *Endurance* expedition. New equipment never tried before was designed, and backup equipment was the best that money could buy. The food brought on board was fit for a king; unusual treats that were capable of being stored for years were taken. In the bleakest moments Shackleton presented his men with a treat that would say to them, "There is more of this when we get home."

Lack of provisioning for team members is a common failing of many managers. They expect their teams to work "flat out" without the correct equipment. Rarely have I seen a CEO who has put the staff's need for equipment high up on his or her agenda.

Focus on Learning and Innovation

Constantly Innovate

Shackleton always learned from prior experiences. His experience of Captain Scott showed him the type of leader he did *not* want to be.

Shackleton designed special clothing, the equivalent of GORE-TEX® today. He also designed a tent that could be quickly erected in a blizzard. These two innovations no doubt saved the lives of his men.

The *James Caird* lifeboat that made the crossing to South Georgia was modified, and these modifications saved them all as a 40-foot-plus rogue wave swamped the boat during the journey. The wave was so large that Shackleton at first mistook it for a cloud!

Leadership Is Task Specific

A leader needs to have experience in the enterprise he/she is running. I firmly subscribe to the theory that a CEO from outside the company and outside the sector has a slim chance to succeed. She will find it extremely difficult to win and hold the staff's trust.

Shackleton was a brilliant leader of an expedition but was spectacularly unsuccessful in business. His skills were at the fore on an adventure where there would be no bailout from others. Would he have been able to lead a massive enterprise successfully? His track record says no.

Leadership Can Be Learned

While truly great leaders are probably born, not made, many good qualities can be embedded in one's makeup. Shackleton trained himself from being an ordinary man to becoming an exceptional leader. He learned from prior mistakes, he was a student of other explorers' experiences, and his hero was the Norwegian, Roald Amundsen. He admired and sought to emulate the skill, preparation, and attention to detail displayed by Amundsen in the 1911 race to be the first to the South Pole.

It is thus important for leaders to be carefully prepared for their role. Too often today a young, bright-eyed executive is thrust into a leadership role totally unprepared, the board mistakenly confusing technical competence with leadership and management acumen.

Finishing What You Start

Many initiatives fail because the leader does not get behind the projects enough. Many leaders have an attention deficit disorder that rivals any teenager's. An additional problem is that some projects are started that, with proper counsel, never would have left the drawing-board.

Some ways you can make a difference in this area include:

- Monitor all late projects each week and make it career-limiting for project managers to be on the "late project list" on a regular basis.
- Have a projects-in-progress summary and review it at least twice a month thus ensuring the projects are finished as fast as new ones are started.
- Set up a focus-group workshop to assess the feasibility of all new major projects—these focus groups typically are comprised of experienced individuals across the organization. During the day they discuss the main problems, discuss the technology that is being proposed, see a presentation of the proposed new systems, and brainstorm the main hurdles the project team will need to clear. If at the end of the workshop the focus group gives the green light, you then have 20 or so sales agents for the new system around the organization. (See the focus-group meeting agenda in Appendix E.)

Develop, Engage, and Trust

Removing Barriers of Rank to Build Cohesion

Shackleton was anti-establishment. He would have loved the changes of open-plan offices and rotational teams. Tasks were assigned based on an individual's skills. All members, including Shackleton, did the dishes, cleaned the floor, and so forth. When it came to rationing the fur-lined sleeping bags to the team, straws were drawn. The three main leaders drew the short straws, in a rigged draw which benefited the younger men.

The Boss always minimized status differences and insisted on courtesy and mutual respect between all members of the team.

"Energize" Others

Jack Welch[7] puts this trait in his top-five must-haves for leaders: the ability to release the team members' positive energy "to take any hill." Shackleton had the ability to energize others. The team was prepared to take on any task he wanted as they knew he would be working beside them. He energized them to; spend weeks in the futile task of trying to break the ship free from the ice, haul the lifeboats over the ice-floe, and make the seemingly impossible traverse of South Georgia's snow peaked mountain range.

Giving Recognition Freely

Recognition is more important than most of us understand. I believe it is one of the most important driving forces in performance. Yet so many companies, managers, and leaders believe it has to be given sparingly, as if too much recognition would water it down. There appears to be a tax on recognition. McDonalds and other companies have taken this tax on recognition to the ultimate by having an *employee of the month*, indicating that only one staff member can achieve this. What does this say to the rest of the staff? Surely, if four staff members have succeeded, then four staff members should be given the award!

I will never forget my daughter at the age of eight-and-a-half, traveling on Christmas Day, as she was given a cardboard origami paper-plane kit by the flight attendant, turning to me and saying, "Dad, will you make this for me—nobody else will be able to do it as quickly as you!" Throughout the flight she watched my progress, encouraging me by

(Continued)

> saying, "Dad, you are ahead of everybody else—it looks fantastic." I
> knew then, as if struck by lightning, that my daughter will grow up to
> be a successful leader whose staff will go the extra mile. She has a
> special and important gift—the realization that giving recognition costs
> so little yet makes such a lasting impact.

As a leader, when did you last:

- Send a signed memo of thanks to a staff member?
- Ask team members up to your office to offer them thanks for going the extra mile?
- Send a letter of thanks to a major customer, appreciating the continued relationship?
- Send a letter to a major supplier, appreciating their faultless supply record?
- Attend the orientation program of new recruits, asking questions that show you have taken the time to read their curriculum vitae and look forward to their contribution?
- Walk around the offices and factory talking casually to staff?

See Appendix D for some examples of recognition letters.

Fitness and Health of the Team

Great leaders care about their staff. Shackleton devised many activities on the ice-floe to keep the team in good health. I am sure some of the team would have had more serious health issues had they been marooned in the United Kingdom in 1914-1915!

Health, fitness, and general well-being of staff are core values some pursue vigorously and to which other CEOs merely pay lip service. I know of one organization where teams are in competition vying for the greatest weight loss. Each person in the organization has been given a walk counter. This is encouraging people to walk at lunchtime, walk up the stairs instead of taking the elevator, walk to work, and so on. The team says it has made a big improvement in staff satisfaction.

Set the Mission, Values, Vision, and Strategy

All levels of staff need to understand the organization's mission, vision, and values. If they do not know or understand the journey how can they be engaged?

Organizations are waking up to the fact that this linkage must be understood if staff are to be "focused, fast, and flexible" as Bruce Holland, a Wellington strategic planner and communicator, has advocated. Strategic planning processes must be much more inclusive if your organization is to reap benefits.

Holland says, "If you have done your job properly, you should be able to rip up the final document as staff and management have the linkage imprinted in their memory." He has found that achieving this level of understanding is much quicker and easier than most managers believe. There are tricks to getting people across the organization involved that can generate enormous amounts of understanding, energy, goodwill, and commitment.

I have to admit to a bit of confusion here, so I set down the *linkages* as part of a learning and reinforcement exercise for us all.

The *mission* is like a timeless beacon pointing to something that may never be reached—for example, Walt Disney's mission is "to make people happy" and 3M's mission is "to solve unsolved problems innovatively."

The *values* are what your organization stands for: "We believe ..." For example, a Public Sector Entity has the values, "Seek innovation and excellence, engage constructively, ask questions, support and help each other, bring solutions, see the bigger picture."

The *vision* is where we want to go. The vision is the tool to galvanize your organization if it is stated with enough clarity and commitment. There are some very famous examples. The one that sticks in my mind is when President John F. Kennedy said, "I believe that this nation should commit itself to achieving the goal, before this decade is out, of landing a man on the moon and returning him safely to the earth."

This simple statement galvanized the whole American scientific community for a herculean effort. Each day, week, and month, employees around the United States were working toward this vision. From the moment it had been uttered, NASA experts were planning backward to see how the millions of building blocks needed to be put together.

Strategy is the way an organization intends to achieve its vision. In a competitive environment, your strategy will be a distinguishing feature between you and your competition. In the public sector, your strategy is the way you can best marshal your resources to achieve the desired outcomes.

Communicate the Organization's Critical Success Factors Clearly to the Staff

Ensuring all layers of staff have an understanding of the linkage between the organization's critical success factors (see Chapter 19) and the mission, values, vision, and strategy is fundamental.

Shackleton knew the importance of getting the team totally aligned. He recognized intuitively that this would happen through understanding the critical success factors (CSFs) and ensuring each day that the team planned its daily duties with this in mind.

Truly great companies know their CSFs and communicate these to their staff (see Chapter 19 for more information about CSFs). Yet many organizations have not distinguished their *critical* success factors from the myriad of success factors. Teams are thus often traveling in a direction very different from the intended path.

Cross-Train and Rotate Teams to Develop Staff

Shackleton broke down the barriers that would get in the way of a cohesive team. He devised a staff rota where all team members, including himself, were involved. He changed all the given rules of past expeditions to arrive at a team that was multi–skilled e.g., the doctor could also skipper the *Endurance*.

Sir Edmund Hillary also used cross training successfully in his Antarctic expedition.

Matching Tasks to Individual Capabilities and Personalities

Shackleton went to great lengths to suit the tasks to individual capabilities and personalities. While stuck on the ice, he ensured that the entire team was occupied in relevant activities: "He never expects one to do more than one is capable of."

This model is very different from "Throw them in the deep end and see who can swim." Not surprisingly, this philosophy is very common in organizations that can be heard complaining about high staff turnover!

Know Your Staff Inside Out

Shackleton spent time with each member of his team to find out what made them tick, how he could best lead them, and how he could serve them. It is no wonder he was called the "Boss."

Valuing Results and People

Shackleton valued life. No goal or target was worth the loss of life. History proves that Shackleton would never attempt a goal if the return journey was not guaranteed. He could have been the first to the Pole, but he knew that he and his men would have died doing it.

Captain Scott, on the other hand put his goals before his men's safety. Frank Wild, in an early expedition, at one point had to disobey Scott's orders—otherwise five men would have died. Scott in a later expedition managed to kill all of the advance party, including himself.

Many senior managers and CEOs have killed staff or been killed through presiding over a system whereby staff had to take unnecessary risks, such as making staff drive home after working 12 hours, demanding that a chartered flight go when the pilot has warned that it is too risky, or sending staff to war-torn countries with inadequate support, training, or a functional escape plan?

As Edmund Hillary once said about George Mallory and Andrew Irvine's attempt on Everest, "I always thought conquering mountains meant coming back alive."

When viewing Margaret Thatcher's leadership one comes to the conclusion that "develop, engage, and trust", and "valuing results and people" were not areas of focus for her. Whilst she was fearless, incredibly intelligent, and operated on only five hours' sleep, her leadership qualities were flawed in many respects. Lord Tibbet is quoted as saying "like me, Margaret Thatcher works best under pressure—pressure that causes more discomfort to one's aides than oneself!"

Accumulate Experience

From an early age, Shackleton looked for experience. At the age of 14, he was a cabin boy on his first sea voyage. He learned from working with both great and not-so-great captains. He sought to go on as many polar adventures as he could, to prepare himself to get to the South Pole. This level of preparation can be seen in the lives of Edmund Hillary, and Winston Churchill, and in many of the leaders in the book, *In Search of Leadership*.[8] You are never too young to take on some form of leadership, as all experiences, whether good or bad, create valuable learning opportunities. The same cannot be said about those sitting in front of the television watching endless sports coverage.

A Viking with a Mother's Heart

Shackleton looked after the comforts of the team. He was a mother hen. He genuinely cared for his team members as if they were his own flesh and blood. He saw a leader as one who served rather than one who was served. He dutifully took his turn performing the most menial of chores and expected his leadership team to do the same. A member of the *Endurance* expedition described him as "a Viking with a mother's heart." This sums up beautifully what a serving leader is.

Ken Blanchard's book, *The Secret*,[9] neatly records the fact that a leader exists to serve others rather than being the one who is served. Shackleton would be the first to nurse an ailing member, he would be the first to brew a cup of tea if he knew his staff were at the end of their tether.

Leaders need to perceive this kind of voluntary servitude as an *asset*, not a weakness.

Notes

1. Robert K. Greenleaf and Larry C. Spears, *Servant Leadership: A Journey into the Nature of Legitimate Power and Greatness*, Paulist Press International (U.S.), 25th Anniversary Edition, 2002.
2. Jan Gunnarsson and Olle Blohm, "The Art of Making People Feel Welcome," *Dialogos*, 2008.
3. Ernest Shackleton, *South: The Endurance Expedition*, Penguin Classics, 2004.
4. Margot Morrell and Stephanie Capparell, *Shackleton's Way: Leadership Lessons from the Great Antarctic Explorer*, Nicholas Brealey Publishing, 2003.
5. Tom Peters, "Thriving on Chaos: Bold Leaders Gain Advantage," *Leadership Excellence*, February 2010.
6. Jack Welch and Suzy Welch, "Leading People: Inventing the Future Now," *Leadership Excellence*, February 2010.
7. Ibid.
8. Phil Harkins and Phil Swift, *In Search of Leadership: How Great Leaders Answer the Question, "Why Lead?"* McGraw Hill, 2008.
9. Ken Blanchard and Mark R. Miller, *The Secret: What Great Leaders Know and Do*, Berrett-Koehler, 2009.

CHAPTER 33

Part Four Progress Checklist

Twelve-Week Change Program

New methods and practices can be locked in if you perform the task each week for a twelve-week period. The checklist in Exhibit 33.1 will help you make the changes that you choose to make relating to servant leadership, discussed in Chapter 32. The checklist in Exhibit 33.2 will help you make the changes referred to in Chapters 25 through 31.

EXHIBIT 33.1 Checklist for Locking in Good Leadership Habits

	1	2	3	4	5	6	7	8	9	10	11	12	13
1. Have you done a few walks around the office this week? (target daily when in the company of staff)													
2. Have you found out about a staff member's life, needs, ambitions this week? (target one staff member a week)													
3. Have you looked at one team member this week to see how you can suit tasks to his or her capabilities and personality?													
4. Have you demonstrated, by an action/deed, your concern over the welfare of your staff this week?													
5. Have you demonstrated "*bostmansbip*" this week??													
6. Have you thanked someone this week?													
7. Have you shown your humorous side to staff this week?													
8. Have you read a management article, a chapter in a development book this week?													
9. Have you met your mentor this week? (target at least every two weeks during change process)													
10. Have you approved an innovation to be implemented this week? (target is ten a year per every staff member)													
11. Have you set realistic and acheivable goals for your staff this week?													
12. Have you performed tasks this week to improve public perception? (speaking engagement, press release, acted on a professional body or charity, etc.) (target at least two actions a month)													
13. Have you had a one-to-one with all of your direct reports this week?													

Question								
14. Have your supported your second-in-command this week?								
15. Have you been conveying positive energy and optimism this week?								
16. Have you personally orchestrated a celebration this week?								
17. Have you been involved in some future-gazing this week to ensure you have thought of options if circumstances change?								
18. Have you ensured that difficult and complex assignments have a few "old dogs" in the team?								
19. Have you promoted any health initiative? (target at least one per month)								
20. Have you invested time developing your staff? (target one person a week whose training will be influenced positively by what you have actioned)								
21. Have you taken measures to reduce risk of injury in your organization by observing and thinking about safer alternatives?								
22. Have you practiced this week any new understanding of psychology? (e.g., in the way you act with your staff)								
23. Have you been active in recruitment process of staff? (weekly involvement)								
24. Have you "energized" any of the team this week, using a Shackleton approach?								
25. Have you coached any young leaders this week? (target two a month)								
26. Have you introduced the book *Shackleton Way* to your direct reports? (quarterly reminder)								

EXHIBIT 33.1 (Continued)

	1	2	3	4	5	6	7	8	9	10	11	12	13
27. Have you spent time this week thinking about the future?													
28. Have you undertaken actions this week that clearly demonstrate the values the organization has?													
29. Have you met an adversary this week to develop a better understanding?													
30. Have you consulted with your *sandpaper* mentors this week?													
31. Have you spent some time developing your safe heaven this week?													
32. Have you managed any crisis well this week?													
33. Have you abandoned something in the last fortnight/month?													
34. Have you been "*young at heart*" this week?													
35. Have you avoided emotional outbursts this week?													
36. Have you been bold in planning but careful in execution this week?													
37. Have you practices a leadership trait this week?													
38. Have you ensured the activities for next week/next fortnight are aligned with the organization's mission, vision, values and strategy?													
39. Have you linked into the critical success factors of the organization this week?													
40. Have you thought more about what is your "*legacy*" this week?													

EXHIBIT 33.2 Checklist for Getting Things Done (Part IV)

	1	2	3	4	5	6	7	8	9	10	11	12	13
1. Some learning happened in the week.													
2. Monitored the key performance indicators (KPIs) in week.													
3. Made progress with implementing winning KPIs in week.													
4. Assisted in finding the organization's critical success factors (CSFs).													
5. Assisted with the marketing of wining KPIs in the organization.													
6. Assisted with the introduction of balanced performance measure reporting.													
7. Implemented one practice from the *special organizations* in Chapter 20 this week.													
8. Most days had four plus hours of *service delivery* time.													
9. Have made some progress with the streamlining of board reporting.													
10. Have made some progress with the implementing rolling planning.													
11. Implemented some of the reporting suggestions in Chapter 26.													
12. Next staff opinion has been planned and is to based on Chapter 27.													
13. Coordinated well with the human resources team this week.													
14. Progress was made with embedding the foundation stones into the performance bonus schemes.													

In-House Customer Satisfaction Survey

A survey is available from www.davidparmenter.com. The Web site will refer to a word from a specific page in this book which you can use as a password.

 xxxx Team User Satisfaction Questionnaire

The purpose of the user satisfaction survey is to aid the xxxx team to deliver a quality service. In this questionnaire we are seeking to investigate your satisfaction with your relationship with the xxxx **team since** xxxx. Your response (in the shaded areas) will help us ensure we deliver a quality service.

The comment fields are a very helpful part of a feedback to the xxxx **team. Invest time in making the comments as specific as possible and give examples where this is appropriate.** Your ratings and your comments are totally confidential. xxxx Limited (the company conducting the survey) will prepare the statistical data and display comments so as to conceal the identities of respondents. Return no later than xxxx by email to xxxx@xxxx.

How satisfied are you with the xxxx team's systems

Rating

5 = Very satisfied, 4 = Satisfied, 3 = Neither satisfied nor dissatisfied, 2 = Dissatisfied, 1 = Very dissatisfied, X = cannot rate

System Name	Cannot Rate	Ease of Use	Ease of Accessing Data You Need	Adequacy of Reporting	Usefulness of Manual/ Quick Reference Guide	Adequacy of Help Desk Support
xxxx						
xxxx						
xxxx						

How satisfied are you with the following xxxxx team's activities?

•• Activities	Cannot Rate	Timeliness	Accuracy (including quality assurance)	Proactive/ Responsiveness	Expertise of Staff	Output (fit for purpose)
Processing of ••						
Processing of ••						
Coordination of ••						
Coordination of ••						
Advice to ••						

How satisfied are you with the following xxxx team's activities? (Continued)

•• Activities	Cannot Rate	Timeliness	Accuracy (including quality assurance)	Proactive/ Responsiveness	Expertise of Staff	Output (fit for purpose)
Monthly •• report to senior management						
One-to-one training						
Other (please specify):						
Other (please specify):						

Rate your satisfaction with ••'s working style (only those teams you have contact with)

<u>Rating</u>

5 = **Very satisfied**, 4 = Satisfied, 3 = Neither satisfied nor dissatisfied, 2 = Dissatisfied, 1 = **Very dissatisfied** X = Not applicable, cannot rate

How satisfied are you with the:	Insert team name	Insert team name	Insert team name	Insert team name	Insert team name	Insert team name
Team's accessibility and promptness in replying to your queries?						
Proactive role of the team in anticipating issues?						
Team's understanding of issues from your perspective?						

(Continued)

Rate your satisfaction with ••'s working style (only those teams you have contact with) (Continued)

How satisfied are you with the:	Insert team name	Insert team name	Insert team name	Insert team name	Insert team name	Insert team name
Team's service ethic? (friendliness, approachability, positive attitude, supportiveness, commitment to continuous improvement)						
Degree of respect the team demonstrates toward you? (e.g., arriving on time for meetings, delivering to deadlines, honoring promises, responding to emails)?						
Willingness to take ownership of issues? (including responding constructively to criticism)						
Teamwork and ability to redirect key issues to the appropriate person within the team?						
Decision making within the workgroup (prompt, stand the test of time, rarely rescinded)						
Team's follow-through/ability to close issues?						

Rate your satisfaction with ••'s communication (only rate those teams you have contact with)

How satisfied are you with the:			
Frequency of face-to-face communication? (e.g., not hiding behind emails)			
Way we communicate operational/routine issues?			

Rate your satisfaction with ••'s communication (only rate those teams you have contact with) (Continued)

How satisfied are you with the:					
Way we communicate complex issues?					
Overall effectiveness of our communication?					
Meetings that we host? (keeping the meeting on track and on time)					
Contribution we make to meetings you host? (being prepared, our level of participation, and the follow-up action we undertake)					
Presentations we deliver?					
Content of the business group's intranet site?					
Reporting					

Provide a comment, **in this section**, to explain a 1 or 5 rating.

What do you consider to be the three main strengths of this service? (If you have used the "5" rating, give examples).

1.	
2.	
3.	

(Continued)

What do you consider to be the three main areas for this service to develop? (If you have used the "1" rating, give examples. Please also give suggestions of specific changes you would like, if appropriate.)

1.	
2.	
3.	

Insert your name. Your name will only be used for administrative purposes	
If the findings of this survey were to be presented, would you be interested in attending the presentation?	*Yes/No* *(Delete as appropriate)*

List of Success Factors

The checklist is available from www.davidparmenter.com. The Web site will refer to a word from a specific page in this book which you can use as a password.

Note: Success factors do not neatly fit within one balance scorecard perspective, they typically impact more than one perspective and thus could easily be included under a different perspective heading.

Success Factors: Environment and Community Focus

1. Positive public perception of organization   □ Yes   □ No
2. Seen in the community as a viable employer   □ Yes   □ No
3. Supporting minorities through employment   □ Yes   □ No
4. Minimizing pollution and waste   □ Yes   □ No
5. Supporting educational institutions (share knowledge via organization's website)   □ Yes   □ No
6. Encouraging voluntary assistance by staff to the local community   □ Yes   □ No
7. Recognition by industry for environmental endeavors   □ Yes   □ No
8. Good working relationships with key community organizations   □ Yes   □ No
9. Supporting local businesses (percent of purchases to have local content)   □ Yes   □ No
10. Enhanced community interaction (favorable reputation in the community)   □ Yes   □ No
11. Environmentally friendly culture and reputation (use of environmentally friendly materials)   □ Yes   □ No

Success Factors: Internal Process Focus

1. Delivery in full on time, all the time, to our key customers   □ Yes   □ No
2. Finding better ways to do the things we do every day   □ Yes   □ No

(Continued)

3. Product leadership in industry   ☐ Yes   ☐ No
4. Maintaining a safe and healthy workplace   ☐ Yes   ☐ No
5. Enhancing operational efficiency (e.g., reducing cost per   ☐ Yes   ☐ No
   transaction)
6. Increasing linkages with key suppliers   ☐ Yes   ☐ No
7. Optimizing technology that matters   ☐ Yes   ☐ No
8. Completion of projects on time and to budget   ☐ Yes   ☐ No
9. Encouraging innovation that matters   ☐ Yes   ☐ No
10. Enhancing quality   ☐ Yes   ☐ No
11. Occupational health and safety legislation compliance   ☐ Yes   ☐ No
12. Timely, accurate, decision-based information   ☐ Yes   ☐ No
13. We finish what we start   ☐ Yes   ☐ No
14. Timely maintenance of assets   ☐ Yes   ☐ No
15 Paperless information flow between key suppliers and   ☐ Yes   ☐ No
   customers

Success Factors: Finance Focus
1. Reducing supply chain costs   ☐ Yes   ☐ No
2. Optimizing revenue from profitable customers   ☐ Yes   ☐ No
3. Growth in revenue and product mix to our profitable   ☐ Yes   ☐ No
   customers (new products, new applications, new customers
   and markets, new relationships, new product and service
   mix, new pricing)
4. Cost reduction/productivity improvement (reduce unit cost,   ☐ Yes   ☐ No
   improve channel mix, reduce operating expenses)
5. Increasing the gross margin   ☐ Yes   ☐ No
6. Optimal utilization of assets and resources   ☐ Yes   ☐ No
7. Improved risk management (better forecasting, broaden   ☐ Yes   ☐ No
   revenue base, increase brand awareness, etc.)
8. Increase in overall spend by key customers (getting a larger   ☐ Yes   ☐ No
   slice of business from our important customers)
9. Increased repeat business from key customers (leading to   ☐ Yes   ☐ No
   increasing market share)
10. Optimization of working capital (optimizing stock levels and   ☐ Yes   ☐ No
    minimizing debtors)
11. Fiscally responsible management, by all managers   ☐ Yes   ☐ No
12. Improving cash flow   ☐ Yes   ☐ No
13. Maximizing off-season potential   ☐ Yes   ☐ No
14. Being a preferred supplier for key customers (more success   ☐ Yes   ☐ No
    at tenders, more nontender opportunities)
15. Recovery of chargeable hours   ☐ Yes   ☐ No

Success Factors: Customer Satisfaction Focus
1. Delivery in full on time, all the time, to our key customers   ☐ Yes   ☐ No
2. Introduction of new services that add value to our key   ☐ Yes   ☐ No
   customers

3. Increased repeat business from our key customers (increased □ Yes □ No
% of sales from top 10% of customers)
4. Improved turnaround time from order to delivery for our □ Yes □ No
key customers
5. Our customers being active advocates for our business □ Yes □ No
(especially our key ones)
6. Identify and capture the potential of new and emerging □ Yes □ No
markets
7. New and innovative low-cost access channels for our □ Yes □ No
products and services
8. Getting the right product in the right place at the right time □ Yes □ No
9. Seeking excellence in every aspect of our interaction □ Yes □ No
10. Acquisition of profitable customers □ Yes □ No
11. Retention of key customers □ Yes □ No
12. Positive brand recognition □ Yes □ No

Success Factors: Learning and Growth Focus
1. Create an environment where our people are encouraged to □ Yes □ No
meet their full potential
2. Create an environment where our people are encouraged to □ Yes □ No
accept their role in meeting our challenges
3. Culture of continued learning □ Yes □ No
4. Developing internal leadership among managers □ Yes □ No
5. Increasing employee productivity □ Yes □ No
6. Developing strategic skills within management □ Yes □ No
7. Increasing adaptability and flexibility of staff □ Yes □ No
8. More open access for staff to strategic information □ Yes □ No
9. Improved alignment of individual and organizational goals □ Yes □ No
10. Increasing empowerment (delegated decision making) □ Yes □ No
11. Increasing productivity through increase in skills, motivation, □ Yes □ No
and so on
12. Multifaceted support to employees' growth (coaching, □ Yes □ No
mentoring, managed by skilled managers, succession
planning, project opportunities)
13. Innovative ideas from staff encouraged and adopted quickly □ Yes □ No
14. Research and development and knowledge rewarded and □ Yes □ No
encouraged

Success Factors: Employee Satisfaction Focus
1. Rewarding and recognizing our existing staff □ Yes □ No
2. Attracting quality staff to the organization □ Yes □ No
3. "Stay, say, strive engagement with staff" □ Yes □ No
4. A pleasant physical work environment for all staff □ Yes □ No
5. Positive company culture (supported by survey, active and □ Yes □ No
well-supported social club, etc.)

(Continued)

6. Provide opportunities for staff to grow   □ Yes   □ No
7. Supporting balance in working and home life (respect   □ Yes   □ No
   different working styles/working hours)
8. Appropriate reward and recognition structure for all   □ Yes   □ No
9. Increasing recognition throughout the organization (e.g.,   □ Yes   □ No
   recognition being a daily activity for managers and staff,
   celebrating success, etc.)
10. Promoting open decision making   □ Yes   □ No

Intranet Content Checklist

A checklist is to help organizations develop a thriving intranet and is available from www.davidparmenter.com. The Web site will refer to a word from a specific page in this book which you can use as a password.

Intranet Content Checklist

GENERAL

1. **Email:** Employees should be able to access their email via a web interface and view attachments. ☐ Yes ☐ No

2. **Calendar management:** Employees should be able to manage their calendar via a web interface and the ability to schedule meetings with other users should also be available. ☐ Yes ☐ No

3. **Electronic meeting:** Voice and videoconferencing via the intranet should be available. This will dramatically reduce long-distance phone and travel charges. ☐ Yes ☐ No

4. **Personalized intranets:** Each user has their own view and access to information. Dynamic web pages based on user profiles and database contents deliver customized content. A database is used to manage the content. ☐ Yes ☐ No

5. **Online support center:** The computer help-desk should be accessible via the intranet with questions answered dynamically via a knowledge database, or via a chat session with a computer support person. This person could remotely access the user's PC, if needed, to fix the problem. ☐ Yes ☐ No

6. **Access to all applications:** Provides the portal for access to all systems such as the general ledger, customer relationship management, and so forth. This means that software does not have to be loaded onto individual PCs and that staff treat the intranet as the one-stop-shop. ☐ Yes ☐ No

(Continued)

DECISION SUPPORT INFORMATION

1. **Executive management site**: Executives should have their   □ Yes   □ No
   own customized area to view daily and see real-time key
   business statistics. This enables them to conduct a daily
   "audit" of the performance of their company.
2. **Balanced scorecard measures** reporting back on the   □ Yes   □ No
   six sections: (1) financial, (2) customer satisfaction,
   (3) employee satisfaction, (4) community and environment,
   (5) learning and growth, and (6) internal processes.
3. **Other performance measures** such as outstanding performance   □ Yes   □ No
   reviews by manager (shown in the four-to-six-week
   performance review period), weekly listing of overdue reports
   by manager, weekly listing of late projects by manager.
4. **Weekly report on all "late reports"**   □ Yes   □ No
5. **Search engine**: Allow employees to search the intranet for   □ Yes   □ No
   information and automatically save their past searches for
   future use.
6. **Knowledge management**: Establish shared communities of   □ Yes   □ No
   interest, where employees can meet and exchange
   knowledge. This can include technology research and
   development, discovery and dissemination of successful
   strategies and tactics, and core discipline best practices
   exchange.
7. **Push-technology**: Relevant information is automatically   □ Yes   □ No
   delivered to the desktops of employees. For example,
   marketing department employees will automatically receive
   competitor news flashes, the engineering department
   employees will automatically receive news regarding new
   technologies, and the human resources employees will
   automatically receive news regarding labor law changes.
   This significantly reduces the need for employees to have to
   surf the Internet for this information.

CONTINUOUS IMPROVEMENT

1. **Progress reports**, so that all staff who are interested can see   □ Yes   □ No
   achievements in the continuous-improvement loop.
2. **Success Express**, a weekly, biweekly, or monthly newsletter   □ Yes   □ No
   about success.
3. **Innovation ideas**, a place where staff can put ideas to   □ Yes   □ No
   improve processes, products, and services.

DOCUMENT MANAGEMENT SYSTEM

1. **Centralized electronic filing** of all records, sharing a common □ Yes   □ No
   index.
2. **Centralized hard-copy filing** secure, bar-coded, and thus   □ Yes   □ No
   eliminating multiple-copy filing.

PROJECTS OFFICE	□ Yes	□ No
1. Project documentation	□ Yes	□ No
2. Project plan, sponsor, budget, milestones, Individual task lists	□ Yes	□ No
3. Problem log	□ Yes	□ No
4. Progress reporting (weekly updates on all major projects)	□ Yes	□ No
5. Lessons learned (output from projects office)	□ Yes	□ No
6. Project conferences: Enable collaboration between project team members via news groups, online conferences, or chat sessions.	□ Yes	□ No
HUMAN RESOURCES		
1. Employee handbook	□ Yes	□ No
2. Benefits information	□ Yes	□ No
3. Organization charts	□ Yes	□ No
4. Company newsletters	□ Yes	□ No
5. Company calendar	□ Yes	□ No
6. Employee directory: Have an online, searchable database for employee's telephone number, location, email address, photo, short-form CV. Allow supervisors to add new employees or change information for existing employees.	□ Yes	□ No
7. Benefits enrollment: Allow employees to sign up online for their benefit options.	□ Yes	□ No
8. Pension information: Allow employees to view account information.	□ Yes	□ No
9. Employee surveys: Have employees complete surveys online, automate the tabulation of results, and distribute the results via email to decision-makers.	□ Yes	□ No
10. Recruiting: Allow employees to view internal job openings and complete self-nomination form online. Automatically route the form to the employee's manager for electronic signature approval and then email the form to the appropriate human resources contact.	□ Yes	□ No
11. Payroll: Have hourly employees submit timesheets via the intranet and automatically calculate payroll information. Allow employees to change withholding information and direct deposit information online.	□ Yes	□ No
12. Travel planning: Have employees schedule their business trips online and automatically email their completed itinerary to them.	□ Yes	□ No
13. Employee performance reviews: Provision for both 90-degree feedback (from supervisor) and 360-degree feedback (from supervisor, peers, staff, self, third parties, etc.). With automatic email reminders sent to supervisors who are late in completing them.	□ Yes	□ No

(Continued)

14. **Employee expenses reimbursement process:** Have employees   ☐ Yes   ☐ No
    submit reimbursement forms online.
15. **Training:** Web-based simulations and computer-based   ☐ Yes   ☐ No
    training classes should be accessible via the intranet.
16. **Employee classifieds:** Allow employees to post classified ads.   ☐ Yes   ☐ No
    This helps build a sense of community and improves morale.

SALES
1. Sales presentations   ☐ Yes   ☐ No
2. Art libraries with product images and logo images   ☐ Yes   ☐ No
3. Price lists   ☐ Yes   ☐ No
4. Market research   ☐ Yes   ☐ No
5. Competitor information   ☐ Yes   ☐ No
6. Company announcements/press releases   ☐ Yes   ☐ No
7. Product demos   ☐ Yes   ☐ No
8. Catalogs and brochures   ☐ Yes   ☐ No
9. Product specification sheets   ☐ Yes   ☐ No
10. **Multimedia tour of the manufacturing plant to "bring the**   ☐ Yes   ☐ No
    factory to the administration staff and customers (via extranet)"
11. **Product availability:** Sales reps should be able to access   ☐ Yes   ☐ No
    product availability information from anywhere in the world
    to be able to communicate to their customers.
12. **Sales data:** Real-time sales information should be available at   ☐ Yes   ☐ No
    all times and this information should be compared against
    sales goals and sales forecast data. This information should
    be obtainable at a corporate level, region level, territory
    level, and sales rep level.
13. **Contact management system:** Provide a central database to   ☐ Yes   ☐ No
    match potential customers to sales reps and when potential
    leads are identified they are entered and automatically
    routed to the appropriate sales rep.
14. **Sales force training:** Provide online training of products and   ☐ Yes   ☐ No
    sales skills, which sales reps can access whenever they have
    time available.
15. **Opportunity management system:** Helps to identify untapped   ☐ Yes   ☐ No
    revenue opportunities based on comparing sales information
    at a corporate level, region level, territory level, and specific
    customer level.
16. **Design products onsite with the customer:** If there is any   ☐ Yes   ☐ No
    customization to product design, allow your sales reps to
    design the product onsite with the customer via an intranet
    application that automatically calculates cost and
    manufacturing completion time. One might consider
    providing portable scanners and digital cameras to their
    sales force to allow them to customize products with
    customer logos, colors, picture, and so forth.

17. **Sales force collaboration:** Provide a means for all of your sales reps around the world to collaborate via news groups, online conferences, and chat sessions. □ Yes □ No

MARKETING

1. **Feedback system:** The marketing department should solicit feedback from the sales force regarding products, promotions, pricing, and so on. This could be done via surveys, news groups, online conferences, or chat sessions. □ Yes □ No

2. **Marketing calendar:** A calendar highlighting when trade shows, seminars, new product launches, promotions, and so on are being held. This should be viewable at a company level, product level, and geographic level. □ Yes □ No

TECHNICAL (ENGINEERING)

1. **Engineering library:** Central repository of code, specs, configurations, utilities, etc. □ Yes □ No

2. **Standards and methodology manual online** □ Yes □ No

3. **Technical papers online** □ Yes □ No

4. **Shared development:** Enable sharing of work in development, making it available to the testing, quality assurance, and documentation departments. □ Yes □ No

5. **Engineering change order system:** Tracking system for change requests being worked on by engineers. This would provide a description of the request, status, and who is working on it. □ Yes □ No

CUSTOMER SERVICE AND SUPPORT

1. **Order entry and tracking** □ Yes □ No

2. **Customer relationship management—information entry and update** □ Yes □ No

3. **Product returns** □ Yes □ No

4. **Warranty claims and processing** □ Yes □ No

5. **Tracking location of freight** □ Yes □ No

6. **Tracking progress of manufacture of tailor-made product** □ Yes □ No

7. **Problem/complaint entry and tracking** □ Yes □ No

8. **Accounts receivable information** □ Yes □ No

9. **Product manuals** □ Yes □ No

10. **Pricing information** □ Yes □ No

11. **Frequently asked questions** □ Yes □ No

12. **News flashes:** Provide quick notification of important news, such as a customer being put on credit hold, or a product being put on back order. □ Yes □ No

LINKAGE WITH SUPPLIERS □ Yes □ No

1. **Key suppliers accessing stock levels** so they become responsible for just-in-time stocking. □ Yes □ No

(Continued)

2. Access to their sales ledger   □ Yes   □ No
3. **Suppliers providing 1-800 service**, and providing direct   □ Yes   □ No
   service to customers having accessed customers' records
   (e.g., processing and repairs broken window screens).
4. **Suppliers providing consolidated invoices electronically** in a   □ Yes   □ No
   format that is directly "uploadable" to the general ledger.
5. **Contact management system**: Provide a central database to   □ Yes   □ No
   match suppliers to key company personnel and to log major
   discussions and agreements.

LINKAGE WITH GOVERNMENT AND LOCAL BODIES

1. Submission of **taxation returns** details   □ Yes   □ No
2. Submission of **consents**   □ Yes   □ No
3. Control over waste   □ Yes   □ No
4. **Contact management system**: Provide a central database to   □ Yes   □ No
   match staff at local bodies to key company personnel and to
   log major discussions and agreements.

LEGAL

1. **Contract system**: Allow your sales reps to close deals onsite   □ Yes   □ No
   by providing a contract system for them to enter the deal
   into, which automatically updates sales information and
   forwards the sale to the production scheduling department
   to begin production of the product.
2. **Contracts-in-progress**: Monitoring progress of contract   □ Yes   □ No
   between the different interested parties.

FINANCE

1. **Financial reports**, at a company level, division level, and   □ Yes   □ No
   department level
2. **Accounting policies and procedures manual**   □ Yes   □ No
3. **Financial delegations**   □ Yes   □ No
4. **Accounts receivable information**   □ Yes   □ No
5. **Accounts payable information**   □ Yes   □ No
6. **Budget system (including forecasting)**: Enable departments to   □ Yes   □ No
   enter their budget information and automatically route the
   information for approval.
7. **Department reporting and forecasting**: Enable departments to   □ Yes   □ No
   enter their financial information and forecast data.
8. **Expense claims**: Automate the collection of expense claims   □ Yes   □ No
   information by having employees submit claims online and
   automatically route the information for approval.
9. **Asset management system**: Enable departments to view the   □ Yes   □ No
   current list of assets assigned to their area and allow them
   to enter new assets and receive asset tag numbers and
   depreciation information.

10. New venture investment guidelines   □ Yes   □ No
11. Procurement system   □ Yes   □ No

MANUFACTURING

1. **Production schedules**: This ensures that everyone has access   □ Yes   □ No
   to the most current scheduling information.
2. **Inventory control system**: Track raw material, work-in-   □ Yes   □ No
   progress, and finished goods inventory location.
3. **Bills of material**: This ensures everyone has access to the   □ Yes   □ No
   most current bills of material used for producing products.
4. **Part ordering system**: Enable ordering of parts online.   □ Yes   □ No

INTRANET TOOLS

1. **Self-Publishing**: These tools enable business users to create □ Yes   □ No
   web pages without the need for them to know HTML. This
   puts the responsibility of creating and maintaining web
   content in the hands of the actual business owners, instead
   of the IT department.
2. **Link validation**: Automatically checks links in web pages to   □ Yes   □ No
   assure they are valid.
3. **Document control**: Provides version control and revision   □ Yes   □ No
   tracking of web pages.
4. **Security**: Provides access control to the intranet itself and □ Yes   □ No
   different levels of access control within the intranet.
5. **Site statistics**: Provides statistics on who is using the intranet □ Yes   □ No
   and which pages within the site are being viewed.

SERVICES TO ENSURE STAFF USE INTRANET DAILY

1. Links to **local traffic** information (e.g., links to AA traffic cam □ Yes   □ No
   on highway, etc.)
2. **Rumor factory**, a place where staff can place rumors; these   □ Yes   □ No
   are answered within the day from the internal
   communications team.
3. Links to **local weather** information, including links to   □ Yes   □ No
   weather cams from other sites on highway, etc.
4. **Breaking news**: These services can be purchased from news   □ Yes   □ No
   providers.
5. **Clubs, personal classifieds, and so forth.**   □ Yes   □ No

Recognition Letters

 Memo for a Member of the Team for Going the Extra Mile

Date

Re: Completing project xxxx

I would like to comment on the exceptional skills you demonstrated in completing the xxxx project on time and within budget. You managed all this while maintaining the routine day-to-day tasks.

Please accept this voucher as a small token of the organization's appreciation. I have discussed the recognition with the CEO who also would like to show his appreciation, in person. I have arranged a morning coffee, in the CEO office, next Tuesday at 10.30 A.M.

Kind regards

xxxx

Letter to a Supplier Who Has Gone the Extra Mile

Dear xxxx

Re: Breathtaking improvement

I would like to comment on the exceptional skill your staff and your contractors have demonstrated in the recent installation of xxxx. The finished product has exceeded my expectations and has been well worth the wait.

Should you need a reference site please feel free to give potential customers my number.

Kind regards,

xxxx

Focus Group Meeting Workshop

A focus group meeting is a very valuable exercise to undertake when you have a major project. The format of this one day meeting could be used step for a variety of projects and is available from www.davidparmenter.com. The Web site will refer to a word from a specific page in this book which you can use as a password.

One day focus group on implementing a scorecard—and getting it right the first time.

Objective:
- To ensure a key group of staff and management are fully aware of what is required to implement performance measurement that works.
- To fully understand the required level of involvement, the necessity for speed and the inherent hurdles this project will face.

Requirements:
A focus group selected from 15 to 30 experienced staff covering the business units, teams, area offices, head office, and covering the different roles from administrators to senior management team members.

Workshop administrator to help coordinate attendees.
At least three laptops, data show, screen, three electronic whiteboards, quiet workshop space away from the offices.

9.00	Introduction from CEO
9.10	The new thinking on key performance indicators (KPIs) presentation covering: • The difference between the three types of performance measures • The characteristics of a winning KPI: two stories • The 10,80,10 rule for performance measures • Critical success factors • Case studies • Why so many performance measurement initiatives fail • The difference between the organization's current performance measurement and that proposed **All major budget holders are invited to join the focus group. Any SMT staff who missed the senior management team (SMT) workshop should attend this session. They leave after this session.**
10.00	Commence workshop 1 on brainstorming a collection of critical success factors of the organization. All work that has been already done in this area will be tabled to attendees (e.g., CSFs from last few year's strategic plans)
10.30	Morning break
10.50	Re-commence workshop 1 short listing the CSFs to come up with five to eight CSFs
11.20	Commence workshop 2 design some key result indicators for the Board (this task will take an additional 10 to 16 week period to finalize)
12.00 pm	Lunch
12.45 pm	Commence workshop 3 brainstorm in different groups some performance measures for a couple of business units and a couple of selected teams (this task will take an additional 10 to 16 week period to finalize for all business units and teams)
2.00 pm	Feedback from groups
2.20 pm	Afternoon break
2.40 pm	Commence workshop 4 brainstorm some performance measures for the organization (this task will take an additional 10 to 16 week period to finalize)
3.40 pm	Short presentation on the way forward: the implementation program
4.20 pm	In-house team complete workshop documentation on laptops (covering CSFs, some measures worth pursuing, the first draft of the next steps, resource requirements etc.)
4.40 pm	Focus group states its opinion on whether to go forward, the key issues to address, and resources required **SMT invited to come back to hear the focus group.**
5.00 pm	End of workshop

Putting Your Support Behind Initiatives

 Memo from CEO to Selected staff

Date

Re: Invitation to attend a one-day focus group

It is important that we have a focus-group workshop to kickstart the xxxx project as:

* There are many pitfalls in such a project and many have failed to deliver in other companies.
* A wide ownership is required and a focus group can have a huge impact on the selling process.
* The foundation stones for this project need to be understood and put in place early in the project.
* The focus group will give valuable input as to how the implementation should best be done to maximize its impact.

We are seeking a focus group selected from experienced staff covering the regions, branches, and head office, and covering the different roles from administrators to the senior management team. I believe you would offer much to this exercise and request that you set aside the time to assist.

I welcome your support on this important project. The project team of xxxx, xxxx, xxxx, and xxxx will need and appreciate your support.

(Continued)

Please confirm availability to attend this focus-group workshop, having discussed it with your manager. I look forward to meeting you at the workshop.

Kind regards

CEO

Memo from CEO to All Budget Holders

Date

Dear

Attending xxxx training

You will all be aware that we have decided to implement a new accounting package. According to research, this is a high-risk activity as many implementations do not "deliver the goods."

The xxxx licenses and associated costs will be over $xxx,xxx and thus it is imperative that we make this project a success—first time!

We are also using this implementation to radically alter the way we process xxxx transactions. This means that we are implementing processes that will mean you are spending fewer nights and weekends working on administrative matters.

You will need to attend the training in person. So please select one course and email back today. I will be taking a personal interest in this and will be monitoring course take-up and no-shows.

Should you feel that you are unable to attend, please first contact me so we can discuss the reasons.

Kind regards

CEO

Staff-Satisfaction Survey

The survey is available from www.davidparmenter.com. The Web site will refer to a word from a specific page in this book which you can use as a password.

 Confidential Employee Survey

Rate each question to show how much you agree or disagree with the following statements.

Rating
5 = **Agree strongly**, 4 = **Agree**, 3 = Neither agree nor disagree, 2 = **Disagree**, 1 = **Strongly disagree**, X = cannot rate

About your organization	Enter Rating
1. I understand the strategic objectives the organization is currently working towards	
2. This organization delivers excellent goods/services to its clients	
3. This organization values employees for the full diversity of their backgrounds, views, and contributions	
4. People in this organization cooperate and support each other	
5. This organization treats people fairly	
6. This organization encourages innovation and creativity	
7. This organization recognizes good performance	
8. Managers represent the organization responsibly and professionally	
9. People in this organization adapt flexibly to change	
10. People in this organization feel free to put forward their ideas	
11. This organization values employees' life outside of work	
12. I work for an organization that makes a valuable contribution to the community	

About what is important to you in your job and working environment	Enter Rating
1. I am rewarded fairly for the job I do	
2. I have job security	
3. I have a safe, ergonomic, and well-equipped workspace	
4. My workload and manager's expectations of me do not prevent me from being able to balance my job with personal/family needs	
5. I know what is expected from me	
6. I have a job that is interesting and challenging	
7. My contribution to the team is valued and recognized	
8. My manager keeps me informed about what is going on in the wider organization	
9. I have the scope within the organization to progress my career	
10. I have at least monthly feedback from my manager on my performance	
11. I am receiving adequate training	

The comment fields are a very helpful part of a feedback. Please invest time in making the comments as specific as possible and give examples where this is appropriate.

What do you consider to be the three main strengths of this organization?

1.	
2.	
3.	

What do you consider are three main areas for this organization to develop?

1.	
2.	
3.	

In what ways could this organization help you do your job better, which you have not already mentioned?

A 360 Degree Feedback Questionnaire Suitable for a CEO

The survey is available from www.davidparmenter.com. The Web site will refer to a word from a specific page in this book which you can use as a password.

A Confidential 360 degree feedback on the CEO

Please indicate which category represents you.

Board Member	Major Clients
External Peers (other CEOs)	Other
Senior management team	CEO (self assessment)

Rate each question to show how much you agree or disagree with the following statements.

About the CEO's leadership

Rating

5 = **Agree strongly**, 4 = **Agree**, 3 = Neither agree nor disagree, 2 = **Disagree**, 1 = **Strongly disagree**, X = cannot rate

---

The foundation stones of leadership

Question	Rating
1. The CEO is a well rounded person, having handled any personal traits that might cause upset to staff and management?	
2. The CEO exhibits a "Love for the Common Man".	
3. The CEO is a good host.	
4. The CEO demonstrates humility.	
5. The CEO demonstrates integrity.	
6. The CEO communicates openly with the staff.	
7. The CEO helps ensure clear and effective reporting to other leaders.	
8. The CEO runs meetings that are purposeful.	
9. The CEO is persuasive and compelling when communicating her vision.	
10. The CEO works actively to develop a "positive" culture in the organization.	
11. The CEO can motivate employees from diverse, backgrounds, experiences, and beliefs.	
12. The CEO maintains an "open door" and keeps staff informed.	
13. The CEO is seen by staff on a regular basis e.g. on walkabout.	

The focus areas of leadership

Question	Rating
14. The CEO is cool headed in a crisis.	
15. The CEO is flexible with their tactics in a crisis.	
16. The CEO can maintain a sense of humor when all looks lost.	
17. The CEO can and does abandon initiatives if they are not working.	
18. The CEO invests their time in the recruitment process.	
19. The CEO has an abundance of positive energy.	
20. The CEO is known for their "never give up" attitude.	

Question	Rating
21. The CEO promotes the **celebration of success** in the organization.	
22. The CEO is **young at heart**.	
23. The CEO **develops and maintains relationships** with key stakeholders, key suppliers, and major customers.	
24. The CEO is a good "reader" of people understanding what makes them "*tick*".	
25. The CEO seldom has **emotional** outbursts.	
26. The CEO invests time in **understanding the future** for the organization.	
27. The CEO **plans carefully** ensuring all bases are covered.	
28. The CEO ensures that all projects are **provisioned adequately** thus giving them the best chance of success.	
29. The CEO demonstrates a commitment to "**continuous learning**".	
30. The CEO gets behind **innovation** and champions it in the organization.	
31. The CEO **initiates change**, and is able to address resistance to change.	
32. The CEO is good at "**finishing what she starts**".	
33. The CEO creates **opportunities to grow and develop staff**.	
34. The CEO demonstrates a **commitment to empowering staff**.	
35. The CEO demonstrates **empathy** with staff.	
36. The CEO would never place results ahead of staff welfare and safety.	
37. The CEO gives **recognition** freely.	
38. The CEO cares about the staff's **fitness and health**.	
39. The CEO has communicated the **Mission, Values, Vision, and Strategy** clearly.	
40. The CEO inspires the senior management team members and staff to share in a **vision** and to commit to the project or task.	

About your CEO's leadership

The comment fields are a very helpful part of a feedback. Please invest time in making the comments as specific as possible and give examples where this is appropriate.

What do you consider to be the three main strengths that the CEO brings to her work?

| 1. |
| 2. |
| 3. |

What do you consider are three main areas for the CEO to develop?

| 1. |
| 2. |
| 3. |

In what ways could the CEO work better with you, which you have not already mentioned?

| |
| |

Index

Printed and bound by CPI Group (UK) Ltd, Croydon, CR0 4YY

16/04/2025

14658516-0004